THE
PHANTOM
VOYAGERS

EVIDENCE OF INDONESIAN SETTLEMENT
IN AFRICA IN ANCIENT TIMES

For Ben & Henriena —

Robert

By ROBERT DICK-READ

© 2005 Robert Dick-Read

Typeset by Q2A Solutions,
New delhi,
India.

Printed in the United Kingdom by Hobbs the Printers Ltd.

For

Thurlton Publishing,
5 St James Villas,
Winchester,
SO23 9SN
England

Email: thurlton.publishing@ntlworld.com
Website: www.phantomvoyagers.com

British Library Cataloguing in Publication Data.
A catalogue record for this book
is available from the British Library.

ISBN: 0-9549231-0-3

CONTENTS

PREFACE

This book is about the Indonesian mariners who came to Africa in ancient times, long before Europeans knew anything of Africa beyond the Sahara, and long before Arabs and Shirazis sailed down the coast in their *dhows* to found exotic cities such as Kilwa, Lamu and Zanzibar. We don't know with certainty who these Indonesians were, where they came from, or even why they came. But though they left no records and few visible traces of their voyages, their legacy in Africa is far greater than generally recognised: for beneath the surface of the Africa we know today, the footprints and fingerprints of those phantom voyagers are legion.

My own researches date back to a brief period I spent at London University in 1959/60 when Professors Roland Oliver and John Fage conducted a prolonged seminar on 'Indonesia and Africa' at the School of Oriental and African Studies. But my interest in the subject goes back even earlier, to the months I spent in northern Moçambique in 1957 when I first heard how people from Madagascar, speaking a strange language, used to make frequent trips to Africa in their big outrigger canoes to raid the coastal *shambas* and villages for food and slaves. Like so many people living in Africa, I had never until then given a minute's thought to Madagascar; but curiosity about these raiders - who apparently spoke an Austronesian language more like those of the Pacific Islands than to any African languages – aroused my interest in the Indonesian connection.

Despite a 'star cast' at the S.O.A.S. seminar sessions, the results were inconclusive. Yes, everyone agreed, Indonesians with yams, coconuts, and plantains, playing happily on their xylophones as they sailed their outriggers lazily across the ocean, must at some stage have come to Africa and Madagascar. But anything more than that was hard to *prove*. Thus Fage and Oliver and the rest of the 'African' fraternity – faced with the whole vast, virgin territory of African history to explore - thereafter seemed to let the subject lapse.

I was in a different position. I was not a professional. I was therefore free to explore my own interests in whatever way I pleased; and as I always felt there was much more to the 'Indonesian' and 'Madagascan Connection' than was obvious, the subject became a life-long hobby.

Part One of this book – roughly a third – barely touches on Africa. First of all I felt that a good grounding in what was going on in the Southeast Asian islands and the northern Indian Ocean from the earliest times to the end of the first millennium AD was essential. So the book starts off with a

1

brief look at the maritime history of the islands; how the people must have had boats of some sort to cross the seventy kilometres of open water (as it was then) to reach Australia 50 or 60,000 years ago; the absolute necessity of a boating culture for survival in a region of 30,000 or more islands; how subsequently they discovered virtually every spec of land in the Pacific ocean; and the intriguing thought that mariners with much the same technology as the Pacific islanders probably came west into the Indian Ocean even before the region was explored by Egyptian, Indian, Greek and Roman sailors – even before the Dravidians came down into southern India.

Taking a leap forward, I then cast an eye over Rome's trading relations with India and the far east, in particular the spice trade and the mysteries surrounding Indonesian cinnamon and cassia which seem to have bypassed the markets of India and Ceylon, yet found their way to Rome via the Horn of Africa; and how this may have been the catalyst for Indonesian settlement on the African coast. China obviously had a role to play in the Mediterranean trade; but was she a major maritime player? Surprisingly, it seems, the Chinese relied largely on Indonesian ocean-going shipping until well into the first millennium AD. Similarly, the Persians and Arabs were not going to be left out of the lucrative Indian Ocean bazaar; but relatively speaking they, also, were late-comers in the long-distance voyaging stakes.

The opening up of sea-born trade between the west (Mediterranean) and the east (China) inevitably effected all those living in between, and apart from India and Sri Lanka, the greatest effect was around the coast of Southeast Asia, and in those islands that commanded the sea-lanes through which all shipping had eventually to pass. And it was as a direct result of this that the trading states of Funan, Kan-to-li, Ho-ling and others came into being in mainland Southeast Asia and the Indonesian islands, and eventually the most powerful state of them all – Srivijaya.

From the 7th century onwards, Srivijaya ruled over much of Java, Sumatra and most of the Malay peninsular, maintaining its authority over this vital strategic area not only with strong land armies, but more decisively, the first well organised navy the region had seen. Part one ends with an excursion through the mangroves and islets of Indonesia seeking out the most likely 'sea nomads' to have made up the rank and file of the Srivijayan fleets, who, it later transpires, are also those most likely to have carried Indonesians to Africa and Madagascar.

In the second, main, part of the book I switch to Africa where the people collectively called the 'Zanj' dominated the east coast for much of the first millennium AD. Who were these mysterious 'Zanj' from whom

Azania, Zanzibar and Tanzania take their names? Not a lot is known about them; but numerous pointers – not least their relationship with the Zabag or Zanaj who were from Java or Sumatra – points to a close connection with Indonesia, and the probability that the Zanj were an Afro-Indonesian race entrenched in eastern Africa long before the genesis of the Arab influenced Swahili. But why should the Zanj have been there at all? What was the main attraction? It is noteworthy that Zimbabwe's ancient gold mining era was contemporaneous with the flowering of Srivijaya, based in Sumatra (*Suvarnadvipa*, 'the Island of Gold') whose political need for gold was huge. So in this section we look also at what is known about Zimbabwe's ancient gold mines and the part they may have played.

The strength of African genetic and cultural elements in Madagascar being so strong, and the number of African words in their vocabulary so numerous, together favour the notion that the island was first peopled - not by pure-blood Indonesians sailing directly across the ocean - but by Afro-Indonesians, i.e. Zanj, after a lengthy gestation period on mainland Africa. Two chapters are devoted to an attempt to fathom out just who the Malagasy are. And this culminates in some detective work that points to the origins of the Indonesian element being originally from south-western Sulawezi – a link that ties in with conclusions hinted at in Part One.

If Madagascar's first inhabitants were Afro-Indonesians, was there a continuing relationship between the island and the mainland in later years? What did Africa give to Madagascar, and did Malagasy culture give anything back to Africa? Can we learn anything from this today? The answer to all these is: Yes. And the strongest links seem, unsurprisingly, to have been with the area that must have been the most important to the Srivijayans, the gold-producing regions of Zimbabwe. I stick my neck out reinterpreting some sacrosanct elements of African culture based on relationships with the 'Great Isle'.

This leads us on to music – perhaps the field in which there has been the widest acceptance of Indonesian influence in Africa. The core of this acceptance lies with Africa's pre-eminent xylophone players, the Chopi, who, according to their own oral histories, may once, in ancient times, have entertained the Lords of the Goldfields in their fortress-like Great Zimbabwe with stunning orchestral music played on their essentially 'Indonesian' instruments. But other instruments are brought into the equation, too, including the African panpipes that bear such striking resemblances to those once played in some Southeast Asian islands.

Did the Indonesians round the Cape of Good Hope and sail up to West Africa? They certainly seemed to have sailed down the East African coast beyond the limits of the Arab *dhows*; and after the epic journey of the reproduction 'Borobodur boat' in 2004, there can be no doubt whatsoever they had the capability to do so. What's more, there is evidence that they left substantial and important imprints on West African culture, especially in the region of the lower Niger, where some of Africa's highest cultures developed far removed from the trans-Saharan trade routes. More than a third of the book – the last third – digs into the evidence of Indonesian involvement in Western Africa where, once again, the origins of some of Africa's most revered institutions come into question.

Acknowledgements.

Apart from my wife, Sally, who as always has been enormously supportive throughout, I have, quite literally, hundreds of people to thank for their help while writing this book. First must come the authors of the many dozens of books and papers on African and Oriental history without which the enterprise would have been impossible. I started compiling a list of people (many of whom are now dead) who have taken the trouble to reply to correspondence – sometimes negatively - but more frequently with positive suggestions and ideas. It would be too much of a rigmarole to list them all here, but a few individuals stand out.

The fact that I was able to get into London University for a post-graduate course without any a previous degree of any sort was entirely due to the efforts of that great Africanist, Mel Herskovitz of Northwestern University, who pulled strings on my behalf. From her lovely house in Broadway, archaeologist Gertrude Caton Thompson, who always felt her conclusions regarding the origins of the Great Zimbabwe had been distorted by 'subsequent commentators', gave me more encouragement than I believe she realised. I owe a huge debt to the enthusiasm and knowledge of Rev Paul Gebauer, a very good friend who helped me when I was setting up the museum in Bamenda (then still part of Nigeria); and likewise to the Rev Jim Hardyman whose remarkable collection of books on Madagascar filled every spare corner of his house and garage in Bromley when he finally came to roost 'back home' after years in 'the Great Isle'. (The collection is now housed in the S.O.A.S. library in London). More recently I have to thank Sir Mervyn Brown, one-time British Ambassador in Madagascar and High Commissioner in Nigeria, for reading the manuscript; he is the author of two excellent books on Madagascar's history. Finally, Professor Roland Oliver… I was nervous about sending him an early copy of the manuscript because, as he barely mentioned Indonesia in any of his writings since those heady days in 1959, I thought he might give it a massive 'thumbs down'. But he read it in detail, gave me good advice and encouragement; and I am most grateful to him.

Website and contact addresses.

I make no claim to have all the answers! Constructive comments and criticisms will therefore be very welcome. These will be published periodically on our website – www.phantomvoyagers.com - along with any counter-comments that might be relevant. Send these either to: thurlton.publishing@ntlworld.com OR robert.dread@ntlworld.com. If you wish to contact us by mail, write to:

Thurlton Publishing,
5 St James Villas
Winchester
SO23 9SN
England

THE
PHANTOM
VOYAGERS

PART 1

THE
INDIAN OCEAN
AND
SOUTHEAST ASIA

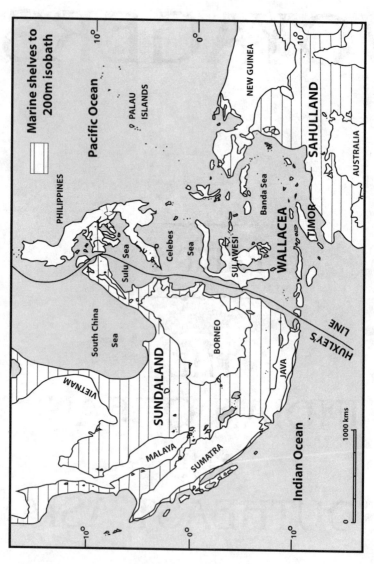

The Indonesian Islands in the Pleistocene era

CHAPTER - 1

Drifting like spectres through the sea-mists of Southeast Asia's ancient past float the barely discernible outlines of some of the world's earliest and greatest mariners. Their form has been dimmed by time; they are too vague to be described with precision. But from the ghostlike ripples of the sea and phantasmal footprints across sandy beaches and muddy shores we know they travelled far and wide, not only over the Pacific swells, but also to the horizons of the setting sun. Who were they? ... Where did they come from? ... and where did their brilliant seamanship lead them?

ANCIENT MARINERS OF THE EAST

Geologically the water-washed world of insular Southeast Asia, or 'Indonesia', is divided into two disparate regions. To the West lie Sumatra, Java, Borneo, and thousands of smaller islands. All the islands of the western group, many of which have living volcanoes thrusting through their crusts, lie on a geological shelf known as the Sunda Shelf – or 'Sundaland'. During the glacial periods of the late Pleistocene the frozen polar ice-caps sucked water from the tropical oceans, lowering the sea as much as a hundred metres below today's levels. Sundaland then formed a single land-mass with mainland south-east Asia sharing much of its rich plant and animal life. Sundaland was the habitat of one of the oldest humans -*homo erectus* or 'Java Man' - who prowled the jungles around the Solo river in eastern Java between a million and a million and a half years ago.

Immediately to the east of Sundaland, separated by a trough of deep water known as the Huxley or 'Wallace' Line, is 'Wallacea'. Here are Sulawezi, the Philippines, Timor, Flores, Sumba, Sumbawa, Lombok, the Moluccas, and myriads of smaller islets extending eastward to the rim of the Pacific Ocean. Unlike Sundaland, Wallacea never became a single land-mass even at the height of the Pleistocene; and there are no signs that *homo erectus* ever managed to cross the trench from Sundaland to Wallacea.

This isolation from the mainland has resulted in the *flora* and *fauna* of Wallacea being far less diverse than those of Sundaland: though from Australia, coming in the other direction, some forms of life - marsupials of

9

several sorts, and some varieties of *eucalyptus* trees - did manage to infiltrate several islands from the Philippines to southern Sulawezi.

Even with the seas at their lowest levels in Pleistocene times anyone from Sundaland wanting to travel to Wallacea would have had to make open-water crossings, none of which would have been less than 45 miles or 70 kilometres wide. Nevertheless, about 60,000 years ago, when the seas were still fifty metres lower than today, dark skinned 'Australo-Melanesian' hunter-gatherers from Sundaland, somehow crossed the deep waters that had up till then proved to be an absolute barrier. They settled all the main islands of Wallacea, and eventually the uninhabited vastness of 'Sahulland' – a third landmass comprising Australia and New Guinea which were once joined together. Those who reached Sahulland were the ancestors of Australia's Aborigines and the secretive people of Papua New Guinea.

Some 35,000 years ago mariners from New Guinea managed to reach the Solomon Islands, where they remained for several thousand years without further exploration. About 13,000 years ago, they took another stride across the 200-kilometres of water from New Guinea or New Ireland to the Admiralty Islands in the Bismarck Archipelago. Comparing these discoveries against the fact that Crete and Cyprus – about 80 kilometres from mainland Europe - were first settled only 8000 years ago, the seamanship of the early Indonesians was astonishing. (1)

Around 3,000 BC there appeared on the Indonesian scene a Mongoloid race of seamen moving south from their homeland in Formosa (Taiwan). These newcomers to the islands practised slash-and-burn agriculture which is notoriously destructive of land – a fact that may have been a reason for them seeking new lands to cultivate beyond the relatively narrow Luzon Strait. They built seaworthy canoes, and may, at that early stage, have invented 'outriggers' to steady their boats in the choppy seas; they made pottery, practised different types of fishing, cultivated millet, and grew sugarcane, coco-yams, bananas, plantains and *taro*. The last of these, *dioscorea alata*, was a plant of major importance that had its homeland in the monsoon regions of mainland Southeast Asia, and may even have been cultivated during the Formosans' pre-history. Along with the other vegetatively reproduced tubers and tree-fruits – particularly bananas and plantains (*musa*) which were native to Indonesia, the Moluccas and New Guinea – yams were to become of fundamental importance to them on their transoceanic explorations; and, as will be seen later, wherever they went, so went *musa* and taro. They almost certainly did not use any metals, but they had domestic animals including pigs, dogs and maybe chickens; and early on in their migrations through the islands they added bread-fruit, sago and coconut to their diet. Above all they introduced a new language, 'Austronesian'. The ancestry of the Austronesian languages, of which there are now some 40 sub-divisions, is difficult to trace; but, although none are still spoken on the mainland, it is possible that there is a distant relationship with Thai.

There is no precise evidence to explain the spread of the Austronesian languages. Most of the conclusions are based on 'glottochronology', an imprecise technique of mapping the changes in speech patterns that have taken place over the centuries. Archaeology can help to some extent by tracing the spread of the red-slipped pottery and ground adzes (quite different from the flaked stone tools of the more ancient inhabitants of the islands) found in rock-shelters and caves in the Philippines, Borneo, Sulawesi and Timor; but the archaeological evidence alone is insufficient to prove or disprove the course of their migrations with precision. In the course of their expansion from island to island the Mongoloid Austronesian speakers must have come into regular contact with the much earlier Australo-Melanesian peoples of what had once been Sundaland, creating complex genetic, linguistic, and cultural mixes of lighter and darker skinned people that still complicate the racial patterns of Indonesia. By the mid-second millennium B.C. Austronesian mariners had spread through the Philippines, Sulawezi, all the small islands of 'Wallacea'– but not to New Guinea, which still speaks Papuan languages – and on to Java, Borneo and Sumatra, and the coastal parts of Peninsular Malaya - though not the central highlands where people still speak Austro*asiatic* dialects.

Then, 3,500 years ago – roughly coincidental with the western spread of Austronesians - there appeared a new and remarkable culture in eastern Indonesia, that of the 'Lapita' people, known for their distinctive pottery and named after the type-site where it was first found in the Bismarck Archipelago off the coast of New Guinea. The Austronesian-speaking Lapita people were the forebears of the Polynesians, who, over the next five hundred years, colonised Tonga and Samoa and dozens of other small islands. These journeys were no mere single voyages of 'accidental' exploration. They were the organised and co-ordinated voyages of people who maintained contact with one another across vast areas of ocean. Even in the early years they were trading obsidian (for manufacturing spear and arrow heads) from volcanic New Britain to islands 1,650 miles distant. By 1,000 B.C. the trading range was even greater: obsidian from the same source has been found in sites ranging from Borneo to Fiji, across a distance of more than 4,000 miles. So, clearly the Lapita people maintained contact with fellow Austronesian mariners as far away as Borneo which lies as far to the west of the Bismark archipelago as Fiji is to the east.

By the turn of the first millennium A.D. the western Polynesians, whose colonies in Tonga and Samoa were by then 1000 years old, were ready for the greatest voyages of all – across the remaining open waters of the Pacific. Large double canoes carrying food plants and domestic animals sailed against the prevailing winds and currents to settle and colonise the Marquesas Islands by (at the latest) 300 A.D, then - perhaps a century later - Easter Island, one of the most isolated places on the face of the earth. Towards the end of the 1st millennium the Polynesians had colonised the Hawaiian chain and finally, by perhaps A.D. 900, the two great southern islands of New Zealand.

Why should we assume that Austronesians with the amazing skills of the Lapita mariners sailed only eastward, into an unknown ocean? With favourable winds behind them and lush islands on the horizon the lure of the setting sun must surely have been irresistible. Isn't it therefore reasonable to believe that they might also have explored beyond Borneo, where they were in some way or another involved in the obsidian trade, to Malaya and Sumatra, and beyond – even to India?

In 1920, James Hornell, at one time a fisheries officer working for the Indian government, and later one of the 20th century's most respected marine ethnographers, wrote an article asserting that *Polynesians*, having crossed probably from Sumatra, had became established in southern India at the latest by 500 BC, in pre-Dravidian times. (2) His opinion was based on the geographical distribution of outrigger canoes and 'brachycephalic' coastal people. "… a point of the highest importance in this connection is the fact that in common with Polynesians, they employ a single outrigger on their canoes, in striking contrast to the double form so characteristic of Malaysian small craft."

'Polynesians' - if they can be so called in India - would have been attracted by the rich fishing grounds along the west coast of Sri Lanka; pearls and *chank* shells in Palk Bay and the Gulf of Mannar; and the beaches of the Bombay Coast. "It is not surprising that there we find the Polynesian boat forms in great variety," said Hornell, "and, in common with peculiar Polynesian fishing devices, in continued high esteem by the local fishermen and divers." To which he might have added that the *blow-pipe*, once a weapon used throughout Austronesian-speaking Indonesia and parts of Melanesia, was also once used in precisely the same parts of India as the single-outrigger canoes.

Hornell went on to support his conclusions with anthropometric evidence which these days would be considered 'politically incorrect', and which may be one reason why his 'Polynesian hypothesis' seems to have been unceremoniously consigned to the 'crazy bin'. But although 'measuring heads' has been unfashionable for years – not just unfashionable, but positively eschewed - common sense suggests that differences in physical appearance must at times be valid indicators of origins. If you were to see a Fijian and an Eskimo walking down a street together in Surbiton, you would not have to be an anthropologist to spot the obvious differences between the two. However absurdly 'incorrect' it might be to point them out, these differences are not going to go away, and will always provide answers about origins. Thus to discredit Hornell's guardedly proffered evidence, as some have tried to do, would be foolish. In a nut-shell this is what he said: (shown in his own words on the web-site):

He pointed out that his 'head measurements' were confined to the Parawa fishing cast in South East India, and admitted the difficulties on account of the heterogeneity of the Austric-speaking people. He then compared the broad-headed (brachycephalic) Tulu, Canarese and Marathi-speaking people of the Kanarese coast who "are distinguished by *strong adherence to the outrigger design*" with the long-headed Dravidian Malayalis of the Malabar coast among whom the outrigger is "*singularly conspicuous by its absence...*". After detailed discussion he concluded: "I incline to think that these Parawas represent a part of that fierce Naga race described by ancient Tamil writers as in possession of the coast districts and with Negapatam as their chief town when the Tamils first ar rived in the south". If so, "*I would then identify the Nagas with an ancient coastal people of Polynesian affinity.*" (3)

Though this conclusion may seem 'way out' to many people, it received support from several contemporary 'stars' including the archaeologists Nicholas Krom and Stein Callenfels and the influential Southeast Asian historian, Heine-Geldern. (3) Hornell thought the Maldive islands may also have been peopled by his 'Polynesians' at a very early period – 'much earlier, I believe, than is generally supposed', for the Maldivians used fishing methods otherwise restricted to New Guinea and parts of the Pacific. He compared: (a) the way in which they lure sword-fish with a wooden model of a flying fish dangled from a rod, (b) the methods of attracting, catching and curing bonito, and (c) a method of catching small octopus by sinking a long rope from which hung numerous shells or narrow-necked earthenware jars into which the octopi crawled. (4)

In short, there is no reason to doubt that as long as 2,500 or 3,000 years ago brothers of the Polynesians were as active in the Indian Ocean as they were in the Pacific.

CHAPTER - 2

INDIA, ROME AND THE MEDITERRANEAN WORLD

The Old World of India.

Hornell's startling suggestion that 'Polynesians' settled in Peninsular India raises numerous questions. First and most important, were the Indians themselves ever great sailors? And, surely, if they were, why didn't their own boat designs supersede those of the archaic outrigger-people early on in their history? Was it that the outrigger concept was so brilliant that Indians embraced it as their own? Or did they, as some people would claim, actually invent the notion of the swift, versatile, aesthetically beautiful outrigger independently of any 'Polynesians'?

For answers to the boating history of India we have to begin by looking back at life about four thousand three hundred and fifty years ago, when the great King Sargon of Akkad was ruling in Mesopotamia; and the Indus Valley civilisation was in full flower around its centres at Mohenjo-Daro and Harappa. Both these civilisations drew their life-blood from the great rivers that sprawled through their fertile lands, with multifarious riverboats of wood, reeds, and skins criss-crossing their broad water highways. Even in those early days the Indus people traded regularly with the Mesopotamians, some goods being carried overland, and some in fleets of ships voyaging hesitantly along their coasts.

For the Mesopotamians the Persian Gulf was their lake, and their ships probably didn't venture far beyond the Indus. But the Harappans, when they were at their height, are known to have sailed far to the south, to the well constructed harbour of Lothal, at the head of the Gulf of Cambay, and to the most southerly of all the Harappan cities, Bhagatrav, 500 miles down the Indian coast from the Indus. Did they go further to gather ship-building timbers from the coastal forests beyond Bhagatrav as Arab sailors did centuries later? They may have done; but if they did there is no indication that they established permanent settlements far down the western Indian coast.

The Indus cultures began to decline around 1,800 B.C. for reasons that are not fully understood and which may have varied in different parts of their huge empire. In some places there is evidence of severe flooding; but Sir Mortimer Wheeler, writing of Mohendro-Daro, believed that the end, when it finally came about three thousand five hundred years ago, was dramatic and violent. (1) Ferocious invaders are thought to have swept through the city slaughtering men, women and children at random, leaving their bodies to rot in the ruins that were never to be rebuilt. Who the ransackers of Mohenjo-Daro were, and how the city finally met its end, is not entirely clear. But if Wheeler's scenario was right, those who plundered it are likely to have been an early wave of Indo-European speaking invaders who moved in from the northwest, the immediate precursors of the pastoralist Aryans who began their overland migration southward into India around 1,500 BC ... at roughly the same time as Austronesian sailors were nudging their canoes into the sheltered coves and mangrove forests of Borneo, Java, Sumatra and Malaya at the western limits of Indonesia.

It is generally held that these Indo-European newcomers were the founders of modern India. They brought with them their sacred language, Sanskrit, and over the centuries they created a treasure-trove of literature around which was built the Vedic philosophies and - subsequently - Hinduism, Buddhism and India's other great religions. By 1,000 BC the Aryans had begun to settle the Himalayan foothills, and the Ganges river. They learnt how to produce iron, they developed agricultural technology, and the use of iron tools. Their tribal organisations gradually gave way to powerful regional kingdoms. And by 500 BC – when the Austronesians on the far side of Indonesia had already begun to settle all the tiny islands of Micronesia, and when they may possibly have been settling in southern India also – the Aryans were poised to move southward into the Deccan and beyond.

The Aryans came originally from the steppes of what is now the Ukraine and had never known the sea. Their society was clearly defined by a variety of castes:- *brahmins*, the priests: *kshatriyas*, the warriors and aristocrats; *vaishyas*, merchants, artisans and cultivators; and the *shudras*, serfs and landless peasants. Though there was no specific mention of a *mariners* caste, riverine water-transport in various forms was clearly of importance to them. From an early date all the rivers of north west India had been important highways on which a number of sturdy river-craft were developed. When Alexander the Great, in 325 BC, needed to convey his army down the Indus to the ocean - some 8000 soldiers with their equipment and supplies - he was able to commandeer 800 – 1000 - 2000 vessels (depending on which authority one reads!) at very short notice.

Mauryan records from the turn of the third century B.C. relate that the Emperor Chandragupta established a Board of Admiralty, and a Naval Department headed up by a Superintendent of Ships who was entrusted with all matters relating to navigation in his kingdom. The Board of Admiralty's responsibilities included the control of inland navigation on rivers and lakes, the enforcement of regulations regarding the fording and crossing of rivers and collecting harbour dues. But the overall impression gained is that his duties were confined to inland and inshore coastal shipping, and that his office had little to do with serious, ocean-going, navigation. So the question arises once more; were the Mauryans or any other Indians, ever ocean-going mariners?

The expert on Indian maritime history, Radha Kumud Mookerji, writing in the early nineteen hundreds, was confident that Indians had indeed sailed across the oceans. "I have already said," he wrote, "that though Indian literature furnishes rather meagre evidence directly bearing on Indian shipping and shipbuilding, it abounds with innumerable references to sea voyages and sea-borne trade and the constant use of the ocean as the great highway of international intercourse and commerce..."(2)

But what sort of references was he alluding to?

In his book he delves deeply into ancient works such as the Buddhist *Jatarkas*, the Hindu *Mahabharata*, and a treatise on astronomy/astrology - the *Binhat Samhita* - all of which were written or up-dated as recently as the 5th and 6th c. A.D.. He comes up with dozens of obscure poetical myths and legends of great maritime feats, including one from the *Digha Nikaya* which is unusual for the fact that it "distinctly mentions sea voyages out of sight of land" – seemingly a rare and special occurrence. His stories are shot through with countless references to shipwrecks and other dramatic disasters such as; "His ship, however, sprang a leak in mid-ocean, but he is miraculously saved by a kind fairy in a magic ship filled with the seven treasures...." And on the evidence of just one Sanskrit work, the *Yukti Kalpataru*, Moorkerji makes a case for there having been huge ocean-going ships built in ancient India, carrying seven and eight hundred, even a thousand, people. But surely these were ships of fable? Collectively the references to early ocean-going shipping leave frustrating question-marks, and suggest that even if the ships of Aryan India did venture far out to sea, they were poorly built, and their sailors were inadequate for the task.

Mookerji depicts one of the large ships painted on the walls of the sixth or seventh century A.D. caves at Ajanta in northwest India. The Ajanta boats tell nothing about truly 'ancient' shipping. Furthermore several

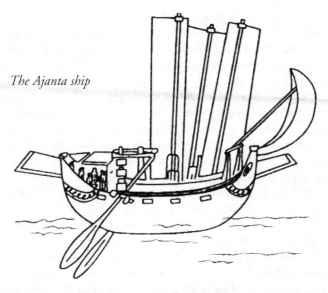

The Ajanta ship

features on the boats that are depicted – for instance the *artemon* foresails - suggest that they could have been strongly influenced by Greek or Roman ships, and offer less than no proof that they were 'Indian'. The high-point of Mookerji's work, 'proving' India's maritime proficiency, is his description and portrayal of the magnificent 'Indian' ships carved on the famous 'Indian' temple at Borobudur in Central Java. But though Indians may have played a major part in designing and building the famous Buddhist temple, it has subsequently been shown, beyond any doubt, that the seven beautiful outrigger ships depicted on it walls were not Indian – but Indonesian. We will come back to these Borobudur reliefs later.

On their slow, steady, thousand year migration overland through India, the Aryans encountered numerous hostile, aboriginal tribes amongst whom were the Tamils, speakers of Dravidian languages, who, according to the Mahabharata, had themselves begun to migrate south from Mongolia in the 13th century B.C. (3) Though the individual identities of the early Tamil tribes have been blurred in modern times, they too were once divided into castes with special expertise:- the *Villavar*, bowmen, from the Dravidian word *vil* meaning a bow; the *Minavar*, fishermen, from *meen*, meaning fish; and the *Thereat*, or "Sea Kings", the "Riders of the Waves". These last were further divided into several far-flung families:- the Thirayar of Bengal; the Thirayar of China; the Thirayar of Burma; the Thirayar of Ceylon; and the Thirayar of 'Pallavam'. They were said to be "... a great seafaring race, whose home appears to have been lower Bengal and who travelled by sea to Burmah, Cochin China, Ceylon and Southern India."

But surely this last claim is spurious. Like the Aryans, the Dravidians' by all accounts were primarily pastoral people whose migrations were overland into country occupied by various primitive neolithic tribes, which included one of particular interest called the 'Nagas'. Aside from Hornell's hypothesis mentioned in the last chapter, there seems to be confusion as to precisely who, or what, the Nagas were. Some notable authors on India do not even give them human form, but have seen them as mythical creatures: "The snake-spirits, half human but with a serpent's tail ..."(4) or "...harmless snake worshipping savages..."(5) They may, or may not, be related to the modern Nagas of the Assamese highlands, a collection of tribes whose roots stem from different places, some from the hinterland of India, some from western China and others from the coast of Southeast Asia,. But V. Kanakasabhai, a noted Tamil author, saw the Naga as very real people: "a very numerous and civilised race ... who at one time or another ruled a great portion of India, Ceylon and Burma". Likewise, S.U. Deraniyagala, referring to Naga in Sri Lanka, thought they might have been the "protohistoric Early Iron Age" peoples of the island, adding that: "It is significant that the chronicles refer to a settlement of the Nagas at Kelaniya (in Sri Lanka) at ca. 600-500 BC (ie. in the time of Buddha)." (6)

Tamil poems of the 1st century A.D. relate how the people of Indra sent five giants to Muchukunta, the Chola king, to help him defeat the Nagas of Kaviripatanam. Is it pure chance that Kaviripatanam was a coastal city south of Pondicherry, close by modern Nagappattinam? ... the city which Kanakasabhai had singled out as the chief Naga port when the Tamils came south? ... and the city that James Hornell believed to have been the centre of the 'Polynesian' incursions along the Indian coast? As there is no mention anywhere else of *Tamil* sailors in Cochin China, Burma, or other places to which the *Thirayar* were supposed to have sailed, the odds must be heavily on the phantom 'Riders of the Waves' having been Austronesian outrigger men whom the Tamils met on the coast, and who, over the centuries acquired Tamil identity and became absorbed into Tamil culture. The point made by G.R. Tibbetts, who wrote extensively about Indian Ocean sailing in pre-European days, that: "The majority of nineteenth century scholars ... were quite definite that the Indians were not sailors" has a solid ring of truth about it. (7)

The Mediterranean World.

Increasing trade between Mesopotamia and the Indus valley four thousand years ago may have caused the Egyptians to sit up and take note. For in the reign of the twelfth dynasty Pharaoh, Sesostris 3rd, they began to look seriously for better ways to reach the Indian Ocean than with camel caravans across the desert.

The Egyptians had long been importing myrrh, ebony, electrum (a natural alloy of gold and silver), frankincense, ivory and other good things, from the mysterious land of 'Punt', but precisely where that was is still not clear. Did the son of Cheops' black Puntite' slave come from somewhere down the African coast? Was the 'dwarf' brought back on one of the expeditions a Bushman from East Africa? Or might Punt have been somewhere even further afield – in northwest India perhaps, where according to Basil Greenhill, a past director of The National Maritime Museum, there are river boats still in use even today that closely resemble those of ancient Egypt? Wherever it was, an expedition to Punt involved the Egyptians in much tedious effort. Having no useful timber of their own, wood with which to build the 'Puntite' ships had to be brought from the Lebanon; barged hundreds of miles up the Nile; and *portaged* across the desert to ship-building yards on the Red Sea. Likewise, any booty procured on expeditions to 'the land beyond the rising sun' had to be carried back over the same hot and tedious desert route on the backs of men and camels.

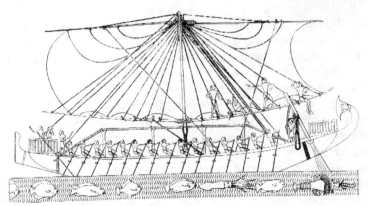

A ship of Queen Hatshepsut's reign for making the journey to Punt. C 1,500 B.C.

One senses that Sesostris must have been frustrated by these cumbersome problems, persuading him to order a canal to be cut to link the Nile Delta with the Red Sea. Not much is known about this first 'Suez' canal or the sort of ships that might have sailed through it. There is solid evidence that Egyptians were by then master ship-builders, and had been for centuries. Proof of this can be seen in Cairo, in the elegant vessel built for the Pharaoh Cheops more than six hundred years before Sesostris came to power. The famous Cheops ship was discovered carefully dismantled in over 1,200 separate pieces in a special tomb beneath his pyramid where, in the dry, airless, desert conditions they had remained in pristine condition for over four and a half thousand years. (8) As the pieces were reassembled, they gradually materialised into an exquisite vessel 141 feet long, with a 19 feet beam, made from planks of Lebanese cedar, some of which were 70 feet

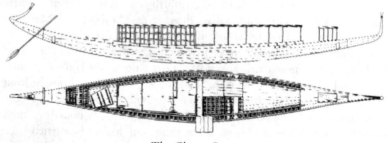

The Cheops Boat

long, all immaculately sewn together with *halfa* grass. Though the Cheops boat was not an ocean going vessel, the technological mastery its builders displayed suggests that it must have been well within the power of Egyptians to build ships to sail around the shores of the western Indian Ocean to India had they wanted to.

During the few centuries following Sesostris' reign the Indus culture began to decline; and alas, so too did the Pharaoh's canal. Once it had filled with wind-blown sand, no further effort was made to link the Mediterranean with the Indian Ocean for nearly another thousand years. But Sesostris had pioneered an idea that would not be forgotten; and when Pharaoh Necho - the man whose Phoenician fleet circumnavigated Africa – came to power in the 6th century B.C., he set about building a new canal (purportedly at a cost of 100,000 lives) from the Pelusian branch of the Nile to the Bitter Lakes. This canal, in its turn, was rebuilt and extended by Darius 1st from the Nile to the Red Sea sometime between 521 and 485 B.C. Having silted up yet again, it was re-opened by the Athenians; and two hundred years later by Ptolemy Philadelphus.

Though surprisingly abandoned during the early Roman rule, when they were certainly building fleets of transport ships in the Red Sea as well as the Persian Gulf, another effort to reopen a canal was made by the Emperor Trajan at the end of the 1st century A.D.; and this time the canal was maintained by Hadrian and the Antonines until the end of the 2nd century. As Roman power declined the sand again took over, until in the early days of Islam, the canal was re-opened for the purpose of transporting Egyptian grain to Mecca: but by the 8th c. it was deliberately closed by the ruler Al-Mansur on grounds of 'national security', to stave off a perceived threat of invasion from the east... and there the idea rested for another thousand years until Ferdinand de Lessep's day.

It is likely that sea/land trade between the Mediterranean and the Indian Ocean had been an established fact for a thousand of years. Apart from the flow between the Indus and Babylonia, Egyptian goods were certainly reaching the Middle Euphrates by 1700 BC, maybe even earlier. However, to suggest that sea-trade between the Old World and *Southeast Asia* has been going on for as long might seem to many as stretching the limits of credulity too far. Yet there is even solid archaeological evidence for just that.

While excavating a merchant's house in a 1,700 B.C. site at Terqa on the Middle Euphrates, archaeologist Giorgio Buccellati was amazed to find a jar that contained what looked like *cloves*. Sounding almost as though he distrusted his own eye, he wrote: "The plant remains which we called cloves are ostensibly so at first look, and were also so identified by Kathleen Galvin, who was our palaeobotanist at the time."(9) But what if there *were* a few cloves? Why was this so extraordinary? Simply because there was only one place on earth where cloves grew in those days, which was in the Moluccas, a group of small islands on the far side of the Indonesian archaepelago.

This in itself was an extraordinary discovery. But counter-balancing it on the Indonesian side in a find that matched it for weirdness, British archaeologists found sheep or goat remains in habitations of roughly the same age (1,500 B.C.) on the even more remote island of Timor several hundred miles south of the Moluccas. (10) As it is generally agreed that sheep and goats were first domesticated in the Middle East where they are indigenous, how on earth did they get to Timor so long ago? One obvious way might be that they were driven overland to Southeast Asia, then by sea. But as the British archaeologist Julian Reade has pointed out, it is almost inconceivable that such animals would have survived months of travel through hundreds of miles of dank, wet, tropical forests. And even if they had, someone would still have had to carry them across hundreds of miles of water from the mainland to Timor. So how did cloves get from the

Moluccas to Mesopotamia? … and how did animals get from the Middle East to Timor at such an early date?

There is only one viable possibility, which brings us straight back to Hornell's 'Polynesian' hypothesis:- that it was 'phantom' Austronesian boatmen who, soon after their exodus from Formosa, had moved through the islands to the west.

According to *1 Kings ix*: in about 1,000 B.C.: "… Hiram sent in the navy his servants, shipmen that had knowledge of the sea, with the servants of Solomon. And they came to Ophir, and fetched from thence gold, four hundred and twenty talents, and brought it to King Solomon" and "…once every three years, the ships of Tarshish came bringing gold and silver, ivory, apes and peacocks…" Talk of peacocks, in particular, suggests that some of the goods must have come originally from India; and the linguistic evidence points specifically to southern India. The names adopted in the Middle East for apes (*kapim*), and peacocks (*tukim*), for instance, and later the words for rice (*oryza*), and ginger (*zingiber*) were all adaptations - not of the Sanskrit or Pali languages of Aryan India - but of *Dravidian* words from the Tamil south.

Because, to this day, no one knows for sure where Ophir or Tarshish were, and what sort of ships were used, we are left with a big question mark, wondering: 'Where, exactly, did these things come from?' and 'Who brought them?' With the interchange of goods between the furthest islands of the Indonesian archipelago, southern India, and the Middle East, does it not look as though it might have been Indo-Polynesians or Indonesians who were the most likely carriers?

Greeks and Romans and the Spice of Life.

By 500 BC rich Greeks had peacocks in their gardens, disturbing their neighbours' peace. Canal or no canal, long before the end of the first millennium B.C. trade between Greece, Rome and India had become an essential part of life. Oriental silks, cottons, and other luxuries, were in great demand among the urban upper classes in the Mediterranean. The seaways as well as the overland routes to the East were a hive of activity. Just prior to the turn of the Christian millennium Strabo wrote:- "I found that about one hundred and twenty ships sail (regularly) from Myos Hermos (in the Red Sea) to India". Ships that the Romans were using on this route were probably of medium size – maybe 500 tons – and their strong, jointed and iron–bound construction gave them an advantage over the Arab and Persian boats in that they could sail in all but the worst weathers, and their strength made them less vulnerable if attacked. In the mid-1st c. A.D.

Hippalus, a Greek captain, is credited with having 'discovered' the 'monsoon' routes from southern Arabia to India. (11) From then on, if Roman ships left Myos Hermos in July they could sail with the summer 'northerlies' down the Red Sea in time to catch the southwest monsoon to take them through the Gulf of Aden, across the Arabian Sea and directly across the Ocean to the Malabar coast of India. The return trip would have been scheduled for some time in November, when the 'gentle north-easterlies' provided a favourable breeze through to the entrance to the Red Sea. This not only shortened the journey, but added immensely to the security of cargoes which were no longer threatened either by pirates hugging the Hadramaut coast, or by desert Arabs on the overland caravan routes.

To guard against pirates on the high seas, Greek and Roman vessels habitually carried archers on board. The discipline and efficiency of these *Yavana* archers (*Yavanas* = *Iaones*, the Greek's name for themselves; i.e. 'foreigners') impressed the Tamil rulers, many of whom subsequently employed them as guards in their own cities and palaces. In the northern

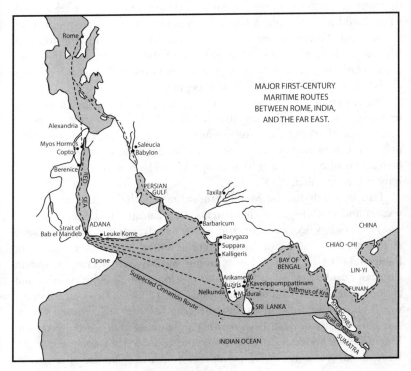

MAJOR FIRST-CENTURY
MARITIME ROUTES
BETWEEN ROME, INDIA,
AND THE FAR EAST.

part of India, the strength and efficiency of the Roman legions came to be looked upon as an essential bulwark against Parthian and Sassanian incursions, and close diplomatic relations developed between several Indian rulers and Rome. As early as 20 BC, so Strabo tells us, the Indian king of the Pandyas on the Coromandel coast sent an embassy to Augustus to seek an alliance - the first of many such embassies from India. Indian elephants were used in Syrian warfare

For over five hundred years, from the time of Mark Anthony to that of Justinian, a substantial community of colonial Romans thrived in several southern India ports. In some places on the Coromandel coast brick lighthouses were built in which fires blazed at night to guide ships safely into port. In 200 A.D. it is said there were 1000 Roman troops stationed in Muziris to protect their merchants. Here also they erected a temple to Augustus; and Tamil poets wrote glowing descriptions of the 'Romanised' town. "Fish is bartered for paddy," wrote one, "which is brought in baskets to the houses; sacks of pepper are brought from the houses to the market; gold received from the ships in return for articles sold, is brought to shore in barges at Muchiris, where the music of the surging sea never ceases, and where Kudduvan (the Chera King) presents to visitors the rare products of the sea and the mountains." Another wrote of "...the thriving town of Muchiris, where the beautiful large ships of the Yavanas, bringing gold, come splashing the white foam on the waters of the Periyar which belongs to the Cherala, and return laden with pepper."

Pepper, an item of particular value, was to remain of major importance for many years, a fact that Pliny the Elder found odd:- "It is quite surprising that the use of pepper has come so much in fashion ... pepper has nothing in it that can plead as a recommendation to either fruit or berry, its only desirable quality being a certain pungency; and yet it is for this that we import it from India!" (13)

Lists of goods for the Mediterranean trade included food and drink, textiles and clothing, household items, tools, unspecified *raw* materials, *costly* materials, spices and aromatics, drugs and dyes, slaves, and items such as the exquisite 1st c. A.D. ivory figurine found buried in the ashes of Pompeii. (14) Huge demand arose among wealthy Romans for fine Indian cloth, unguents, perfumes, pearls, and precious stones. Silks, muslins and cottons were sold at fabulous prices; the first of these - silk - being literally worth its weight in gold during the reign of the 3rd century Caesar Aurelian. A papyrus describes a typical consignment of goods shipped from Muchiris (near modern Cochin) to Alexandria, for a rich Roman merchant. It included over a thousand pounds of aromatic spikenard, over 4,700 pounds of ivory, and nearly 800 pounds of textiles with a total value of 131 talents, which, at the time, would have been sufficient to purchase 2,400 acres of Egypt's best farmland. And if these goods were shipped on a 500 ton vessel, there might have been as many as 150 such consignments on board for that one journey.

In AD 77, lamenting the extravagance and reckless spending of Rome's rich and famous, Pliny wrote despairingly that there was "no year in which India did not drain the Roman Empire of a hundred million sesterces … so dearly do we pay for our luxury and our women." Tiberius grumbled that "the ladies and their baubles are transferring our money to foreigners." And even during Christ's lifetime, the emperor Augustus, shamed by the widespread lowering of standards, passed a law forbidding the wearing of transparent Indian silks on the grounds of indecency.

The trade between Rome and India may have reached its peak during the reign of Augustus (27B.C.- 14 A.D.), although archaeological evidence from Arikamedu (Pondicherry) the great bead-making centre in south-eastern India, suggests it was a little later. Under the emperor Vespasian,(69– 79), a man of military discipline and down-to-earth tastes, a new era in social manners was ushered in, and "the simpler habits of the Plebeians and the Provincials prevailed over the reckless luxury and dissipation in which the highest classes had so long indulged." Rome's inhabitants began to spend less on perfumes, ornaments, and precious stones, and after the death of Caracalla in 217 Indian trade began to decline still further. The importation of spices and commodities such as pepper, however, continued for many more years. Indeed, such was the demand for it that when, in 408, the Barbarians were at the gates of Rome, Alaric, agreed to spare the city in return for a ransom that included 3,000 pounds of Indian pepper.

It was not a one-way trade from India to Rome. There is abundant textual evidence of the *Roman* goods that were shipped to India, supported by physical evidence in the form of amphorae, which carried wine and oil from several parts of the Mediterranean, Italic Arretine wares from Arezzo in Tuscany, and classical intaglios and seals – many of which have been found throughout Southern India and at Mantai in Sri Lanka. Large amounts of Roman coinage – including gold *aurei* - have been found, with the majority in the far south of India where the locals sometimes used them as their own local currency. Even Roman lead was imported for use in the minting of local coinage in Satavahana.

Some of the earliest of the copper coins, which were locally minted at end of the first millennium BC in the Bay of Bengal, had images of high-prowed ships, and vessels with two stubby masts on one side.(15) Were these Roman ships, or Indian? The depictions were so crude that the ships could have been from practically anywhere. Indeed, such was the extent of the Indian Ocean trade that one scholar has argued that the period "when the Classical civilisations of the Mediterranean encountered Buddhist India and Han China" should be looked upon as the beginning of the 'World System'! (16)

All this traffic seems to have been carried in Greek and Roman ships. The classical people of the Mediterranean seem to have ruled the waves unopposed. The Persians and Arabs still clung to the coasts; and there is no evidence whatsoever that *Indian* ships ever conveyed goods across the ocean to the Red Sea for onward shipment to Rome.

There was, however, one grey area. There were one or two spices that reached the Mediterranean after transhipment in the Horn of Africa which were *not* carried on Roman ships. So how did they get there?

CHAPTER - 3

"All these stories are nonsense. In fact cinnamomum, which is the same thing as cinnamum, grows in 'Ethiopia', which is linked by intermarriage with the Cave Dwellers. These buy it from their neighbours and bring it over vast seas on rafts which have no rudders to steer them, no oars to push them, no sails to propel them, indeed no motive power at all but man alone and his courage. ... They say that their traders take almost five years there and back, and that many die. On the return journey they take glassware and bronzeware, clothing, brooches, bracelets and necklaces so here is one more trade route that exists chiefly because women follow fashion."
Pliny the Elder, Natural History. 23 – 79 A.D.

CINNAMON AND CASSIA

Women and fashion? Would those poor chaps really have slogged all that way, risking life and limb for five years, on unwieldy rafts, propelled at best by paddles, just to fetch a few inferior dresses and some mixed costume-jewellery? Nonsense! The compelling reasons, the driving forces, the real value of their voyaging must surely have been in the taste-buds of rich Romans' tongues, for the finest fragments of nubile cinnamon bark and flowers that they lovingly carried on their out-bound journeys from the East.

There were three varieties of cinnamon important in the Mediterranean world: Cinnamon leaf, or *malabathrum*, course cinnamon bark, called *cassia*; and the more delicate bits of bark and the flower tips, which, to the Romans, was the true *cinnamon*. The first of these, *malabathrum*, was the most common, and had the lowest value. It came from a tree variety that grew in China and India, and when harvested, the leaves were bundled and tied up in large balls for export to Rome by various routes, overland as well as by sea on Roman ships. It was used as a condiment; in making aromatic unguents; and for flavouring wine. The trade in *malabathrum* was open, and the Romans knew where it came from. (1)

It was the other two varieties, *Cinnamomum cassia* Blume, and *Cinnamomum zeylanicum* Nees; which were the best, and which for centuries were surrounded by mystery and misconception by all the Western writers. Herodotus thought they came from Arabia, and so did Theophrastus: Agatharchides said Sabaea; Philostratus, India; Strabo simply said the 'cinnamon-country', probably meaning India; an anonymous papyrus said from 'Trogodytica' (meaning North-east Africa somewhere). Although Pliny said 'Ethiopia', neither *cassia* nor true *cinnamon*, nor anything like them, ever grew in Arabia, Ethiopia, Somalia, or India. Both were only obtainable from Southeast Asia and some of the Indonesian islands where in those days they grew wild.

Pliny's description, odd though it is, does give us a few clues as to who the courageous mariners might been. First the 'Ethiopians' and the 'Cave dwellers' - two sets of people who live apart, but are related by marriage. Recent archaeology has confirmed that there were indeed 'cave dwellers' on the island of Mafia, off the Tanzanian coast, as long ago as the third century BC. They had domesticated chickens (chickens came to Africa either from India or Malaysia). They hunted and fished, and cultivated several food plants. (2) They had grey/black glazed pottery like that of the Indian early iron-age; also pots of a marl clay similar to those of the Nile delta. Mafia island being some miles off-shore, the cave-dwellers, must have had boats. And as Mafia lies opposite the Rufiji delta where Rhapta, a town associated with sewn boats, is said to have been located their craft may have been more than mere dugout canoes hacked from a single log. Bushmen, who would have been the people living in the hinterland at the time, are never known to have been seamen: so who were these cave-dwellers on the island of Mafia?

Pliny knew the Berbers and Arabs well enough, and if his 'Ethiopians' and 'Cave Dwellers' had been either of them he would have said so. They obviously differed from any other people he knew. Likewise, Pliny must have known about the Arab boats that sailed regularly in the Red Sea and around the coasts of Arabia; thus the extraordinary rafts on which the cinnamon arrived obviously weren't Arab vessels. That they were unlike any other boats he had previously seen or heard about is plain from the way he wrote about them. Compounding the mystery in Pliny's eyes must have been the fact that his extraordinary raft-people did not deliver their cargoes directly to Roman merchants. We know that they brought their goods to entrepots in the Horn of Africa; to Opone (Ras Hafun); to Socotra; to Mosylon and other ports on the Berber coast opposite Aden. In these ports their cargoes were purchased by Arab traders who took them up the Red Sea to Egypt, and finally to the Mediterranean.

On the other hand there are good grounds for arguing that the 'raft-men' may have been Indonesian voyagers. The 'rafts' were probably some

*Hawaiian Canoe
(J.Cook 1773-74)*

*Double Canoe.Tonga
(J.Cook 1773-74)*

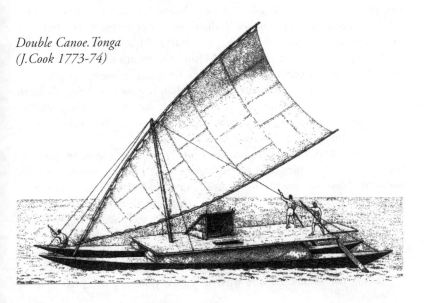

sort of multi-hulled canoes with platforms, not dissimilar to some of the large voyaging canoes used to explore the Pacific. (3) Absence of 'rudders to steer them' might simply mean that they had *prahu*-style steering-oars rather than axial rudders such as Pliny would have known. Like so many Indonesian and Polynesian boats, even in modern times, in contrary winds or still air they would have been propelled – fast - by banks of sailors with paddles – not long oars such as the Romans would have used. As there is every likelihood that the sort of Indonesian sailors who made such a journey would have been dark-skinned, his description of them being 'Ethiopians' would be justified. If they *were* Indonesians, they probably came across the ocean with favourable winds directly from northern Sumatra to the Horn of Africa via the Maldive Islands (see Hornell's comments in Chap 1), avoiding the ports of southern India and Ceylon, thereby remaining unobserved by Roman merchants. Pliny said they were 'linked by intermarriage' with the 'cave men', which means they probably spoke the same or similar languages. If so, this fits well with the hypothesis that there may already have been Indonesians residing on Africa's coast. All this is feasible, even probable; but we are getting into a guessing game based on the evidence of one Roman writer; and it would be risky to be dogmatic without further support.

So what other alternatives are there? Despite what has been said about Indian shipping, could these rafts possible have been Indian? The Greek 'master' who wrote the *Periplus of the Erythraean Sea* in the mid-1st c. A.D. mentioned four specific types of 'Indian' ships. Two of them, the *trappaga* and the *kotymba* were obviously pilot boats: "They manoeuvre (ships heading up the river to Barygaza) right from the mouth of the gulf through the shoals and tow them to pre-determined stopping places; they get them under way when the tide comes in and, when it goes out, bring them to anchor in certain harbours and basins." They were probably the ancestors of the dhow-like Indian *batellas, dhangis* and *kotirs* – sturdy ships which, in those days, hugged the rivers and coasts.

But the author of the Periplus also wrote of two larger ships in southern India. "Kamara (modern Kavirippattinam), Poduke (Pondicherry), Sopatma (Madras?) are the home ports for local boats that sail along the coast as far as Limyrike (Malabar) and others called *sangara*, that are very big dugout canoes held together by a yoke, as well as for the very big *kolandiaphonta* that sail across to Chryse and the Ganges region." ... 'Chryse' here referring to the Indonesian islands and the rich coast of Southeast Asia. (3)

Taking the *kolandiaphonta* first, it is now generally accepted that far from being an Indian name for an Indian vessel this was a straightforward transcription of the common Chinese term '*Kun-lun-po*', meaning 'a ship of Kun-lun', the Chinese name for Sumatra or Java. The sturdy *Kun-lun-po* were not Indiamen, but Indonesian ships which plied across the Bay of Bengal and up both the east and south-western coasts of Southern India.

As for the other vessel, Lionel Casson in his translation of the *Periplus Maris Erythræi* pointed out that in Tamil-form, *sangara* equals *shangadam*, which the Portuguese borrowed as *jangar* or *jangada* meaning a 'raft', or more specifically, a "double platform canoe made by placing a floor of boards across the two boats." One of the 20th century's leading writers on the Roman/Indian trade, E.H. Warmington, was very specific about southern Indian seafaring when he wrote:- "The Tamils of the south did not sail across to the West, but instead supplied foreign ships in Cochin backwaters (from large canoes, etc)…" He went on to comment on the *sangara* that it was apparently "… very large, made of single logs bound together, apparently double canoes either Malay in origin or corresponding to the *jangar* of Malabar today."(5) Rather than contradicting him, most pundits seem to agree that the *sangara* is likely to have been derived from an Indonesian twin-hulled design: and obviously it sounds suspiciously like the cassia-carrying 'raft' so eloquently described by Pliny.

Some writers have claimed that Arab and Sassanian Persian boats sailed to the southern Indian ports. George Hourani, the expert on Arab shipping, says the furthest the Persian Gulf *dhows* went was to a few anchorages on the Malabar coast to fetch hardwoods for building their ships. Warmington said "North-west India traded in its own ships with North-east Africa, freely to Cape Guardafui, and then in conjunction with Greeks and Arabs … (and) by an understanding with Arabians dating from very ancient times Indian ships could and did trade freely with the Somali coast". But Hourani denies categorically that Indian ships were ever in evidence down the coast of Arabia, which would have been inevitable if they had been *en route* to Africa.

Then Warmington contradicts himself: "From what we have said above, it is clear that the activities of Indians by sea after the discovery of the monsoons by a western power did not increase to any large extent, except in the matter of local navigation round their own coasts." He says that a few Indians did come in pursuit of trade, but that they were not in high repute among their countrymen, adding "just as Brahmans of high caste today suffer penalties if they cross the sea." The *Periplus* refers to vessels sailing from North-west India to 'far-side ports' (i.e. ports on the Horn of Africa) carrying cotton cloth, grains, ghee, sesame oil, cane sugar and other items (notably absent from the list are cassia and cinnamon.). But the *Periplus* makes no specific mention of *Indian* ships, leaving open the more likely probability that this trade was handled entirely by *Arabs* who, with the Romans, covered the Gulf of Aden and the entrance to the Red Sea.

CHAPTER - 4

CHINA AND THE KUN-LUN-PO

If, two thousand years ago, Rome was the dominant power in the West, the unquestioned masters in the East were the Chinese. Apart from being the political power-house, China had the edge on everyone in industry, technology, commercial acumen, culture, literature – in fact, in virtually every field except one: nautical.

China's nautical history is enmeshed in curious enigmas and contradictions. All too often amazing technology was frustrated by the iron hand of politics - of what could-have-been or might-have-been if her Admirals and Master-mariners had ever, except on the rarest occasions, been given a freer hand. For a brief period China built some of the largest sailing ships that have ever put to sea. Yet throughout most of its history, China's ever inward-looking, self-devouring attitudes meant that it played only a minor role in the maritime affairs of the world - a state of affairs that had a direct effect on political developments in Southeast Asia.

By 500 B.C. China had already developed a wide variety of vessels. Ships of all sorts and sizes plied up and down it's immense river systems: huge sailing-rafts traded close inshore from Siberia to Indochina: fleets of up to 2000 war-canoes, each 70 or 80 feet long, propelled by paddlers and with deck-castles for archers, were undertaking punitive expeditions against fractious states up and down the coast; the inshore-seas and rivers must have been abuzz with vessels of a thousand varieties. (1)

But however fine the boats, or courageous the sailors, they never ventured far out to sea.

Some stories suggest that by the 4th century B.C. there may have been glimmers of change on the horizon. They tell of the kings of Chhi, Wei, Hsuan and Yen who successively sent people abroad to seek fabulous islands where it was said that life-prolonging drugs and other secrets of immortality were to be found. Many of these expeditions, such as that of Hsu Fu in the service of Chhin Shih Huang Ti the Prince of Huai-Nan, sailed away never to be heard of again. There is scholarly speculation that he and the 'three thousand young men and girls at (his) disposal' found an idyllic life in Japan; or that Hsu Fu and his band might even have reached America, and been unable to return. And despite all the uncertainties and risks of contrary winds and sea-monsters that invariably led to failure, it seems the Chinese persevered with these expeditions, continuing to despatch them from time to time until the turn of the millennium.

When Hsu Fu set off with all his young men and girls, the Lapita people had long since occupied all the islands of Melanesia, and had already been trading obsidian over vast distances for nearly a thousand years. Cloves shipped from the far away Moluccas, had been known to the Chinese since several centuries B.C; and as they must until then have been brought to China by merchants-sailors from the islands, could it be that cloves were one of the life-prolonging drugs the kings of Chhi, Wei, Hsuan and Yen sought to obtain directly from source in their own ships? The same went for other spices and rare products for which the Chinese were dependent upon merchants of Java, Sumatra, Borneo, and Sulawesi, who delivered their goods to Chinese cities in their own ships.

The world knew about China, and China knew about the world; but while others dominated the inter-island trade, and were successfully exploring further and further afield, China, despite sporadic efforts to seek the elixirs of life, seemed to be hugging her navies close to her bosom, letting others risk the wrath of pirates and the elements to do the long-distance fetching and carrying for her.

The fact that, even in the first few centuries of the Christian era, Chinese ships did not venture into the Indian Ocean cannot be seen as a reflection on their *technical* genius. By the late 6th century A.D., when Britain was subsiding into the dark ages, Chinese ship technology was so advanced that, so it is said, warships were being constructed with as many as five decks, standing more than a hundred feet from the water, carrying 800 marines in addition to the seamen to man them. Nevertheless as late as the 5th and 7th centuries – according to the records - most Chinese travellers to the Indian Ocean seem to have travelled on *Kun-lun* ships rather than their own.

The 6th century saw the development of an important trade between Sassanid Persia and China. Cargoes from Persia included aromatic resins, pistachio nuts, drugs, perfumes, and brocades. Oliver Wolters, in his book on *Early Indian Commerce*, (2) seemed quite clear about who was doing the shipping:- " ... what is known of Asian shipping in the fifth and sixth centuries has indicated that at least in respect of the voyage between Indonesia and China the Chinese knew of Indonesian and not of Persian and Indian shipping. Nor does the evidence at present available from other sources contradict the Chinese evidence. The conclusion must be that the shippers of the 'Persian' cargoes were for the most part Indonesians." Cosmas Indicopleustes, in the first half of the 6th century, recorded that Ceylon held a 'central position' in the Persian trade, their goods being carried from there to China - not in Persian ships at that time, but in *Kun-lun* ships from the islands.

In the 7th century the famous Chinese pilgrim, I Tsing, went, with others, to India on vessels provided by an Indonesian ruler. The same I Tsing refers to Tongking being visited by peoples of the *K'un-lun* countries, by which he means Indonesia. And by then *K'un-lun* merchants were also sailing annually to Canton where, with a striking display of confidence on one occasion, they are said to have killed an uncooperative and unacceptably corrupt governor. By way of additional confirmation that *K'un-lun* ships were involved in the Persia/China trade, there were occasional complaints from customers (nothing much has changed over the years!) that the shippers were adding cheap, second-grade *Indonesian* resins to the higher quality Persian goods to swell the profits! (3)

By the middle of the 8th century merchant ships of nearly 600 'tuns and tunnage' were being built in China; rather larger than the average ships of the Spanish Armada 800 years later. The writer Wang Tang said they were mostly owned by merchants trading up and down the Chinese coast. Sailors lived on them with their wives and families; there were 'gardens' on board, as well as the owner's slave-girls, and musicians. But clearly these large merchantmen still didn't venture far from the coast, for Wang Tang describes the ships that did:- "The sea-going junks (*hai po*)" he said, "are *foreign* ships. Every year they come to Canton and An-i. Those from Ceylon are the largest, the companion-ways alone being several tens of feet high. Everywhere the various kinds of merchandise are stacked up. ... When these ships go to sea, they take with them white (homing) pigeons, so that in case of shipwreck the birds can return with messages." (4)

The largest vessels may have *sailed* from Ceylon, but they would undoubtedly have been Indonesian:- a) because, so far as we know there were no such large Ceylonese ships existing at the time, and b) because Indonesians controlled the Strait of Malacca and the Sunda Strait – the only seaways between Ceylon and China. As there is at least one Chinese record specifically referring to Indonesian vessels being chartered to merchants from other parts of Asia and as every merchant doing business with China should not necessarily be seen as being an 'Indonesian' (as Wolters said, the Indonesian contribution should be seen as supplying *transport* facilities), this may have been the case with the ships Wang Tang referred to. The conclusion must be that shipping to and from China and Southern India was handled, if not 100%, predominantly by Indonesian sailors in Indonesian vessels in the employ of, or on charter to, Chinese, Persian and Indian merchants.

If, then, the bulk (if not all) the 'Indian' shipping early in the first millennium A.D. was, in reality Indonesian, it would not be unreasonable to assume – as already suggested - that it was *K'un-lun* – Indonesian – ships that were involved in the Mediterranean trade, bringing cinnamon and cassia and other spices directly to Ras Hafun and the Berber ports, either via the Maldive islands; or straight across from Sumatra.

There is also a hint of corroboration of this in Chinese literature.

By the end of the 1st millennium B.C., when the Greek and Roman trade was at its height, China was already recognised as the region's super-power. Her influence was inexorably spreading; and despite the predominance of Southeast Asian and Indonesian shipping, Chinese vessels were already coasting to the Malay Peninsular, as well as Java and Sumatra.

But if that was the limit of the known world for her *mariners*, her *envoys* were beginning to explore the world beyond. The *Chhien Han Sha*, written about this time, described how Han traders were spreading their fingers into new markets in Indonesia and beyond, despite being unable to rely entirely on their own Chinese shipping for conveying them and their goods:- "There are superintendent interpreters belonging to the civil service personnel who recruit crews and go to sea to trade for brilliant pearls, glass, strange gems and other exotic products, giving in exchange gold and various silks. In the countries where they come the officials and their followers are provided with food and handmaidens. Merchant ships of the barbarians (may) transport them (part of the way) home again. But (these barbarians) also, to get more profit (sometimes) rob people and kill them. Moreover (the travellers) may encounter storms and so drown. Even if nothing (of this kind happens, they are) away for several years."

Finds of Chinese pottery and coins of this period in Borneo, Java, Sumatra and Dong Son (Annam) support this text, and stone sculptures in southern Sumatra (Pasema) bear a close resemblance to the Han style. "...It is arresting to think" wrote Jo Needham, the great British expert on China, "that Chinese merchant-officials walked with Roman citizens from Greece, Syria and Egypt on the quays of Arikamedu" on the Coromandel coast of India. Once again, however, it must be stressed that they did not get there in Chinese ships. It was the merchant ships of the 'barbarian' Indonesians that transported them across the Bay of Bengal, from Sumatra or the

Isthmus of Kra, to India – and possibly even further...

"It may have been not only the Indies." wrote Jo Neeham. "The possibility is still open that Han trading envoys got as far as the Axumite kingdom of Ethiopia: 'In the Yuan-Shih reign-period (+1 to +6) under the Emperor Phing Ti, (the minister) Wang Mang, assisting the government, desired to glorify his majestic view. He (therefore) addressed rich presents to the King of Huang-Chih enjoining him to send an embassy with a rhinoceros as tribute. From the kingdom of Huang-Chih, going by ship about eight months one reaches Phi-Tsung. Going on further by ship about two months, one gets to the frontier of Hsiang-Lin in Jih-Nan. It is said that south of Huang-Chih there is the country of *Ssu-Chheng-Pu*. It was from there that the envoy-interpreters of the Han returned.'"

Ssu-Chheng-Pu, according to Needham, equals Tzeng-Po or 'Zanj'-people of the East African coast. "In which case Ssu-Chheng-Pu would be the oldest mention of East Africa." But Needham warned; "Most sinological geographers have frowned upon this view, though not all, and it is still on the agenda."

It is hard to find fault with the view that K'un-lun sailors dominated the sea-lanes from China to Sumatra, and from Sumatra to southern India - and probably from southern India to the Horn of Africa as well. Who they might have been working for in the early part of the 1st millennium is not known. As the seamen of the day might as easily have been 'blood-thirsty pirates' as 'honest merchants', they could have been working for their own account in different 'tribes' or *sukus*; but more likely they were in the employ of one of the burgeoning States - Funan, Ko-ling, Ho-lo-tan or Kan-to-li, the State of Funan. However they were organised, their importance to the pattern of trading at the time must have been enormous, and in many instances they must have been able to wield considerable power. We will see how this affected the growth of Statehood in the region; but first of all it would be useful to find out what sort of ships they might have used that enabled them to become so important in the region.

CHAPTER - 5

Bugis Prahu

JONQUES AND PRAHUS
AND OTHER LITTLE SHIPS

During the past few decades a number of extraordinary ship-remains have been unearthed by archaeologists in western Indonesia. The oldest are pieces of a plank-built boat found at Pontian, on the south-west corner of the Malay peninsular carbon-dated to the 3rd – 5th century A.D. Parts of a similar boat have been found in southern Thailand that are, from associated bead evidence, probably from about the same period. And in southern Sumatra, near Palembang, strakes clearly belonging to a large and sturdy hull, dated to the 5th – 7th century have been found. Chinese sources of the same era mention stitched-plank ships from the islands that were the equivalent of 162 ft long; but so far no direct evidence of such huge boats has come to light. A remarkable aspect of all of these relics is that the same stitched-plank, lashed-lug and dowel techniques appear to have been used in Indonesian boat construction for the next fifteen hundred years.

Also from Palembang and Sambirejo in southern Sumatra archaeologists have found two quarter-rudders measuring 27ft and just under 20ft long respectively – much the same as those still in use on large boats today and probably dating from the first half of the 1st millennium A.D. A reconstruction of some other bits of timber at Sambirejo has produced a single strake over 47ft long from which it has been estimated that the vessel was 65–70feet long, and narrow. It is thought that both this, and a similar boat found at Mindanao in the Philippines would have been unstable unless they had outriggers. It is worth noting that throughout the whole period no significant remains of ancient ship-building have been unearthed in southern India. (1)

The slender Sambirejo remains may have been from a vessel similar to the swift and elegant outrigger called a *kora kora* that prowled the islands and remained in use as a fighting ship long after the arrival of the Portuguese. In the sixteenth century every local chief in the Philippines and the Moluccas had his own fleet of warships, his status depending on the number he could muster for expeditions to distant islands to capture slaves. Each ship, paddled by up to 300 men ranged in double banks on each side, supported a raised platform for warriors armed with spears, blowpipes, bows and swords. Steersmen manned the ship's two lateral rudders as the tilted rectangular sail set from a tripod mast helped drive it through the water at great speed. The high stem and stern-posts curving upwards at each end were decorated with streamers; and, in earlier times, the heads of defeated enemies. (2)

A Kora-Kora from Roding 1798.
(After Horridge.)

The larger, bulkier, remains such as those found near Palembang seem to have been from mono-hulls without outriggers, probably the forerunners of the famous Indonesian *jongs* or *jonques*, cargo-carrying vessels that still existed in large numbers early in the 16th century. Though the name brings to mind the Chinese '*junk*', the *jonque* was a specifically *Indonesian* design, and - if the history of trans-oceanic sailing is anything to go by, its ancestry maybe even older than that of the Chinese *junk*.

The two differed in several important respects, most significantly that the *jonque's* planks were held together by wooden dowels, whereas a *junk* was constructed with iron nails and clamps. The *jonque* had quarter rudders – features that single out a typical Indonesian *prahu* - whereas a '*junk*' was steered by that great Chinese invention, an axial stern-post rudder.

There was one particularly remarkable boat-building technique that was shared by both the Indonesians and the Chinese. *Jonques*, like their Chinese counterparts, had hulls made up of four, possibly even as many as six thicknesses of timber, a completely new outer sheath being built over the previous timbers when they began to age. Such hulls, 6 or 8 inches thick, made both *junks* and *jonques* incredibly heavy and robust. It would seem almost certain that this technique was borrowed by the Chinese, *from* the Indonesians at some stage, given that China did not possess ocean-going ships before the 8th or 9th c. when, only after the Sung came to power, they started building a powerful, ocean-fairing navy.

Two Chinese Buddhist pilgrims who boarded Indonesian ships in Sumatra for passage to India left records which, though widely spaced in time between the 3rd and the 8th centuries, compliment each other in their descriptions. The ships were 160 feet long, and some 600 tons burden; they were built of several layers of planks; no iron was used in their fastenings (confirming that they were not Chinese); they were sewn with sugar-palm fibres, and were rigged with multiple masts and sails. As neither writer made any mention of outriggers it must be assumed they didn't have them, suggesting that they were probably ancestral to the *jonque* rather than any ship such as the *kora-kora*.

But the most vivid impression of a *jonque* was that of a Portuguese chronicler, Gaspar Correia who described the first visit to the Straits of Malacca of Governor Alfonso de Albuquerque early in the 16th century:-

"Seeing that the *junco* wanted to start fighting, the Governor got close to her with his whole fleet. The galleys started shooting at her, but this did not affect her in the least, and she went on sailing ... The Portuguese ships then shot at her masts ... and she dropped her sails. Because she was very tall, our people did not dare board her and our firing did not hurt her at

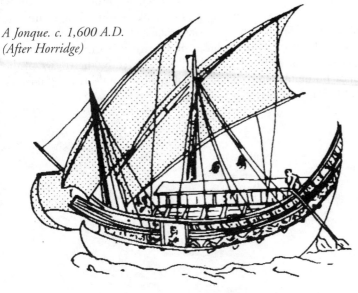

A Jonque. c. 1,600 A.D.
(After Horridge)

all, for she had four superimposed layers of planks, and our biggest cannon would not penetrate more than two… Seeing this the Governor ordered his own *nau* to come alongside her. This was the Flor de la Mar, which had the highest castles of all. When she managed to board the *junco* her aft castle barely reached her bridge. … The crew of the *junco* defended themselves so well that they had to sail away from her again. [After two days and nights of fighting] the Governor decided to have the two rudders she carried outside torn away."

It was only then that 'The *junco*' finally surrendered.

There was one other famous Indonesian ship design which can be seen in seven low relief panels on the walls of the 8th-9th century *stupa* at Borobudur that have already been mentioned. Like so much else, not everyone is in agreement as to what they represented. Mookerji's belief that they were Indian ships has now been discarded. Adrian Horridge thinks they show vessels that are ancestral to the *kora kora*. James Hornell saw them as being descendants of the *kolandiaphonta*, or *kolandia*, which he said:- "probably had a close kinship with the two-masted Javanese outrigger ships of the Boro-Budur sculptures seeing that the Periplus distinctly states that the *kolandia* traded to Chryse." And Anthony Christie of the School of Oriental and African Studies in London, having equated the *kolandiaphonta* with the *kunlun-po*, believed that both they, and the Borobudur ships, were the ancestors of the lumbering, cannon-ball-proof *jonques*. From their sturdy construction, they were probably capable of lengthy voyages, and the very fact that they are the only ones depicted suggests that they were probably the Boeings or Airbuses of the age that carried Indonesian influences so far and wide... a possibility proved by the voyage of the 'replica' Borobudur ship which arrived in Ghana in February 2004 after an 11,000 mile voyage from Indonesia.

CHAPTER - 6

THE EARLY INDONESIAN STATES

Although, at the turn of the Christian era, Indonesians were unquestionably the main merchant-mariners of the Far East, the bulk of all the exotic goods carried from Rome and India to Southeast Asia were destined for China - not for the princes and potentates of Sumatra and Java, as one might expect; for in general the islands were still backward, poor, and politically disorganised. Whereas the Chinese silks so sought after by Greeks and Romans were generally exchanged for comparably 'luxurious' western goods, the more ordinary spices and resins from the islands were paid for in common 'specie' or, with luck, gold.

Indonesian sailors did not have a monopoly on the Chinese trade. When possible, the preferred route for China's riches was overland, either along the silk-road through Turkistan to Roman Syria; or by overland caravan to ports in north-western India and from there by sea up the Persian Gulf. In the second century A.D. however, the central Asian overland routes were severely disrupted by incursions of nomadic steppe people, suddenly making the sea route a more attractive alternative. And as the nomad incursions continued there was a massive flight of rich and privileged Chinese from the north to regions south of the river Yangtse which in turn spurred the demand in southern China both for western and Indonesian products coming in by sea. Following China's partition in the post-Han period in the 3rd century, the routes through Turkistan were closed off completely, giving the sea-route an even greater fillip.

For two reasons - the extra distance around the Malay Peninsular, and the ever-threatening risk of pirates - the sea-route from India to China involved two separate voyages. The first leg took ships across the Bay of Bengal to the Isthmus of Kra in Malaya; then after portage overland, by sea again to the final destination in China. The journey was long and laborious, and was to an important degree governed by the monsoons. The first, east-bound, stretch was dependant on the *westerlies* that blew across the Indian Ocean from April to July: the return journey relied on the

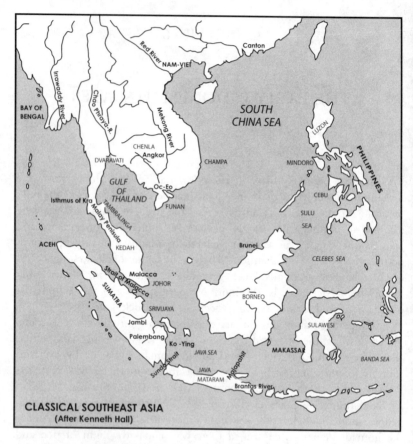

CLASSICAL SOUTHEAST ASIA
(After Kenneth Hall)

easterlies that came with the northeastern monsoon in January. Being therefore impossible to complete the whole journey to China and back within a single year, most crews found it expedient to return home from Kra after travelling the first leg rather than wait around for the return cargo. The discontinuous journey was thus slow and expensive.

With its strategic position on the route between Kra and China, it was on the back of this sea-trade that the State of Funan was founded sometime in the first century A.D, with its most important *entrepot* and commercial centre at Oc-Eo in the Mekong Delta.(1) Funan's founding legend reflected its close ties with India and the Indian trade at the time. It tells of a great Brahman, shipwrecked on the coast, who married a local *naga* princess, the spirit-daughter of the ruler of the water-realm, which lead through devious stories to his own royal status – very similar in many ways to the legends of many Indian states. In fact Funan may represent one of the earliest instances in Southeast Asia of a local ruler importing elements of Indianisation – a move that probably had as much to do with boosting the ruler's personal image as it did to lending the State enhanced mystical power and an aura of civilisation. It was all part of a process that in later years was the main driving force behind the Indianisation of coastal areas in many of the larger Indonesian islands, leading the outside world sometimes to see them as 'colonies' of India - the 'Islands of Hind'.

Despite a gradual increase in traffic across the South China Sea and temptations for merchant-ships to by-pass Oc-Eo, Funan continued to grow rich from its commanding position straddling the east-west trade for several centuries. In 240 A.D. a Chinese envoy to Funan took home a glowing picture of the country, telling the Emperor Wu how the people:- "... live in walled cities, palaces and houses... They devote themselves to agriculture... Taxes are paid in gold, silver, pearls and perfumes ... There are books and depositories of archives and other things. The characters of the writing resemble those of the Hu [people of Central Asia who used a script of Indian origin.]" (2)

Funan was both prosperous and powerful, and remained so until well into the fifth century when growing harassment from Cham pirates began severely to disrupt the sea-lanes between the Isthmus of Kra and southern China. By the end of the 5th century Funan was becoming increasingly desperate, appealing to the Chinese rulers in Tongking for help against the Cham. But by then the opening of alternative sea-routes round the Malay Peninsular and across the South China Sea by-passed not only the Cham problem but also Oc-Eo, radically diminishing Funan's importance. The final blow to Funan came when Khmer insurgents swept down from the mountains in the north overrunning the once powerful state.

There is no reliable evidence of precisely when the sea-route through the Strait of Malacca began to acquire greater importance than the sea/land/sea route across the Isthmus of Kra, but from the ship remains found at Pontian in southern Malaya and the maritime sites in Sumatra, one is tempted to think that the Malacca Strait must have been opened up as a regular shipping route at the latest by the 2nd century A.D. As mentioned in the previous chapter, the remnants of the Pontian and Palembang ships appear to have been sturdy cargo vessels, while those of Sambirejo in Sumatra (albeit 7th – 8th C.) were sleek, narrow ships of the *kora-kora* type – fast, heavily manned, fighting vessels with multiple out-riggers, such as might have been used by pirates. Then, as now, piracy in the archipelago was a major factor and probably presented on-going problems for merchant-seamen using the Malacca Strait. Indeed it is very possible that the need to control piracy might have been a major catalyst in the consolidation and organisation of larger trading centres, which led eventually to the formation of more authoritative and powerful States.

For whatever reason, during the 2nd or 3rd century, doubtless with an eye on Funan's burgeoning trade, alternative commercial zones began to emerge in the Java Sea. Prominent among these was one referred to in Chinese commercial records as 'Ko-ying'. Not much is known about Ko-ying... in fact the difficulties of being absolutely certain about any of the early Southeast Asian States was well illustrated by O.W. Wolters when, in his *Early Indian Commerce*, he discussed the problems encountered by scholars trying to interpret Chinese imperial histories.

"One illustration" said Wolters, "will reveal the working in this field. P'o-li has been located in Borneo by Bretschneider, on the southern coast of Sumatra by Groeneveldt, and at Asahan on the north east coast of Sumatra by Schegel. Pelliot identified it with Bali, Gerini with the west coast of the Malay Peninsular, Moens with southern Sumatra and also with Java, Obdeijn with Banka off the south-eastern coast of Sumatra, and Hsu Yun-ts'iao with Panei on the north-eastern coast of Sumatra. Sir Roland Braddell identified it with Borneo and thus completed the cycle of identifications where Bretchneider began as long ago as 1871". Wolters himself located P'o-li somewhere in the eastern part of Java!

The consensus is that Ko-ying was somewhere in south-eastern Sumatra where it would have been well placed to control traffic plying between India and China through both the Malacca and the Sunda Straits. More precisely, it may have been in the region of Palembang which years later became the capital of the great Srivijayan empire.

Apart from giving some protection to ships *en route* around Malaya, it is probable that one of Ko-ying's main functions was as a terminus for *Kun-lun* ships carrying cargoes from the spice-islands, destined for China and India. According the Chinese records, it was mainly involved in the traffic of cloves, nutmegs and mace from the Moluccas, and exotic timbers such as sandalwood from Timor, in return for which Indian merchants exchanged pearls, gold, jade, pistachio nuts, horses and glassware. (Was this Roman glassware? ...or Indian glass from Arikamedu? We don't know). In any event, although it was one of the polities that marked the beginning of a whole new era in the Indonesian islands, in its infancy Ko-ling appears to have been a lesser state; and whilst Funan still existed, Ko-ying's trade with China probably still passed through the Mekong port of Oc-eo.

Though Ko-Ying was most powerfully placed on the international trade route, it was not by any means the only rising power. Other embryonic 'states' competing for Chinese trade and Chinese favours were soon sending envoys to the Emperor. Chinese texts mention, among others, P'u-lei, P'o-ta; P'o-huang; P'en-p'en; Tan-tan; and Ho-ling all located variously in Sumatra and Java. Though it may have been one of the most successful of the earlier states, Ko-ying was soon superseded in importance by the west Java kingdom of Ho-lo-tan; and then by the first really important commercial centre, Kan-to-li which has been described by O.W. Wolters as "the most important of the trading kingdoms before the rise of Srivijaya ... which deserves an honoured place in the histories of Indonesia."

Kan-to-li, whose recorded history runs from 441A.D. to 563A.D., probably encompassed a huge area of southern Sumatra including the valleys of the Batanaghari and Musa rivers. Chinese tradition has it that 'Kan-to-li' was actually the early name for 'Srivijaya' which ultimately became the greatest kingdom of them all. It is also possible that Kan-to-li grew directly out of its predecessor Ko-ying. If this was so it would have been a link in a chain of organised control that gave Indonesians absolute dominance over the strategically vital Malacca and Sunda Straits for well over a thousand years. The unprecedented power derived from this geographical situation would have enabled those States based in the region of Palembang in southern Sumatra to control all shipping and trade from China and the Indonesian archipelago to India, Ceylon - and Africa and Madagascar.

Kan-to-li was also the first *Buddhist* state to be established in Indonesia. Progressive and ambitious Indonesian rulers highly valued the skills of Brahmans and Buddhists and "other workers of magic", and contrary to popular belief, it was not Indians who *imposed* their 'superior' culture and religions on the Islands, it was the reverse. 'Indianisation' was a *consequence* of the progress Indonesia was making, rather than a *cause*; and the form of Buddhism chosen by the islands' rulers played an important part in their subsequent history.

There are two main schools of Buddhism, Hinayana and Mahayana. Briefly, the difference is that Hinayana Buddhists adhere strictly to those teachings of the Master that have purely ethical content - they do not represent Buddha as a human being; but as 'a footprint, a tree, a throne, an umbrella' or some other such abstract device. The Mahayana school, on the other hand, elevates Buddha to the status of a 'deity', and represents Buddha 'the enlightened one', and a range of Bhoddhisatvas, in human form. "Indeed," said John Keay writing of Mahayana Buddhism in his book *India*, "Buddhist icons of the Pala period are so anatomically exaggerated and so generously provided with extra heads and arms that only a trained eye would identify them as Buddhist".(3) Mahayana Buddhism may well have been favoured by the island states because it viewed commerce less negatively than either Hinayana Buddhism or Hinduism; additionally, it harboured no such misgivings as those held by Hindu Brahmans about sailing far from land. Thus, as a Mahayana Buddhist, to be a merchant and a long-distance mariner was not only condoned, but something of which to be proud.

Indian craftsmen of the Pala dynasty, (which was founded in Bengal c. 750 A.D. and survived into the 11th century), produced bronze Bodhisatvas and effigies of Buddha so numerous that it is almost certain they were mass produced.(4) Thousands of these small images were exported to Indonesia, where they are still being dug up by farmers and treasure-seekers. One of those most frequently found images is the popular *Avalokitesvara*, the Bodhisattva of Compassion, who's head-dress is adorned with a lotus-bud emblem seen by some to have phallic significance. Another common casting was that of the Buddha *Dipamkara*, the "Calmer of Waters" to whom Southeast Asian seamen were particularly devoted, and which was probably carried by them as talismans on their long voyages to China and India, Africa and Madagascar.

Though the greatness of Sumatra and Java may have been helped by Indian creative genius, it has to be seen as a wholly *indigenous* achievement of people who, by their own choice, embraced some aspects of Indian culture. But ultimately, the success or failure of all the early Indonesian states depended largely on their relationship with China whose hegemony in the Southeast Asian islands was undisputed. Hence the records are full of references to embassies to the Southern Chinese ruler-of-the-day - embassies designed to secure the exclusive rights to trade, and seeking protection against warring neighbours. The fact that Kan-to-li sent fewer embassies to China than its rival neighbours is taken to mean that its position was more secure than that of others – hence it had no *need* to send embassies. Thus Kan-to-li's dominant place as the immediate pre-cursor of Srivijaya might have been expected to continue to expand and flourish as the years went by.

But that was not to be. For reasons that have never been fully explained, Kan-to-li suddenly went into decline following the last embassy sent by Vijayavarman, son of Gautama Subhadra, in 519, and by 563 A.D. it had completely disappeared from the map. (5)

Between the time of Vijayavarman's embassy and Kan-to-li's demise there occurred a cataclysmic event that brought about unimaginable changes, not just to Indonesia and China, but to people in East Africa, the Middle East, the Mediterranean, indeed, all around the world. (6)

"From the southwest...there twice was the sound of thunder", said the Chinese *History of the Southern Dynasties* in 535 A.D. And a few months later, from the same document: "Yellow dust rained down like snow". In 536 the Roman Senator Cassiodorus wrote: "The sun seems to have lost its wonted light and appears of a bluish colour ... We marvel to see no shadows of our bodies at noon, to feel the mighty vigour of the sun's heat wasted into feebleness, and the phenomena which accompany a transitory eclipse prolonged through almost a whole year."

In 1999, David Keys, onetime archaeology correspondent of the "*Independent*", published a book called *Catastrophe* in which he put forward some fascinating theories about a series of natural occurrences that may have changed the course of events far and wide. The crux of Key's story is that in 535/6 the world witnessed one of the largest and most violent volcanic eruptions in recorded history – one that virtually vaporised the huge mass of Krakatoa, the volcano in the middle of the Sunda Strait between Java and Sumatra. By the best estimates, 25 cubic miles of sintered rock and molten magma, as well as an even vaster quantity of water vapour and gas were thrown tens of thousands of feet into the air where they were caught up in stratospheric winds that spread them rapidly, like a giant collar, around the world, creating the biggest and thickest sunshade the people on earth had witnessed. It was an explosion large enough to have rumbled through the air-waves and been heard as far away as Nanjing in China 2,800 miles away: one whose consequences spread across the globe.

From an ancient Javanese chronicle written retrospectively several centuries later, (which may have been adulterated in eighteenth century copying), a passage described how, amidst thunder and lightening, a deafening roar emanated from the mountain, that shook the earth furiously, followed by gales and torrential rains that plunged the world into darkness ... "The noise was fearful. At last the mountain burst into two pieces with a tremendous roar and sank into the deepest of the earth". The land in the northern part of Java to the east was flooded, drowning many of the inhabitants, and sweeping away their property. When the water subsided the area where the mountain was had become sea, and the land was divided into two. "This was the origin of the separation of Sumatra and Java."

Whether or not the 535/6 eruption created the Sunda Strait is debatable. There was almost certainly a channel between the islands long before that. Nevertheless the explosion must have been huge, far bigger, even, than the 1883 eruption of the re-born Krakatoa which is said to have been heard 4000 miles away. If the shock of the earlier one had been limited to a radius of fifty or a hundred miles from the centre of the volcano, there would have been unbelievably large waves and massive devastation on both sides of the strait, as there was in the 1880's. But though it may have had an immediate and devastating effect on commerce, it is unlikely that the eruption alone would have been sufficient to threaten the survival of the State of Kan-to-li on the eastern coast of Sumatra.

The massive cloud of water vapour and dust thrown up by the eruption rapidly cast its shadow around the earth having an immediate effect on the world's weather patterns. It was this that ultimately had more far-reaching and disastrous effects on human populations than the Big Bang itself. For several years the earth's climate was changed. In some places the rainfall was many times the norm; in others there were extreme droughts leading to starvation; widespread loss of life; and social unrest. In the once great state of Funan, the elaborate water-works that maintained the country's wet rice production fell into disuse, and the fields quickly reverted to swamp and jungle. Agricultural lands were depopulated. Administrative supervision and central financial support collapsed, leaving the way open for the Khmer invasions which led to Funan's final demise.

In Key's scenario, the climatic changes led to a calamitous outbreak of plague in Africa somewhere between Opone and Rhapta – i.e. between Ras Hafun and the Rufiji delta – most likely focused in an area near the borders of modern Somalia and Kenya. Here, in the equatorial belt, higher rainfall led to unusually rapid growth of vegetation which in turn encouraged an explosive increase in the populations of many kinds of animals, including rats, the most prolific and dangerous carriers of the plague. Though rats may be plague-carriers, in some parts of the world they are naturally immune to the disease, and present little threat. But in exceptional times such as followed the eruption, when rat populations suddenly ballooned, it was inevitable that immune plague-carriers would sooner or later come into contact with other rats that were not immune. These, in turn, spread the disease to the rest of the animal kingdom and so eventually to humans, resulting in the decimation of whole communities over a widespread area.

In East Africa an occurrence such as this may well have been the cause of a major culture-change that is evident in a change in pottery styles about this time. The early iron-age pottery of the East African coast, usually referred to as 'Kwale'-ware (after its type-site near Mombasa) gave way to an entirely new style known as 'Tana'-ware (from its type-site on the Tana river in northern Kenya) suggesting that there had been an influx of new people with different traditions.

Like the earlier Kwale style that had spread with suspicious speed down the East coast almost as far as Durban, the newer Tana-wares soon found their way across to the Comoro Isles and Madagascar. In both cases the rapidity of their spread, and the fact that Tana pottery eventually reached Madagascar, suggests that highly mobile maritime cultures of one sort or another may have been involved.

The plague, spreading rapidly along the coast of Africa, must soon have been carried northwards on ships bound for Arabia and the Red Sea from where nothing could stop it reaching Egypt. It soon broke out at Pelusium in the Nile delta; then in Roman Byzantium from where, having scythed its way painfully, year by year, through the populations of the Mediterranean, it spread to Persia. Unstoppable, the disease moved inexorably on to India; thence overland along the silk-route; and then to Indonesia, probably carried on Persian ships trading to India's southern ports and, beyond there, on Indonesia's own *kunlun-po*. Whatever its precise route, it seems to have taken several years to affect Indonesia and nearly fifty before the full force of the disease was felt in China.

One region to be stricken by severe droughts was southern China. The rains failed, crops shrivelled, and the resultant hunger and poverty led to social upheavals that completely undermined the tax system upon which hitherto stable government had been dependent. Inevitably this led eventually to the collapse of the political and administrative structure of the country. Rebellion broke out; the reins of government of south China were taken over by the army. Power was grabbed by General Chen, a war-lord who imprisoned and executed his fellow military leaders. The aged emperor was captured and left to starve to death in the Imperial palace. A puppet emperor was put in his place; but ultimately the general took the throne for himself, so creating the fragile Chen dynasty in 557.

Some scholars argue that the sudden disappearance of Kan-to-li in the third quarter of the 6th century was due to trade between Kan-to-li and China being interrupted when the weak Chen dynasty came to power. (7) O.W. Wolter's view, for example, was that when the Chen rulers failed to provide an assured market for Persian and local Indonesian products, unemployment among the mariners contracted to Kan-to-li resulted in their dispersal among the islands and estuaries, where they probably reverted to the age old profession of piracy. As the power of Kan-to-li, (and all other trading states in western Indonesia) depended largely on the mariners and merchantmen who serviced the veins and arteries of the kingdom, the essential fragility of the alliances formed with the seamen became a constant problem. Never firmly based on land, forever roaming the seas, and ever fickle if a more advantageous or profitable political alliance was offered them, there was little to stop the free-spirited mariners switching allegiances. As a Chinese writer of the time said: "When they want to go elsewhere, all they have to do is pull up their poles..." If the rulers of Kan-to-li could not offer them a living, well, 'The Jolly Roger' it would have to be...

In this respect Oliver Wolters was probably correct. But was the political weakness and commercial instability of which he wrote the true cause of Southern China's decline, and Kan-to-li's demise? Might not these problems have been the end-results of the eruption of 535? Once it is established, the plague remains in a region for a long time, raising its ugly head in lethal ways after many years of dormancy. Might it not have been the plague that led to the sudden disappearance of Kan-to-li in 563 A.D.? Whatever the reason, nothing more was said of it in Chinese literature. When sailing in the region forty five years later Chang Chun recorded only the state of Malayu on the south-eastern coast of Sumatra. There was not a single mention of Kan-to-li.

CHAPTER - 7

SRIVIJAYA AND THE SEA NOMADS

From the time of Kan-to-li's collapse in 563, over eighty years were to elapse before 'Malayu' in eastern Sumatra sent a mission to China, and trade again showed signs of life. By then the state of Funan had collapsed completely, the overland route across the Isthmus of Kra had lost its importance, and the pattern of trade had shifted to sea-lanes through the Strait of Malacca.

From the earliest days of Ko-ying and Kan-to-li the viability of the Indonesian Island states had been, and continued to be, dependent upon a three-way relationship carefully balanced between:

a) the **rulers**, the hub of whose power was in the seaports near the mouths of the great rivers from where they could control all movements from inland towards the coast, and vice versa;

b) the **producers** in the forests, fields, and mines of the hinterland who created much of the State's wealth;

c) the State's often independently-minded **mariners** who protected the country from rogue pirates, manned the merchant fleets, and, in the case of Srivijaya, formed a highly organised navy.

These relationships – often of people with different ethnic and tribal allegiances - were held together not just by formal alliances sealed with oaths, but as importantly, by the sharing out of the spoils of overseas trade on a mutually acceptable basis. The system was fragile because if, for one reason or another, the balance was upset - if trade declined and profits were poor - producers might withhold their products, or even look for markets elsewhere. Or, as may have happened with Kan-to-li, the mariners might renege on their oaths and sail away in search of better rewards, or back into a happy-go-lucky entrepreneurial life of piracy.

The smaller states were generally dependent upon the productivity of a single river system hemmed in by hills and forests on all sides. The producers would bring down their goods from the fields, forests and mines of the hinterland, to the go-downs in the State's capital, or other big cities on one of the great rivers that connected the interior with the sea. From there the merchant-mariners, under long-term contract with the ruler, or chartered for the purpose, would convey goods to and from the markets in China, India, or wherever else they might be destined. The possibility of peacefully building a large State incorporating several river systems was made well-nigh impossible by the inherent lack of control imposed by the natural barriers of forests, swamps and mountains.

Since the State was an *entrepot* for goods *en route* between the Indian Ocean and China, good relations with China were essential, hence the need for frequent embassies to the Chinese Emperor to secure the necessary protection and trading rights. It was a tight-knit, if potentially fragile, organisation: armed force and organised sea-power were essential.

Kan-to-li's successor in south east Sumatra, Srivijaya, probably began its rise to prosperity just as the others had, in the traditional system of riverine exchange. But one major factor came to differentiate Srivijaya from the rest. Whilst forming strong alliances with neighbours to protect its flanks, it was alone in building up a powerful army of foot soldiers to exercise 'persuasion', and if necessary force the people of the hinterland to honour their commitments.

At the same time, Srivijaya, from its capital Palembang on the Musi river, seems to have built up a more organised and powerful 'Royal Navy of Sea Nomads' than its neighbours, and from the latter part of the 7th century it was in a position to dominate the maritime commerce passing through southeast Asia. (1) An inscription found near Palembang gives some idea of its power. It relates how, on April 23rd 683 the King of Srivijaya embarked on a *siddhayatra* - a quest for 'supernatural power' - and with 20,000 foot-soldiers to call upon, set forth in his ships to conquer his arch rival, Malayu (modern Jambi), and establish hegemony over the people of the Batanghari river network.(2) Such expansionism backed by force had not been seen before: and Srivijaya did not stop at Jambi.

If it were to establish an empire that had absolute control over the sea-routes between east and west, Srivijaya, of necessity, had to control the Sunda Strait in the south and the Isthmus of Kra in the north. But the Srivijayans were not without opposition. Chinese records refer to numerous missions from smaller riverine powers arriving regularly at the Chinese court seeking the emperor's favours and hoping to receive special treatment. One such state was the important emporium of Kedah on the west coast of Malaya, through which passed much of the Indian traffic from across the Bay of Bengal. Its overtures to China, possibly in conjunction with P'o-lo and Barus, two states in the far north of Sumatra, constituted a threat that the Srivijayans could not countenance. With their new-found power on the high seas, they rapidly 'acquired' the dependency of Kedah; and this was soon followed by Kalah, yet further north on the Malayan coast. With the acquisition of these two states Srivijaya's control over the Isthmus of Kra and the Strait of Malacca was finally confirmed.

In time, so states the *HisnT'ang shu* admiringly "...Srivijaya had fourteen cities, and a number of them must have been rivals before Srivijaya struck them down."(3) There had never before been a State in Indonesia with such enormous power and wealth, whose supremacy was based on its alliance with the all important maritime societies between Java and the Isthmus of Kra that controlled the portals to Indonesia and China. In recognition of Srivijayas's indisputable leadership the Chinese granted it "preferred trade status." It had by now acquired such prestige both in Indian and Chinese markets, that - so it is said - merchants looked for any excuse they could find to trade in the name of the Srivijayan ruler.

Though one might think that the Srivijayan navy would have been made up of mariners drawn from the ranks of *orang laut*, or 'sea-people', living in nearby islands, this was probably not the case. If the *orang laut* in the first millennium were anything like the relatively primitive, individualistic, groups of sea-nomads living in the vicinity of the Malacca Strait and the Lingga Islands in recent times, it is unlikely they would have been able to muster the disciplines and strengths to create an organised navy such as Srivijaya needed, and seems to have created.

But if it's navy was not made up of 'local' mariners, who might they have been?

In the island world in which they lived there must have been many Indonesians who, far back in history, had honed their boating skills as a basic necessity for survival. As O.W. Wolters wrote: "The Malays did not become skilful navigators only in the lifetime of I Tsing, who sailed to India in one of their ships. Their accomplishments in the 7th century were preceded by a long period of bold voyaging." Records of the 3rd century tell of ships sailing from the Philippines across more than 800 miles of open water to Funan; three hundred years earlier still, Chinese envoys had made their way to the Malay Peninsular in 'barbarian' ships; and beyond that, as we have seen, Indonesians could draw on an accumulation of literally thousands of years of maritime experience.

Who, then, were the people who crewed these ancient ships?

Chasing two thousand year old ghosts could prove to be a fruitless waste of time: so rather than trying to draw conclusions from inadequate archaeological evidence and obscure Chinese references, it is possible that more might be learned about them from looking at the overall boating scene in historical times, and extrapolating back into the past.

The Phantom Voyagers

There are a number of surviving groups of Sea Nomads throughout the islands whose roots seem to be ancient and who are therefore worth exploring. One well known, and possibly obvious group, are the Mawken, an extensive band of boat-people who, because of their commanding positions along the coast of the Kra Peninsular, might well have had powerful influence in that area. But though the Mawken were described a hundred years ago as "possibly the most expert boatmen in the world", their boats – expanded dugouts - are small, and they themselves, according to eighteenth century accounts, have always been timid folk who scatter and hide in the mangroves at the first sight of strangers. According to one of their own origin stories they originally lived on land where they had plantations of coconuts, bananas, pineapples and breadfruit, amongst other things. But being constantly harassed by Burmese and Malay overlords, they eventually fled the land to live permanently in their canoes which they turned into floating homesteads with *atap* roofs. They have no history of large boats capable of oceanic sailing, and can be discounted.

In the seas around Borneo and in the straits between Singapore and Sumatra there were a host of other '*Orang laut*': the *Orang Tambus; Orang Mantang; Orang Barok; Orang Galang; Orang Sekanak; Orang Posik; Orang Moro; Orang Sugi*, and more . They, and the dozens of smaller *sukus* into which they were divided, undoubtedly had a role to play ... but probably more like that of an infestation of hornets lurking in the mangroves and estuaries of the myriad tiny islands - a constant danger to unwary passers-by, and best avoided. Like the Mawken, they were not, on the strength of what is known about them, likely to have been the sort of people to create an organised body of long-distance traders and explorers who would have been able or willing to cross the oceans to India and Africa. They are more likely to have been like another potential group of *orang laut*, the Ma-lo-nu of Sarawak where, according to a Chinese chronicle, the chiefs bored holes in their gold-plated teeth, and drank and ate from human skulls, and among whom "... savages assemble in large crowds, and having caught the shipwrecked, roast them over a fire with large bamboo pinchers and eat them". Or maybe they were all like the Fenjab described years later by the Arab, Masudi, who "...have frizzly hair and strange figures; mounted on their boats they lie in wait for ships that pass in the neighbourhood and shoot upon them poisoned arrows of a special kind" ... more reminiscent of Conan Doyle's blow-pipe-wielding Andaman Islanders than disciplined long-haul seamen.

Further east in the archipelago, between Sulawesi and Mindanao were the warlike Samals who had large boats of the *kora-kora* type. In 1847 the

British steamer *Nemesis* encountered a fleet of between 40 to 60 of these pirate craft. The largest were described as being 80 feet long with 80 crew, with many others about 70 feet long, 12 feet in beam, with crews of 40 persons, and carrying four to six guns. "A feature of the Illanun and Samal pirate craft" wrote David Sopher in his book *The Sea Nomads* "was the double bank of rowers like the Mediterranean biremes of antiquity, which, being either pirates or warships, had the same requirement of speed and the capacity to carry a large compliment of fighting men as did the Moro pirate ships."(4) Ships like the *kora-kora* would have been capable of open-sea voyages as we have suggested when linking such vessels with the *sangara* of Pliny's day. But their carrying capacity would have been small, and their owners were probably too bound up in piratical pastimes to have become involved in the sort of long distance journeying that the Srivijayans needed.

Then there were the famous Bajau, the mostly widely dispersed of all the sea-nomads.

It seems that for a very long time the Bajau, or Bajo, have been among the most capable and ubiquitous sailors of the Indonesian Islands, who would have been better potential for the Srivijayan navy. Their precise history is vague. But judging from the number of places that have 'Bajau', 'Bajo', Baju, Waju or sometimes Bajoo in their names they must once have been very widespread. Bajo toponyms can be found scattered between the extremes of the Indonesian islands: from Mentawai off Sumatra's west coast, to New Guinea in the east - a vast area stretching over 2,500 miles from west to east and, 1000 miles from north to south. "Their existence is one continuous voyage. Seafaring is second nature to them – they ride the bosom of the ocean like aquatic birds", said a traveller, Raymond Kennedy, years ago.

Importantly, the Bajo's sinuous roots are closely entangled with those of other major seafaring people including the Bugis (sometimes written Bugi or Buki), the Mandar, and the Makassarese, all of whom, if their prowess in modern times reflects their ancient past, could lay claim to having been suitable seamen for the Srivijayan navy a thousand years ago.

The Bajo are said to have originated in Sulawesi in the same region as the Bugis or *Tau-Wugi*, 'the people of Wugi' with whom they have a close relationship. Bastian in 1885, wrote of the part played by the Bajo in the establishment of some of the earliest political states in Sulawesi:- "(Their) traditions refer to the very beginning of Bugis and Makassarese pseudo-history, following the legendary period when the ruling class descended from heaven, ruled for seven generations and then disappeared, an episode which may refer to a period of Hindu-Javanese cultural penetration." From

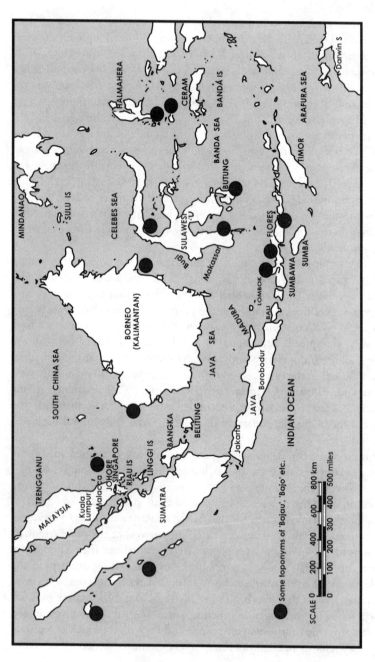

Map showing some toponyms of Bajau. (After David Sopher)

this it would seem they are of ancient stock that would have been well established by Srivijaya's time.(5)

For all their close association with the Bugis and Makassarese, the life-style of the Bajo varied considerably in the different places in which they settled. For many of them, like the Mawken, their small boats were 'home'. They were born, brought up, and died on board, eking out a living in the shallow, crocodile infested fore-shores of remote islands where they caught fish and turtles and dove for shellfish. Others travelled as far as the northern shores of Australia to seek out the much prised sea-slugs, or *tripang*, which fetched high prices as a delicacy in southern China. Yet others, among the richer Bajo, might have been found living in a vessel called a *vinta*, an outrigger with three or four booms slung across several dug-outs supporting a proper house. Like modern stink-pots in marinas around the world, the *vinta* was 'for residential purposes only'; a home in which to raise a family, that never left its well protected anchorage. "No wind, no waves", the Bajo would say with a twinkle, "yet the boat rolls!"

Some of the Bajo formed convenient relationships with higher caste peoples on the larger, more developed islands, providing them with fish, running errands from island to island, acting as porters for trade-goods. These land-based Bajo hunted on land as well as in the sea; they tilled fields, cultivating rice and other crops, and kept gardens of coconuts, bananas and fruits. Some of them built long-houses for their extended families, whereas the true sea-nomads - if and when they lived temporarily ashore - built rougher, single-family shacks on the beach. Often, Bajo villages could be found on isolated islands or promontories a day or two from the nearest markets where they sold their fish. They were by nature peaceful people, often travelling without weapons and frequently harassed by pirates against whom they had no organised defence, a factor that contributed to their wide dispersion. A number of observers reported a tendency for... "the Baju to keep to themselves, melting away to distant settlements elsewhere if harassed." (6)

The languages and customs of the Bajo, like those of their 'cousins' the Buginese, underwent constant changes resulting from contacts with many different people. Their willingness to pick up and use the languages of their 'host' people around the archipelago was a frequently noted feature, and even extended to things at the centre of their life such as boat terminology which one might have thought would be immutable. Adrian Horridge, who knew the area well in the 1970's and 80's wrote "Where they settle it is surprising how quickly itinerant sailors adopt the local language and begin to use local words for their *prahus* and rigs."

Conversely, it has also been said that Bajo, Buginese, Makassarese, Mandar and other closely related culture-groups who dominate the world of the *prahu* have their own terminology for the parts of a *prahu* that are quite distinct in their separate languages. Special vocabularies have formed over the years; thus the rich variety of vessels suggests a gradual development over a very long period, at the same time highlighting the variety of life-styles that characterised the widely travelled Bajo and Bugis.

If the Bajo sailed to far-flung places and were fine fishermen and traders, the Bugis had qualities that made them even likelier candidates for the roll of the region's leading mariners. A sociologist once described the social structure of the Bugis as 'centrifugal'. They "spin off their members away from their own valleys and islands, temporarily or permanently, into the outer world, where they restively strive after new wisdom and wealth. ... For the Bugis it is as normal that people emigrate as it is that most men marry." This 'centrifugalism' sharply contrasted with 'centripetal' societies such as the Balinese or Toraja whose members were "drawn inwards, enmeshed in the web of community, kinship and ritual obligations". It was a perfect social background for voyagers and explorers. (7)

In addition to their acknowledged seamanship the Buginese had a reputation of being both traders as well as staunch and sometimes cruel warriors. For centuries they were the main players in the transport of spices, sandalwood, pearls, ambergris, Dammar resin, edible nests of the cave swallow, sago and dried shark's fin, for trade with southern China. When the Portuguese arrived in the early 1500's the Buginese were renowned also as pirates who sold their captives as far afield as Malacca. Even in the 1970's anything up to two hundred Bugis *pinisi*, each of 120 – 200 tons, might be found lying in the port of Sunda Kelapa near Jakarta, with yet more at anchor in Surubaya or Ujung Pandang. And in the 1980's a fleet of around 800 *pinisi* still carried timber on regular routes from Kelimantan to Java.

The Buginese were also successful sea-borne colonists, establishing trading posts in virtually every Indonesian port. In the seventeenth century they even took over the state of Johore, and within a few years of Singapore's foundation in 1820-30, the Bugis had settlements there. (8) In 1792, a traveller noted that... "The Bugis people who come annually to trade at Sumatra, are looked upon by the inhabitants as their superiors in manners, the Malays affect to copy their style of dress, and frequent allusions to their feats and achievements are made in their songs. Their reputation for courage, which certainly surpasses that of all others in the eastern seas, acquires them this flattering distinction; they also derive part of the respect showed them from the richness of the cargoes they import and the spirit with which they spend the produce." (9)

Forty five years later another author wrote of Bugis who had formed colonies in India: "...in honesty, energy of character and general conduct, they are far superior to the Malays. ... It is supposed by strangers that the Bugis are addicted to piracy. That individuals of the Bugis nation are to be found, who, as the Chinese say, 'indulge in disorderly thoughts and actions, and go about madly scheming irregular profits', I do not pretend to dispute, but during my sojourn in Eastern India I never heard of a single instance of a piratical attack by a Bugis trader; and, on the contrary, several circumstances have come to my knowledge which would go to prove that their inclinations tend the contrary way." (10)

Eighteenth century maps, redrawn by Bugis navigators from Dutch originals, show that these remarkable seamen must have reached the Maldive islands that hang from India like a seine-net to catch all that moves between East Asia and Africa. How long they had known the Maldives is impossible to say; but as Maldivian boats have features that link them to Indonesia rather than India or Arabia such contacts may be very ancient. (11)

From all this it would seem that, as they still are today, the Bugis have been mariners and people of consequence for many years. Good leaders; excellent seamen; honest traders; adventurous travellers; fine warriors. In earlier years they may in addition have been ferocious pirates and perhaps even head-hunters; but if at any time a powerful Indonesian prince had wanted a fleet manned by the best seamen available, it is doubtful whether he could have done better than to choose the Bajo or the Bugis or a mixture of the two. Frequently, when such situations arose, it was the Bugis or their descendants who became the most trusted employees, holding the highest ranks. It is this group of people that has the best claim to have served the classical states of Indonesia, Srivijaya in particular; and as will become apparent, when viewed from an Africa standpoint, they are the most likely Indonesians to have been involved.

There is support for this hypothesis of a different kind. The Old Malay inscriptions from Palembang and Bangka island that tell of the great *siddhayatra*, when the King of Srivijaya set out on his quest for 'supernatural power', may not shed direct light on our particular quest: but the language the inscriptions are written in is highly significant. This fact was spotted by Alexander Adelaar when he was studying the origins of the language of Madagascar. Having first noticed the similarities of Malagasy and Malay, he went on to compare Malay terms for the points of the compass with Malagasy equivalents, concluding that: "The evidence of directional terms

61

shows that the early Malagasy migrants were in contact with South Sumatra …". Furthermore, he continued, "The evidence also strengthens the aforementioned hypothesis that the few lines in an unknown language (showing similarities with the Barito languages) on the seventh century Old Malay inscriptions of South Sumatra are in a kind of pre-Malagasy". (12)

The full importance of this will become clearer when we start to look at Madagascar's relationship with Africa, but in addition to forging a link between Srivijaya and Madagascar, it also strongly suggests a connection between Srivijaya and Sulawesi/Borneo. The *Barito* languages that Adelaar refers to take their name from the Barito river in southeastern Borneo, which have similarities, not only to modern Malagasy, but also to languages spoken in Southwestern Sulawesi, the home territory of the Bugis, Bajo, and the Makassar.

Convoluted though this may appear to be, everything points to the ancestors of the Bugis and Bajo having been the mainstay of the Srivijayans' navy, as well as to a Bugis/Bajo linguistic connection with Madagascar and – by extension – with the East Coast of Africa.

From the 7th century onwards Srivijaya maintained its dominance in the region until, early in the 10th century, faced with growing internal and foreign pressures, its world began to crumble. From 922 it was repeatedly invaded by Javanese who were only repelled only after a century of attacks and counter-attacks. But the respite was temporary, and Srivijaya never fully recovered.

During the Sung dynasty (960 – 1279) Chinese merchants trading with Java and islands to the east began to venture beyond the confines of the inshore waters, by-passing the Srivijayan *entrepots* of Jambi and Palembang thus seriously weakening their hold on trade. (13) The stresses and strains this created inevitably increased the waywardness of many of Srivijaya's smaller vassal states for whom visions of greater independence loomed; and as a sure indication of its growing insecurity, Srivijaya, in efforts to re-affirm its dominant trading status, began sending more frequent embassies to China.

Adding further to Srivijaya's problems, Arabs, who were by then flexing their muscles down the East coast of Africa, also began to threaten the Indonesian monopoly in the Malacca Strait. As early as 902 Ibn al-Fakili reported that "the parrots of *Zabag* (Sumatra) spoke many languages, including Arabic, Persian and Greek". Arab commercial strength - doubtless swelled by the resource-rich shores of Africa upon which the people of Lamu, Mombasa, Zanzibar and Kilwa were about to grow rich - continued to increase, until in the third quarter of the 12th century a

Chinese writer was able to say ... "Of all the wealthy foreign lands which have great store of precious and varied goods, none surpasses the realm of Ta-shih (the Arabs). Next to them comes the She-p'o (Java), while San-fo-chi (Srivijaya) is third". How were the mighty fallen! (14)

With Srivijaya in a weakened state, the hyenas began to gather. Kedah, its vasal state in Malaya, awoke to the possibility of cutting out the monopoly route through the Malacca Strait by re-opening the sea-land-sea route across the Kra Isthmus; and like screeching vultures in search of blood, the Tamils in India began to circle threateningly over the seaways. By 985 the first of the Cola rulers in southern India, Rajaraja the Great, had expanded his empire to include Ceylon and set about building the first and only powerful navy that ancient India ever saw. (15) In 1015 his son, Rajendra, in the hope of opening direct trade links, sent the first of several missions to China. Then, in 1017, only a year after an exhausted Srivijaya had regained pole position by inflicting a defeat over Java in the south, open war broke out between the Colas and Srivijaya. In 1025 Rajendra's navy, almost certainly supported by the Khmer state of Ankor, under Suryavarman 1st, attacked and sacked Palembang, seizing its legendary riches and capturing its Maharaja. (16)

Though Cola influence in the Malacca Strait remained strong for the next fifty years, the World order was about to change forever. Mortally wounded, Srivijaya managed to limp on; but eventually, before the end of the thirteenth century, it had to give way to the expanding Majapahit Empire of eastern Java. By that time the significant role that Srivijaya had played in expanding Southeast Asian influences across the ocean to Africa and Madagascar had been overshadowed by the Arab and Shirazi merchants on the African coast; and the steadily expanding hoards of Bantu-speaking Africans in the hinterland.

The glory days of the most powerful empire that Southeast Asia had ever known fast receded into the dark and vacuous corners of memory that they occupy today.

THE
PHANTOM VOYAGERS

PART 2

AFRICA

Introduction

It goes without saying that when one is trying to trace the history of people who have kept no written records there is bound to be an element of pot-luck when trawling through the sparse evidence in search of footprints, fingerprints and hard facts. In the case of Indonesia and Africa the problems have not always been with the primary actors – the early Indonesians - who left no records; but all too frequently it has been the attitude of latter day researchers.

One of the major conundrums is why academics have failed so dismally to look beyond African shores for answers to many of the mysteries that lie within them. When Roland Oliver and John Fage first took an interest in 'Africa and Indonesia' in 1959, evidence of contacts was thin – so thin, indeed, as to discourage them from further research. Thus forty years later, Roland Oliver, in a telephone conversation, still saw the subject almost as a joke: "...a few outrigger canoes appearing over the horizon laden with coconuts, bananas and yams, and some crew members happily tinkling on their xylophones!": and in his latest and probably last book, The African Experience, which is described as "a work of reflection (covering) the entire span of human history across the African continent", there is - surprisingly - not a single reference to Indonesia, nor any of consequence to Madagascar. (1)

Once having been effectively declared a 'non-subject' by such 'greats' as Oliver and Fage, later and lesser academics, ever fearful to tread where their masters failed to lead, seem steadfastly to have steered away from it, and as the vogue for specialisation has become more entrenched, matters have only become worse. This has been particularly noticeable in the study of Madagascar. Because of Madagascar's French colonial past, and because the structure of its language is Austronesian - closer to that of Easter Island, 14,000 miles away in the Pacific, than to any of the nearby African languages - Madagascan studies long remained the bailiwick of French orientalists, while the predominantly English speaking Bantu/African experts stayed firmly on their own side of the Moçambique channel.

[1]Despite this, Professor Roland Oliver generously read the first draft of this book for me. He made some very useful suggestions and his overall reaction was extremely positive. Many thanks to him!

Added to this were some less attractive factors. With Uhuru hovering over university lecture rooms like a barbed halo it has become very difficult for even the most honest academic to suggest that everything that appears to be African may not in fact be so. The pressures have been great; but they have occasionally led to some diabolically obscure conclusions that have led subsequent researchers up alleys that have only served to compound the mysteries, rather than elucidate them. We will encounter several; but for a starter, there is one that concerns the people who occupied the coast of East Africa for well over a thousand years in what might be called the pre- or proto-Swahili era. They are the people called the 'Zanj', who, despite a number of well defined clues laid throughout the years by Arabs and Arabists, are still relegated to an obscure corner of history that they certainly don't deserve. The Zanj had boats. They were not Arabs; nor – in their earliest manifestation – do they seem to have been Cushitic, Hamitic or Bantu; and being described as big and black, nor were they apparently Bushmen or Hottentots. So who were these mystery Zanj?

CHAPTER - 8

WHO WERE THE ZANJ?

In ancient times the coast of East Africa was known as 'Azania', from which modern Tanzania and Zanzibar take there names. Pliny, for example, wrote of 'Azania', and the people associated with it called the 'Zangenae'. At about the same time as Pliny, in the middle of the 1st century, the Greek sea-captain who wrote the *Periplus* mentioned the 'Small and Great Bluffs of Azania', and – possibly of significance – people on an island who had sewn boats and dugout canoes that are used for fishing and for catching turtles. "The inhabitants of this island also have their own way of going after these with baskets, which they lower instead of nets around the mouths of [?rocky inlets]."(1) The techniques he observed were obviously new to him, and he would have been unaware of their apparent similarities to fishing techniques in Malaya and Indonesia.

Ptolemy Claudius, in the 2nd century, mentioned the 'Zingis' or 'Zanj', which referred to both a place and its inhabitants somewhere south of the 'Barabara', or Berbers. The Sassanids of Persia, around 300 A.D., had dealing with "Zand Afrik Shah", i.e. the king of the Zanj people of East Africa. Cosmas Indicopleustas, writing about 520 A.D. mentioned the 'Zanj' but added little that was new. The Zanj of Azania are mentioned time and again throughout the first millennium, and must therefore have been permanent - and prominent - residents of the coast.

Late in the 7th century, and again in the early part of the 9th century Sassanian rulers in the Persian Gulf (beating Saddam Husain to it by more than 1000 years) employed large numbers of slaves to drain the Euphrates marshes in southern Iraq. Of the many slaves brought in from Egypt and the Nilotic Sudan, and others who were corralled from local populations along the Mesopotamian rivers, all – according to the records - spoke Arabic. But the largest group of slaves, designated 'negroes' from the coast of East Africa were ignorant of Arabic, and required interpreters. They were 'Zanj'; and much has been written of their revolt against slavery towards the end of the 9th century.

Who were the Zanj?

The author of the *Periplus* had written that Azania "...is under the rule of the governor of Maphiritis, since by some ancient right it is subject to the kingdom of Arabia as first constituted." On account of this, many scholars have assumed that the Zanj must have been Arabs of some sort. But if that was the case, why on earth would the Zanj have been unable to speak Arabic?

The British orientalist, Anthony Christie, thought the word 'Zanj' may have originated on the far side of the Indian Ocean. "The Arab word *zang* or *zenj* used for negro may not be Arabic."...said Christie. "An apparent Chinese form occurs as early as 607 AD. There is no doubt that this *seng-ch'i* was typically S.E. Asian. It could possibly be a S.E. Asian word." (2)

In Tang times, [by 618 A.D.], ambergris from Africa was finding its way to China; and soon rhino horn, ivory, ebony, frankincense and myrrh were added to the shopping lists, some of which were transhipped to China via Srivijaya. (3) Writing in 1278, Chou Ch'u-fei, referred to the people of the lands from which these goods came as the *Kuen-luen Tseng-kji*. Normally the term *Kuen-luen* carried implications of swarthiness, and was usually used by the Chinese to describe the dark people of tropical Southeast Asia. (4) Here, however, it links the people of Southeast Asia (*Kuen-lun*) directly with the Zanj of East Africa (*Tseng-kji*). Writing at about the same time as Chou Ch'u-fei, an Arab author placed the 'island of the Zanj' more or less where northern Madagascar would lie, implying that the Zanj lived on both sides of the Moçambique channel. Ibn Said (d.1286) held that the people of *Al-Qomr* – 'the Moon' - gave their name to *djabal al-kamar* - 'the Mountains of the Moon' - which were in the African interior, saying that these people were not Africans but rather the 'brothers of the Chinese'. This was surely another clear indication of blood-ties on the other side of the Indian Ocean.

From Arab writers it is not always clear whether the term 'Zanj' was linguistic, geographical, or racial. Most writers declared the Zanj to be '*sudan*', or 'black'. According to Masudi (mid 10th century) they made iron ornaments, kept cattle, and were in some way connected with the Berbers of the north-east coast. But two contemporaries of his - Istakhri and Ibn Hawqal - reported that in one region of Zanj country the climate was cold, the culture primitive, and the inhabitants were *white*, an overtly racist cover-all term used by Arab writers meaning that though they may have been dusky, they were not 'blacks'. (5) As the East African specialist Nevil Chittick pointed out: "Though (in Arab sources) the Zanj are distinguished from slaves from other parts of Africa, their racial character is not wholly clear."

The Phantom Voyagers

In the 1970's and 80's, using post-Islamic Arab writings as her sources, Marina Tolmacheva, a Soviet researcher at the Institute of Ethnography in Leningrad (later a professor at Washington State University), wrote several articles about the Zanj which helped to build a picture of who they might have been.(6) From what the Arabs had to say, there were clearly different 'kinds', or 'tribes', of Zanj. For instance, Zanzibaris were distinguished from Pembans, and both differed from other Zanj on the mainland. Though the Zanj are described as 'black skinned' the term was never used in the same way as 'Sudan' which was a general Arab term for Black people – in fact, as already stated, al-Istakhri and Ibn Hawqal referred to some of them as 'White Zanj'. They were Pagans, and their conversion to Islam seems to have been a slow process. In the 10th century their rulers were regularly referred to as 'Kings'. Only in the 13th century did they become 'Sheikhs' and 'Sultans': and not until the same century was Mogadishu, which may once have been at the northern limits of the Zanj 'empire', referred to by Yaqut as a Muslim city, or by Ibn Said as 'the glorious city of Islam'.

Several Arab writers referred to the fact that the Zanj were fine orators. In the 9th century al-Jahiz repeatedly described their eloquence: "There is not in the world a parlance easier for their tongue than their language. One of their men would preach in the presence of the king of the Zanj from dawn till sunset without recurring to gestures or interrupting himself until his speech is finished." And a little later al-Masudi noted that: "the Zanj have an elegant language and men who preach in it. One of their holy men will often gather a crowd and exhort his hearers to please god in their lives and to be obedient to him. He explains the punishments that follow upon disobedience, and reminds them of their ancestors and their kings of old." Al-Dimishqi stressed that this eloquence for which they were famed applied mainly to the northern Zanj, saying that the inhabitants of more distant places 'are deprived of any cultural understanding'; and Ibn al-Nadim pointed out that they "do not have any kind of known script or written language".

Referring to their language, Tolmacheva mentioned ten or twelve Zanj idioms in Arab manuscripts some of which she thought might have had Bantu affiliations, though in several cases these links were uncertain, even questionable. Some even appear to have referred to people who were *not* Bantu Africans. For example, as first noted by al-Jahiz in the 9th century, the people of Pemba and Zanzibar respectively were referred to as *ya-nbwa* and *ya-kibwa*. It is possible that these were forms of the Bantu words *mbwa* referring to 'dogs' or *kubwa* meaning 'large', but, in Tomacheva's view, it is more likely they were a version of *batwa*, a word used in Bantu languages to denote 'stranger'; or 'alien' people such as Pygmies, or Bushmen; or to describe 'the smaller races' that they – the Bantu - had displaced. Rather than suggest that the Zanj were Bantu, these names seemed positively to differentiate them, a point reinforced by the fact that as late as the 16th century, when Arabs were well established on the coast, "they still", according to Marina Tolmacheva, "called the language of its people Zanj."

Several other Zanj words in the Arab texts which sound as though they could have had a Bantu origin, may actually have been borrowings from across the Indian Ocean. *Kilari* or *kalari*, refers to root vegetables or 'edible ground plants' of some sort, of which sweet potatoes, or yams are possibilities. But as we shall see, these plants were introduced to Africa from Indonesia a very long time ago. A word that arose in the Arabic texts as referring to bananas was *al-qnd*, which would usually be transcribed as *kundi*. Like yams, bananas and plantains of all varieties were also brought to Africa from Indonesia at some time in the distant past, and names derived from the -*konde* root are widely found from Madagascar to West Africa. There was a fruit, too, described by Ibn Battuta as "... *jammun* which looks like an olive. It has a nut like an olive, but its taste is very sweet". But *jammun* also comes from across the Indian Ocean, being known in Ceylon as *jamb* and in Malay, *djambu*.

If there was a problem with Marina Tolmacheva's research (which she herself recognised) it was that by limiting herself only to post-Islamic Arab references, the earliest of which was in the 9th century, she severely restricted the scope of her conclusions. When al-Masudi said that their orators reminded the people of their ancestors "and their kings of old" he seemed to accept the fact that the Zanj had been on the coast a long time, thus bridging the gap between the earliest mentions of Azania and the Zangenae, and the Chinese *seng-ch'i*.

When the Arabs encountered them, the Zanj already occupied the offshore islands including Pemba, Zanzibar and (according to Ibn Rusta) the Island of 'Barbar' – somewhere off the Somali Peninsular. They must therefore have been mariners; and it is reasonable to assume that their means of getting between the islands would have been the traditional *ngalaua* outrigger canoes that had been introduced by Indonesians, and are still used on inshore waters in Madagascar and from the Bajun Islands to Tanzania further south. If their original language was Austronesian, as we suspect, and the Zanj gradually acquired Bantu languages in its stead, their traditional abilities as seamen would not be entirely surprising. As migrating Bantu became more numerous on the coast, and the Arabo-

Bantu Swahili language took shape, the offspring of the minority 'stranger' community of mainly male mariners would surely have been brought up to speak the language of their African mothers - whoever they might have been.

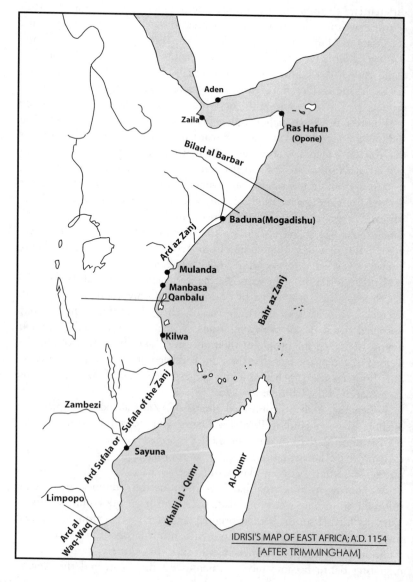

IDRISI'S MAP OF EAST AFRICA; A.D. 1154
[AFTER TRIMMINGHAM]

Who were the Zanj?

One of the earliest and most interesting 'maps' of the East African coast was that compiled by the Arab, el-Idrisi, in 1154. In it he mapped over 2000 miles of the coast - from Mogadishu to the Limpopo – dividing it into several distinct zones. To the Arabs, the whole western part of the *Bahr al-Hind* (The Indian Ocean) was then called the *Bahr az-Zanj*. Idrisi subdivided the *Bar az-Zanj* into the *Bilad az-Zanj*, the "Land of the Zanj" stretching roughly from Mogadishu to Tanga; and the *Bilad az-Sufala* (also referred to as "Sufalah of the Zanj", or the *Ard adh-dhabad*, the "Land of Gold") between Tanga and the Limpopo. Beyond the 'Sufalah of the Zanj' – that is all the country, approximately, to the south of the Limpopo - was the '*Ard al-WaqWaq*', the land of the 'Waq-Waq', another name that in the literature of the day was synonymous with 'Indonesians'.

In the first millennium many people still held to the Ptolomaic notion that southern Africa curved away to the east in a solid strip of land that crossed the southern Indian ocean, 'to places where it was dangerous to go.' Although Al-Masudi had cast doubts on the Ptolomaic geography, the southern seas were obviously a no-go area for the Arabs. The writer Al-Buruni, for instance, was confident that "...The sea beyond Sufalah of the Zanj is unnavigable. ... No ship which ventured to go there ever returned." He was referring, of course, to Arab *dhows* which may have been much less manoeuvrable than Indonesian vessels.

El-Idrisi doubtless shared Al-Buruni's thoughts, and although he did not say so specifically, he may still have harboured the notion of the land extending eastward when he referred to the region beyond the 'Sufalah of the Zanj' as the '*Ard al-Waq Waq*'.(7) Why, one wonders, did he otherwise make this obvious connection with Indonesians? Was he suggesting, or even confirming, that Indonesians were living on the coast of southern Africa? Whatever he had in mind he clearly implied that people from Indonesia sailed far to the south, beyond the limits of Arab navigation.

When Idrisi described the people of Sayuna, an important harbour on or near the mouth of the Zambezi, he wrote: "The Zanj have no ships in which they can travel [the open sea]". This has led some commentators to conclude that the Zanj were landlubbers. But surely Idrisi only meant that they lacked large ocean-going vessels? Surely they must have had vessels for travelling up and down the coast, and for getting to the offshore islands which we know they reached? He goes on:- "... but ships come to them from Uman and other places [concerned with trade with the Zabag islands] that belong to the islands of Hind. They exchange there [in Zanj country] their goods for those of Zanj. The people of the Zabaj islands [also] travel to the Zanj in both small and large ships and engage in trafficking in their goods because they understand each other's language."

As already noted, 'Zabaj', or 'Zabag' was the Arab name for Sumatra and, indeed, for the State of Srivijaya; and 'the islands of Hind' can be read as 'the Indonesian islands'. The phrase '... *because they understand each other's language*' is therefore of great significance. It does more than just imply a connection between the Zanj and the Zabaj. It confirms a close link of some sort. In fact, Al-Biruni had already written of the "Zabaj and Zanj" as one and the same, saying they are very tricky to deal with!

The English Arabist the Rev Trimmingham, seemed to be agreeing with Al-Buruni in a brief footnote to an article about the Zanj. He first explained that the Arabic word '*Zabag*' can be transcribed from Arabic in different ways: "Zabaj/Zanaj, an early Arabic rendering of Java, though actually Zabaj was also Sumatra." He then wrote of an island which lay off the coast of Mombasa that had been described by Idrisi as belonging to the Zanj, or, according to another Arab writer, the Zanaj. "... might it be Zanj?", said Trimmingham, tentatively suggesting that the 'Zanaj' and the 'Zanj' might be the same people.(8)

Zabag, Zabaj, Zanaj, Zanj. The conclusion is compelling, that throughout the first millennium, before the Bantu dominated the hinterland, and before the Arabs were established in strength in their fortified coastal cities, there was a strong Indonesian element implanted on the two thousand miles of coastline from Somalia to South Africa who have come down to us today as the 'Zanj'.

So what happened to the Zanj? We know that Indonesians were the first to colonise Madagascar. It seems certain they had widespread settlements on the African coast. Also, there was regular trade between the Zanj of East Africa and Srivijaya in Sumatra. Now add to this another piece of the jigsaw, pointed out by the Arab writer, Ibn al-Mujawir, which was that from time to time the Zanj had a presence in the port where Aden now lies. If there was continuous two-way traffic between the Zanj and the Zabaj this makes strategic sense. As Shirazi and Arab interference in the trade between Africa and Srivijaya increased, control of Aden might have been as important to the Zanj as it was for the British in later years. In his chronicle, Ibn al-Mujawir, though writing of them as the people of Al-Komr, explains what might have been a key factor in the ultimate demise of the Zanj (at the same time highlighting their brilliance as sailors):

"The Al-Komr (Malagasy) people used to leave Al-Komr to reach Aden in fleets and using a single monsoon ... these people have now disappeared since their power came to an end and since the route of their travel has been closed ... From Aden to Mogadiso there is one monsoon ... from Mogadiso to Kilwa there is a second monsoon and from Kilwa to Al-Komr there is a third one. These people managed to unite the three monsoons into one. A single vessel from Al-Komr thus went .. directly to Aden .. in the year [1228-1229 A.D.]. It was to have docked at Kilwa but it docked at Aden instead. The vessels ... have outriggers because the seas ... are dangerous. [But following the conquest of Aden] these people lost power and the Barabar [people of Berbera] came to them and chased them out of Aden."

There is something about this that makes it sound like the last pathetic gasp of the people who, for a thousand years had maintained a life-line between Madagascar, Africa, and the Austronesian homelands on the other side of the ocean. By the time of the last fateful expedition to Aden, Kilwa and the other main sea-ports of Africa must have become almost wholly 'Arabised', or some would prefer – 'Swahili-ised'. The Zanj would have slowly metamorphosed into the Swahili as we know them today. The last outposts of their empire would have retreated to Al-Komr beyond the Moçambique channel, where they still speak their Austronesian language; whilst their strongholds in Africa had given way to Bantu.

Spencer Trimmingham thought the demise of the Zanj may have been about a hundred years earlier than the period of which Ibn al-Mujawir wrote: "... when the change took place around 1150, it occurred rapidly and simultaneously in all these places and was probably associated with a change of leadership which might have been the result of external or internal stimulus." In increasing numbers, people from the southern coast of Arabia and the Persian Gulf were moving into the centres of commerce on the coast, ousting or intermarrying with the old Zanji ruling classes. "The fact," Trimmingham concluded, "that the rulers of these places do not seem to have followed an indigenous cult simultaneously with Islam implies that the original Zanji ruling class had been displaced by immigrants who were already Muslims and who used Islam both as a cohesive basis for the state and as an important transoceanic link".

CHAPTER - 9

THE GOLDEN DAYS

Sumatra used to be known as 'Suvarnabhumi' – 'the Land of Gold': and on the face of it, there seem to be good reasons for it. First, it is unusual among Indonesian islands in that it has gold mines; and in ancient times it appears that the rulers of Ko-ying, Kan-to-li, and Srivijaya all made good use of them. As early as the 3rd century, Chinese scripts mention gold coming from Ko-ying which is presumed to have been in southern Sumatra; and when an embassy was sent from Kan-to-li to China between 454 and 464 the tribute included gold and silver.(1) The 7th century inscriptions of Bangka Island - those that were written in what Alexander Adelaar called a 'pre-Malagasy' language – referred to the Srivijayan royal court having "a treasury filled with gold and property", and how the king's enemies sought information on the precise whereabouts of the gold and jewels kept in that treasury. A later inscription in southern India describes how Srivijaya-Palembang, sacked by Rajendra Cola 1st in the eleventh century, was noted for its 'golden gates' and 'royal treasury filled with gold.'

Arab and Chinese documents frequently mention Srivijaya's exports of aromatics and forest products; but, apart from a few specific instances such as those already mentioned, they do not say much about gold. Of the thirteen Srivijayan cities conquered by Rajendra Cola's navies, for instance, the annals only mention gold in relation to the capital, Palembang. Gold, it seems, was of such value and rarity that the Midas-like Maharaja alone exercised total control over it.

The Arab chronicler Ibn Khurdadhbih, writing in the 9th century, related just how important gold was to the running of the Srivijayan state. According to him it was customary for the Maharaja to demonstrate his debt to the oceans by communicating with *Tandru n Luah*, "the God of the Waters of the Sea" by daily throwing a gold bar into the water, chanting "Look, there lies my treasure" – a sure indication of the importance of overseas trade to the well-being of the State. When a Raja died, Palembang harbour was dredged, and the gold bars were distributed among the royal family, military commanders, and - if there was any left - the king's other subjects. Indeed, it was said that the greatness of a deceased king was measured by the number of gold bars retrieved from the water on his death. Ibn Khurdadhbih's story was repeated by Abu Zaid a hundred years later, and as there is no good reason to doubt it, there must have been a constant need to replenish the stocks of gold.(2)

But despite Sumatra's sobriquets, *Suvarnabhumi* or *Suvarnadvipa*, 'the Island of Gold', one has to wonder just how much gold was actually produced locally. Though some of the mines were in the far north of the island, possibly beyond the reach of the Srivijayan rulers, the majority lay within their borders, in the mountainous spine that runs down the western side of the island, from which flow the rivers that feed the broad plains that are the lifeblood of Palembang and Jambi. When the Dutch first colonised Sumatra they found numerous ancient gold mines, but in their haste to exploit the known seams for a quick profit they allowed no opportunity for archaeologists to study the mines properly; so our knowledge of them is woefully inadequate.

In the 19th century, geologists working in the western mountains reported traces of ..."advanced mining techniques ...deep vertical shafts, horizontal tunnels, stopes, winzes(sic), aquaducts, and sluices", but with no further elaboration. They also found large stones used to crush the ore, and evidence that the miners knew the use of mercury to extract the gold from quartz and other unwanted minerals. "The extensiveness of the old workings" said the geologists, "indicates a thorough organisation, in which thousands and thousands of men must have been employed. It is evident that considerable quantities of gold have been produced." (3) Taken together, the descriptions suggest that Indians, who exerted a powerful influence on the art and technology of the islands in the first millennium, may have had a hand in Sumatran mining. As India's remarkable mines in Mysore, some of which were several hundred feet deep, were already nearing the end of their useful life by 300 AD. (4) there would have been no shortage of expertise to open up the Sumatran mines.

In the years between 1900 and 1940, using 'modern' technology, the total output of the Sumatran mines, not all of which had been within the borders of 'Srivijaya', accounted for 82% of *all* the gold, produced in the Netherlands East Indies – a total of 101,063 Kg. (5) This works out at an average of about $2^3/_4$ tons a year (which, when compared with the 3 tons stolen in one swoop at London Airport in the November 1983 Brinks Mat robbery, is not a huge amount.) Might far more gold than the $2^3/_4$ tons have been produced using primitive methods? ... almost certainly not. But regardless of how much the ancients produced, human nature being what it is, if they were able to create an even bigger pot of gold from other sources, it is hard to believe that any Maharaja would have turned up his royal nose at an opportunity to do so.

So what other opportunities might there have been?

There is gold in Borneo; but this was not worked extensively until the 17th century. (6) China was a recipient of tributary gold, and therefore not likely to have been an exporter as well. India once produced large quantities; but there is no reason to think that the gold-hungry Indians would have shipped their precious bullion to Sumatra. In any event, as we have mentioned, their own production was declining by the fourth century; and by then also the days of Roman largesse which at one time threatened to deplete Rome's own Fort Knox, were long since over.

But at more or less the same time that Srivijaya was rising from the ashes of Kan-to-li there was one other major source of gold coming 'on stream'– and that was in Africa – in what Idrisi described as the *Ard adh-dhabad*, the country of Gold, or the *Sufalah az-Zanj*. Could it be that the people of the Island of Zabaj or Zanaj obtained gold from their brethren the Zanj in Africa to whose country, according to Idrisi, they travelled in 'both small and large ships', and with whom they were able to engage in 'trafficking in their goods … because they understood each other's language'? Could it even be that, with experience gained in their own mines in Sumatra, the Srivijayans had a hand in developing the mines of Sufalah? Was there, indeed, a golden chain linking the Zanaj and the Zanj?

There has been mining of one sort or another in Southern and Eastern Africa for at least 2000 years. Some iron workings, on the coast and also inland, even as far south as the Transvaal in South Africa, may date back to the 1st or 2nd century AD. (7) Copper mining in Zambia seems to have started around the 4th century AD; (8) whilst gold mining in the highlands of Zimbabwe may have a start-date of around 600 AD. Though some people hold the view that mining technology was independently invented in Africa, (9) most concede that it is likely to have been introduced by outsiders. And as the Zanj people seem to have played a prominent role on the coast for well over a thousand years, and were almost certainly in the southeast long before Bantu speakers reached that part of Africa, Zanj participation in early mining cannot be discounted, particularly as we know (from Masudi) that they were iron-workers. The 600 AD date for the start of gold mining is particularly striking. Following the great 'volcanic interlude' (see chapter 6) the date is roughly contemporary with the first appearance of Tana-style pottery in East Africa and Madagascar; and by neat coincidence it synchronizes well with the rise of the Srivijayan empire in Sumatra and western Java.

Just how extensive was mining in the Zimbabwe highlands?

The records of the old Rhodesian government can help here, although, curiously, 'Rhodesian' law in the 1950's defined an 'ancient mine' as 'any shaft, cutting, tunnel or stope which was made for mining purposes and which was in existence before 1890'. As numerous mines had been opened up by settlers in the years immediately preceding 1890 this was a curious definition which could easily distort the true facts. But discounting those that were probably opened by Europeans, it is estimated that in a wide swathe across Zimbabwe there were over 4000 ancient gold mines varying in age; at least 500 copper mines; and uncountable iron workings some of which, beyond Rhodesia's frontiers near the upper reaches of the Congo, were huge. Although annual output of gold was not likely to have been massive using primitive techniques, the total amount extracted over the centuries was estimated by the Rhodesian archaeologist, Roger Summers and people in the mining industry at between 20,000,000 and 25,000,000 ounces, the bulk of which is likely to have been extracted before the Portuguese arrived at the end of the fifteenth century after reaching a peak between the end of the 9th C. and the end of the 12Th C. (10)

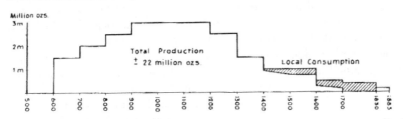

Chart showing suggested annual production figures.

The ancients had many ways of prospecting for gold. Herodotus, in his 'Histories', told some amazing tales of 'Indians' in a land that lay 'Eastward of India' who prospected with ants. His descriptions of the miners were lurid (forgive the digression!); "All the Indian tribes I have mentioned copulate in the open like cattle; their skins are all of the same colour, much like the Ethiopians. Their semen is not white like other peoples' but black like their own skins – the same peculiarity to be found in the Ethiopians". (11) But their use of giant ants for prospecting is worth repeating as it seems, incredibly, that it may contain a few golden grains of truth.

"There is in this desert a kind of ant of great size – bigger than a fox, though not so big as a dog …. As they burrow underground they throw up the sand in heaps … the sand has a rich content of gold and it is this the Indians are after when they make their expeditions into the desert. Each man harnesses three camels abreast, a female, on which he rides, in the middle, and a male on each side on a leading rein…" [Herodotus then describes these camels: 'the camel in its hind legs has four thighs and four knees, and its genitals point backwards towards its tail.']. "They plan their timetable so as actually to get their hands on the gold during the hottest part of the day, when the heat will have driven the ants underground. When the Indians reach the place where the gold is, they fill the bags they have brought with them with sand, and start for home as fast as they can go; for the ants … smell them and at once give chase; nothing in the world can touch these ants for speed, so not one of the Indians would get home alive if they did not make sure of a good start while the ants were mustering their forces."

A lovely yarn; but how might it have applied to ancient Zimbabweans? African termites will burrow down as much as 100 feet to get water for their colonies, and the soil amassed as they excavate will contain samples of all the rocks and minerals through which they have tunnelled. If a prospector panning the spoil from a termite's nest finds evidence of gold, it is a fair bet that there is gold beneath it. This method was put to the test over several years by 'a classically-minded Rhodesian miner' named W.F West and found to work! (12) It was used in India, and is likely to have been one of the methods used in southern Africa.

A second method of prospecting, used universally to this day, would have been the well established technique of panning the rivers.

A third – and possibly the most widely used – would have been careful observation of the vegetation. For instance, land where *Mangwe, Mopane,* and *Msasa* trees grow is unlikely to be gold-bearing. On the other hand Ficus trees are found in areas that may well be auriferous, so it was there that they looked for the telltale signs of reefs.

As the majority of reefs were visible on the surface, the first phase of mining was relatively simple. But the reefs generally dipped steeply and were frequently only 30 cms to a metre wide. If the stope stretched far underground, the miners sank shafts and excavated laterally to the limits of light and air, before repeating the process with another shaft nearby. The system was similar to the techniques described in Sumatra where miners sank 'deep vertical shafts and horizontal tunnels'.

Old mines have been found where the underlying ores must have been barely visible on the surface. Some old shafts were barely 18 inches in diameter and can only have been wide enough for children (or Bushmen?) to pass. For digging they used hardwood sticks and short handled hoes, but in one ancient mine the discovery of a shovel caused a stir, shovels being unknown in that part of Africa when Europeans arrived, but used in India and Indonesia for centuries. When the ore was extracted, the miners left columns of mineral-rich rock to support the ceiling, or – on rare occasions – propped the ceiling with timber supports; and when an area was worked out, the shaft and the *stope* were usually filled in as the next shaft was excavated. No artificial light was used, so as the *stopes* got deeper conditions became more and more difficult. Mines were usually worked until water was reached, which in some cases was as much as 120 feet beneath the surface.

To loosen the ore, fires were set against the walls, and quenched with carefully directed streams of water, but there were dangers in this as they created potentially explosive steam. Carbon monoxide and other noxious gases were cleared by digging special ventilation shafts with charcoal fires set beneath them to create convection currents, as in a chimney, sending the foul air up to the surface and drawing fresh air down the main shafts. Because of the ever present fear of flooding, it is probable that the mines could only be worked during the dry season in August, September and October.

One problem that Roger Summers was unable to figure out was how the miners hauled the broken ore to the surface. Early Indian mines, some of which reached a depth of 600 ft, had fairly sophisticated lifting gear; but there were no signs of this in the African mines. It is, however, conceivable that some form of gantry may have been erected over the tops of mine shafts which would explain the lack of evidence. In modern times the bark of *baobab* trees has been extensively used for making rope, a method probably also used centuries ago.

Having got the ore to the surface the miners were faced with the laborious task of crushing it and recovering the gold, copper, or whatever other metal there might have been. One of the commonest ways of milling the ore was in *dolly-holes*, mortar-like holes made in rock surfaces in which it was bashed with dolerite pestles or hand-held balls of hard stone. Another more efficient method may have been with a large rock weighing maybe 1000 or 1500 pounds onto which a small tree trunk was fixed so that it could be rocked back and forth by two people like a see-saw, as uncrushed ore was pushed beneath it. This ancient but simple piece of machinery, known as a *mullocker*, was still in use in the twentieth century in some Indian mines and there is some evidence that it might have been used in

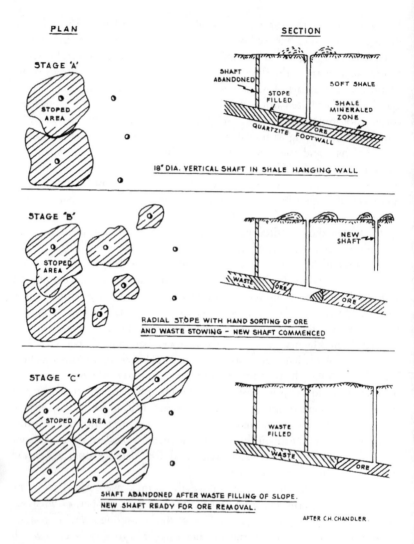

PLAN

SECTION

STAGE 'A'

STOPED AREA

SHAFT ABANDONED
STOPE FILLED
SOFT SHALE
SHALE MINERALED ZONE
QUARTZITE FOOTWALL
ORE

18" DIA. VERTICAL SHAFT IN SHALE HANGING WALL

STAGE 'B'

STOPED AREA

NEW SHAFT
WASTE
ORE
ORE

RADIAL STOPE WITH HAND SORTING OF ORE
AND WASTE STOWING - NEW SHAFT COMMENCED

STAGE 'C'

STOPED AREA

WASTE FILLED
WASTE
ORE

SHAFT ABANDONED AFTER WASTE FILLING OF SLOPE.
NEW SHAFT READY FOR ORE REMOVAL.

AFTER C.H. CHANDLER

Africa. Maybe the 'large stones' that the Dutch geologists described in Indonesia were used in a similar way. Once crushed to a powder, the most likely method of concentrating the metal was by the time honoured technique of 'panning' in wooden trays; but as very few milling and recovery sites have come to light there is scant evidence of precisely how this was actually done. It seems that 'amalgamation' with mercury, as used in India and, apparently, in Sumatra, was not used in Africa.

Some remarkable finds have been reported from the African mines. They include a copper coin of Antonius Pius (A.D. 138 – 160) said to have been found 70 feet below the ground: a silver penny of John of England (1199- 1216) found on the surface near a mine: and a silver sixpence of Elizabeth 1st of England, retrieved from 'fill' 40 ft down. Scholars tend to treat these reported finds with suspicion, maybe because they have neither found them themselves, nor seen them with their own eyes. There is, however, no obvious reason why anyone should have lied about them; and as a large variety of coins were in circulation along the early Indian Ocean trade routes, the fact that they have turned up in Zimbabwean mines may sound surprising, but is by no means impossible. Less questioned by the experts were the discoveries of 9th century blue-green, green, and yellow beads of southern Indian or Malayan origin.

In the 1890's a miner found the remains of "a small brown man with straight black hair done in a short type of pigtail, naked except for a loincloth, found in a crouching position in the bottom of an ancient stope on the Champion mine, Gwanda." As the ore in the region was rich in arsenic, it is presumed it may have been this that preserved the body. Roger Summers commented: "Captain Chick's description of 'long hair tied in a sort of pigtail' sounds as if the miner may have been an Asian rather than an African".

A number of mines in different regions were associated with pottery with a graphitic 'glaze' known to archaeologists from their type-sites as *Ziwa* or *Gokomere*, similar to the early iron age *Kwale* ware of the coast. The earliest pottery in this style dates back to the coming of the iron age in Zimbabwe, thought to have been in about the 2nd century A.D; but as these pottery types remained in use over a period of six or seven centuries – incidentally providing a fascinating thread of cultural continuity over a long period - they cannot really be used as a means of pin-pointing the beginning of mining.

The finger has already been pointed at Indians as the technical experts behind both the Sumatran and Zimbabwe mines. The techniques of mining; the treatment of the ore; the extraction of the precious metals – all (except the absence of mercury) appear to follow the patterns of ancient Indian mines. "Since ancient Rhodesian mining methods differed from those in use elsewhere in Africa but were very close to those used in Southern India, we may postulate a connection", wrote Roger Summers, concluding that Indian prospectors probably came to Zimbabwe in about the sixth or seventh century to look for alternative sources of gold to replace the diminishing reserves in Mysore. As Summers made no mention of

Sumatran mines, it seems that when he was writing in the 1960's he was unaware of them.

If Indians were responsible for the African mines, one has to ask why there were no other signs of Indian settlement in the region and no mention of them in any of the Arab chronicles. And in view of the doubts already expressed about Indian prowess on the high seas, would they really have been able to carry on this trade so far from home?(13) On the other hand as we know that Indonesians were in Africa, and as will see much more evidence of Malagasy/Indonesian involvement in the very same region where the gold mines were located, is it not far more likely that the mines formed an essential part of the Indonesian diaspora?

What happened to all the gold? A few small gold objects have been found scattered throughout the mining region, showing that at least some was used locally; but most of it appears to have been taken down to the coast to be exported.

There were several obvious routes to the sea from the Zimbabwean goldfields. One was overland to the Zambezi valley somewhere near the modern town of Tete, from where there were 300 miles of navigable water to the sea-port described by Idrisi at 'Sayuna'. "Sayuna is medium in size", Idrisi said, "and its inhabitants are a collection of people from Hind, Zunuj, and others. It is situated on the shore of the sea and is the residence of the ruler of the country. He has an army of foot soldiers for they have no horses. This town is situated on an estuary into which the ships of the voyagers can enter." (14) The 'Zunuj' can only have been Indonesians; but were the 'Hind' from mainland India, or the 'Isles of Hind', i.e. Indonesia?

Five hundred miles to the south, between the Zambezi and the Limpopo, the Save valley provided an alternative route to the sea from the majority of the mines, and at the head of the navigable part of the river leading to the ocean there are some fascinating but little known remnants of what must at one time have been a thriving riverine community. Dug into land behind the Save's banks near the village of Marumbene on the Zimbabwe/Moçambique border, archaeologists found what appear to be the remains of ancient boat-docks. (15) According to the local Africans there were several such docks, all located near the confluence of the Save with its tributary the Lundi that flows from the hills near the Great Zimbabwe. The Marumbene docks were visited by Roger Summers in 1959 who described them as being roughly rectangular, about 250 yards long and 40 feet wide. The depth was not great but the presence of a large number of hippopotami and crocodiles prevented him making accurate measurements. The main dock was some 600 yards from the bank of the Lundi, which joined the Save a quarter of a mile downstream. A watercourse (dry when examined) wound through the countryside at a depth of about 10 feet linking the dock with the river. "It seems," said Summers, "as if this donga had been excavated to provide a place in which small ships could moor off the river."

In the course of the 200 miles from Marumbene to the sea the Save drops a mere 350 to 400 feet, and the fact that sawfish, tarpon and an estuarine turtle have all been caught near the village - sustained, apparently, by the exceptionally high salinity of the river fed by the leaching of salts from lands higher up the valley - confirmed that it was navigable all the way from the coast.

It is often assumed that goods brought to the coast down the Save valley would have been destined for Sofala, the most southerly 'port' reached by Arabs in mediaeval times, which tradition claims to have been located near modern Nova Mambone. But did Sofala ever actually exist as a port? In Arabic the word 'Sufalah' simply means a 'shoal' or 'sandbank' and could apply to almost anywhere. 'Sayuna', the town at the mouth of the Zambezi, was described by Idrisi as lying in the 'district of Sufala'. A *region* rather than a *town* may also have been what el-Masudi had in mind when he wrote of Sofala as…"the most distant frontier of the territory that is reached by the ships of Oman and Siraf." To the Portuguese, the name referred to the 'hinterland' south of the Zambezi, and to Idrisi the *Bilad az-Sufalah* was definitely a region. The odds are that there never was an actual town or port called Sofala. So, if they did not go to a port called Sofala, what might have been the coastal destination of the products of Zimbabwe?

Lying between the mouth of the Save and Cape St Lucia, not many miles north of modern Durban, there were a number of other very ancient ports to which goods from the interior might have been sent, some dating from the early iron-age, i.e. first or second century A.D. Two excellent natural harbours within Idrisi's 'Region of Sufalah' were Chibuene, well protected in Vilanculos Bay; and Inhambane, about 100 miles further south, comfortably tucked in behind Cape Correntes - the famous 'Cape of Currents' beyond which lay the Land of the Waq-Waq, where Arab sailors feared to venture in their dhows. Both towns almost certainly existed in pre-Islamic times; 6th century pottery has been found at Chibuene, thus it existed before gold mining in the interior began. But, of most particular interest, it was here amongst the sand-dunes that archaeologists found crucibles for purifying gold, thereby associating Chibuene ineluctably with the gold-mining communities inland. (16)

Though Palembang in Srivijaya seems to have been the most likely destination for Africa's gold, there is an alternative possibility that pops up like a joker in the pack. Might it have been the Javanese, not the Sumatrans, who played the strongest hand in the gold game? Could Sufalah's gold have gone to *Java*?

Far back in history, Java had acquired a reputation for being a veritable El Dorado, supposedly producing huge quantities of gold of its own. In pre-Christian times the *Ramayana* mentioned that Hanuman, the Monkey General, commanded his simian hordes to search for Rama's abducted wife, Sita, in *Yavadvipa* (Java) - "the gold and silver island that is rich in gold mines". Ptolomey (in the 2nd C.) wrote, that *Iabadiou* (Java) is "said to be a most fruitful island and to produce much gold." In the 7th C. an inscription of the *Yava* King Sanjaya proclaimed that the island was "possessed of gold mines". And early *T'ang* sources (618 – 907) to late *Sung* (960 – 1279) refer to Java producing both 'white gold' (silver) and 'yellow gold' (the real thing). One *T'ang* text described how the residence of the king was covered with tiles made of gold, how there were ponds with sides of gold, and how even the oars of the boats were decorated with gold and jewels. A 14th C. writer, Friar Odoric of Pordenone, says of the royal palace of Majapahit in eastern Java (the Hindu State that succeeded Srivijaya):- "It is very great and has great staircases, broad and lofty, and the steps thereof are of gold and silver alternately; likewise the pavement of the palace has one tile of gold and the other of silver, and the wall of the same is on the inside plated all over with plates of gold." (17) And Marco Polo, (whose information was based on hearsay and was not always reliable), said of Java: "The quantity of gold collected there exceeds all calculations and belief. From thence it is that the merchants of Zai-tun and Manji in general have imported, and to this day import, that metal to a great amount". (19)

Modern treasure hunters are constantly finding beautifully crafted rings, hair pins, and other items of personal adornment buried in the soil; but perhaps most mysterious and extraordinary of all the discoveries was in the village of Wonoboyo, near Prambanan in Central Java, where, in 1990, a number of exquisite solid gold bowls, dishes, ladles, shell-like water dippers, etc. weighing in total 440 ounces and dated to about 900 AD, were found buried 9 feet beneath the surface stashed in a large Chinese porcelain jar. (20)

It seems that Java's reputation for being an island with enormous riches in gold might have been justified.

And herein lies the mystery. We have already seen that 82% of gold from Dutch Indonesia, which consisted of 14,000 islands including half

Papua New Guinea and most of Borneo, came from western Sumatra. In support of this, Brian Colless, writing in 1973 on Javanese gold, made the point that a fundamental problem of understanding ancient Javanese civilisation hinged on the question of gold. Most old literary texts characterise Java as having been rich in gold and possessing gold mines, but, while archaeologists have found ample evidence in the form of gold rings and other objects, geologists emphatically deny that Java could ever have produced gold in appreciable quantities. As Colless asked incredulously: "Whence came Javanese gold?"

Several possibilities have been suggested:

a) that ancient writers attributed products to Java that were actually imported, possibly from as far away as the Philippines. A good example: cloves and nutmegs were thought by many people to have been grown in Java, though in reality they were only being transhipped in Java, having come originally from the Moluccas,

b) that a lot of Java's 'gold' objects were in fact wood or brass covered with gold leaf, giving visitors a wrong impression of their value.

c) that Java may have owned gold mines elsewhere, on another island, most likely in Borneo where, in the latter part of the 17th century, Chinese miners started extracting gold in substantial quantities. Prior to that date there may have been some small scale 'panning' by Dyaks and Malays; but there is no evidence that Borneo produced large quantities of gold in ancient times.

So once again, given the relationship between the Zanj of Africa and the Zabaj of Sumatra; given the power of Srivijaya, and its command of the high seas; given that, at it's height, Srivijaya's hegemony extended deep into Java, as far as Prambanan and Borobudur; given the movement of people between Indonesia, Africa, and Madagascar which must have continued over a period of a thousand years, into the eleventh century; surely the most likely answer is that the gold from ancient Zimbabwe was mined primarily to satiate the ravening appetites of both Sumatran *and* Javanese princes. Maybe one day chemical analysis will go some way to proving or disproving this hypothesis.

CHAPTER - 10

WHO ARE THE MALAGASY?

In the patchwork of relationships that link Africa with Indonesia, the Austronesian-speaking people of Madagascar have always been a key element. But the answer to the frequently asked question "Who are the Malagasy?" is complex and convoluted, and there is not always agreement as to their precise origins.

Various hypotheses have been put forward that link the Malgache language to those of the Philipines, the Toba-Batak of Northern Sumatra, different parts of Melanesian, or Malaya.(1) However in academic circles, more often than not, Madagascar's language – and hence one of the core centres of the peoples' origin - is indivisibly linked with that of the Ma'anjan of the Barito valley in South-eastern Borneo. But as academics who hold this view seem to have been untypically lazy about checking their sources, it is a connection that should be treated with caution. For, on a closer look a Ma'anjan origin is highly debatable.

The Malgache/Ma'anjan link was first proposed in 1929 by the Norwegian missionary/linguist Otto Dahl who, during fifteen years in Madagascar had acquired what he modestly described as a good 'day-to-day' knowledge of the Merina and Sakalava dialects. Dahl's choice of Ma'anjan as a comparative language arose from a chance meeting, rather than any broad study of Indonesian languages. He was already interested in the Malagasy/Malayo-Polynesian connection, when, on his way through Hamburg, he happened to run into an associate, Walther Aichele, who in the course of conversation mentioned that he had noticed a remarkable convergence between Malgache (Malagasy) and the Ma'anjan language of South-east Borneo. Encouraged by his friend, Dahl decided to pursue this lead.(2)

Dahl's source materials were minimal: there were at the time just two Ma'anjan 'dictionaries' – 'word-lists' would be more appropriate - one collected by C. den Homer in 1889 with about 350 words; and one with 206 words collected by Sidney H. Ray in 1913. From these brief documents Dahl found a sufficient number of words with parallels in Malgache on which to base his opinion that Ma'anjan must have been its 'mother' tongue.

But, though no doubt a persuasive linguist, Dahl cannot have been all that familiar with South-eastern Borneo and the lifestyle of the Ma'anjan people. If he had been, he might, from the start, have seen how unlikely it was that the Ma'anjan were involved, and been more cautious when formulating his conclusions.

The Ma'anjan, together with the Ngadju, Ot Danum, and Benuaq, are sub-groups of the Languan Dyaks, all members of the Barito language-family in South-eastern Borneo. Such is probably of more interest to western ethnologists than to the Ma'anjan themselves for whom concepts of 'ethnicity' or 'belonging to specific tribal groups' are, as in other parts of Borneo, almost absent. (3) Most of the Dayaks live in relatively small, isolated, inland communities; their languages are Malayic and indigenous to Borneo; and, if not Christians, they practice an animist religion. But the term 'Dyak', or 'Dayak' needs to be used guardedly. According to Judith Hudson and her husband who lived among the Ma'anjan in the 1970's, Dayak has "about the same specificity of meaning as the American word 'Indian', and, like the latter, serves as a cover term for a heterogeneous assortment of named tribes..." Traditionally no Borneo groups call themselves Dayak, since the term is pejorative; roughly the equivalent of 'hick' or 'yokel'.(4)

Despite this, modern ethnographers continue to speak of 'Sea Dayaks', or 'Land Dayaks', the latter group being the one to which the Ma'anjan belong. The available historical evidence suggests that until the mid-seventeenth century the Ma'anjan lived in the fertile alluvial plains in what is now the Hulu Sungai district of South Kalimantan, about 100 miles from the sea. They practiced swidden cultivation at a subsistence level, and grew small quantities of black peppers to exchange with Banjarese traders in the coastal ports of South Borneo.

In the 1850's the Ma'anjan living in the forests of the Padju-Epat area were also well known as the makers of large dugout canoes. Indeed, apart from rice cultivation and the pepper trade, this was their main occupation. "All the canoes that are used on the Barito and in the sultanate", a Dutch report of the time noted, "are made almost exclusively by the Dayaks of Padju Epat." Large canoes 30 – 50 feet in length were hacked from huge trees and broadened with fire. "Hundreds and hundreds of them are brought down the river by them every year in order to be sold." (5)

Builders and salesmen of large dugouts they may have been, but nowhere in their history is there any suggestion that the Ma'anjan have at any time been sea-going people. Indeed there is no way in which it makes any realistic sense to link the simple, family-loving, forest-dwelling Ma'anjan with the great voyages of migration to far away Africa and Madagascar. Even Otto Dahl himself was unable to come up with any convincing maritime parallels between the two languages; the closest connection with the oceans that lay between Borneo and Africa was a Ma'anjan word for 'sea' which bears a very shaky relationship to the name of a lake in the middle of Madagascar. Apart from that there is nothing to suggest the Ma'anjan had any knowledge of lands beyond Kalimantan.

But then, in the penultimate paragraph of his "Malgache et Maanjan", it was, oddly enough, Otto Dahl himself who gave the clearest pointer as to where the Malagasy might have come from, and who they really might have been, when he wrote (my translation): "Nevertheless the resemblances to Maanjan do not resolve all the problems of Malgache. There are in Malgache some elements that seem to point to the Celebes." (6)

As we have seen in an earlier chapter, the south western part of the Celebes, or Sulawesi, was the traditional heartland of the most famous and fearless of all Indonesian mariners, the Bajo and the Bugis, whose ancestors were the most likely of all the Indonesian Sea Nomads to have been able to undertake the trans-oceanic journeys to Africa . Otto Dahl thus opened the door to the possibility that it might not have been the Ma'anjan who were the progenitors of Malagasy, and that it could have been others from Sulawezi who spoke a similar language.

Adelaar's tentative suggestion that the 7th century texts of Bangka and Palembang were a sort of 'pre-Malagasy' from that general region fits well with this assumption; and is particularly interesting in that it creates an ancient link between South-eastern Borneo, Sulawezi, and South-eastern Sumatra, seven hundred miles apart across the Java Sea.

Is there any evidence from the African or Madagascan side of the Indian Ocean to support a hypothesis that it might have been the Bajo or Bugis (see Chapter 7) who – maybe among – others were the phantom voyagers?
Bugi, Bajo, Mandar, Makassar. Are these not names that mingle like distant bells in the susurrating reefs of Africa, as well as the surf-thrashed shores of Sulawezi? *Bajo, Bajau, Bajoo, Badjo, Baju* … Who are the people who inhabit the 500 islands and islets strung out along 170 miles of the African coast between Lamu and Kisimayu? (7) The *Bajun?* or *Bajuni?* Could there possibly be a connection? Is it stretching credulity too far?

The origins of the Bajun of East Africa are unresolved and can justifiably be termed 'enigmatic'. Vinigi Grottanelli, still the best authority on the Bajun, devoted much space to finding the origin of their name – seven pages, to be precise - in his 'Pescatori Dell'Oceano Indiano', but still left the question open. He made a point, however, of saying that the name does not follow the normal Bantu rules. They are never known as the *wa-bajuni*; nor is the singular *m'bajuni* ever heard. Likewise they are not *m'juni, mujuni, wajuni or vajuni* as would be expected if they were north eastern Bantu. They are the 'Bajun' or 'Bajuni' pure and simple. They are said, variously, to have Arab, Persian, Indian, Bantu and possibly some oriental blood in them. They are a mixture; but originally from where? (8)

James Kirkman, the British archaeologist who excavated the early Swahili town of Gedi, believed that apart from the Witu - a tribe of hunters who spoke a click language like that of the San, and were on the coast long before the Bantu - the Bajun were the oldest inhabitants of their namesake islands. He had a theory that the Bajun are the descendants of the lost 'Almozaid' people mentioned by the Portuguese chronicler, Joao de Barros, in *Da Asia*, 1552 who said of them: "From their entrance, like a slow plague, they spread along the coast … The town of Magadoxo gained such power and state that it became the sovereign and head of all the Moors of the coast; but as the first tribe who came, called Emozaydy, held different opinions from the Arabs with regard their creed, they would not submit to them and retreated to the interior, where they joined the Kaffirs, intermarrying with them and adopting their customs, so that in every way they became *mestizes*. These are the people whom the Moors of the seacoast call Baduys" … and it was the Baduys whom Kirkman equated with the 'Bajun'. (9)

It is difficult to claim, from this, that the Baduys were 'Indonesians'; but clearly if they were neither Moors, Kaffirs, nor Muslims, and despite coming under the suzerainty of the 'sovereign' of *Magadoxo*, from what de Barros said, it seems likely that they came originally from somewhere other than the Middle East or the Horn of Africa. So can we see in the *mestizes* a mingling of Afro-Indonesians being put under pressure by the Arabs? We might even speculate that de Barros's term 'Emo*zaydy*' could have been a mishearing of 'Zabag', 'Zanaj', or 'Zanj'.

Excavations on Manda, one of the Bajun islands, have revealed substantial settlements with buildings going back to the late 8th C. – i.e. before Arabs started settling on the coast. Many of the buildings are of brick and *porites* coral blocks, similar to those used in settlements at the southern end of the Red Sea. The archaeologist Mark Horton believed there had been a settlement on Manda for at least 150 years prior to these buildings being erected. He noted, also, that it was the location in which the majority of the items imported to the Bajun islands been found. "Here there lived a trading community, occupying huts of perishable material, but living off fine Chinese porcelain" remarked Horton. "During this period, there is no evidence for Islam, either in the form of mosques or tombs." Sasanian ceramics from southern Persia, Egyptian (or Sasanian?) glass, and Indian pottery were also found in the lowest archaeological levels. So whoever these early islanders were, with their Chinese porcelain and Indian pottery it would appear that they must have had contacts across the Indian ocean. (10)

As already pointed out in the Sea Nomad chapter, the far-ranging Indonesian Bajo were known for acquiring their hosts' languages in their peregrinations through the islands, including words for boat parts and fishing gear. Therefore, if the African Bajun are, by chance, predominantly Indonesian, no importance need be attached to the fact that they have lost their mother tongue. Though the Bajun now speak a Bantu language, their livelihood – apart from a few goats and chickens – is from the sea, and they do not conform to the way of life of the neighbouring Bantu. Nor, for that matter, do they have anything to do with the cows and camels that preoccupy their immediate neighbours, the Somali. The Bajun of Africa are fishermen, and amongst other things they fish for 'sea-cucumbers', or *trepang* – large slug-like creatures that are not everyone's favourite food – but for which the Bajo and Bugis of Indonesia travelled thousands of miles, gathering them in shallow lagoons on Australia's northern coast, and selling them to wealthy gourmets in markets on the Chinese mainland.

Also, the Bajun of Africa have an unusual way of catching turtles using a *remora*, a sucker-fish. Having caught a *remora* - usually about 30 – 90 cm long - a ring and a rope are inserted in its tail. When a turtle is spotted it is released and quickly fixes its suckers on the turtle's shell, by which means turtles weighing 24 lbs or more are hauled in by the fisherman. (11) Exactly the same technique is used by fishermen in parts of Melanesia, Japan, and northern Australia.

The inshore boats used by the Bajuni are double outrigger canoes - *ngalawas* - with two slightly different types of outrigger fitting, both of which are Indonesian in origin. Hornell suggested a Javanese ancestry for these; but the outrigger floats of Makassar canoes in South-west Sulawezi were attached in a similar way. Despite what has just been said about the general loss of boat terminology, there is one outrigger term that may have clung on through the ages, because there would have been no African equivalent to take its place. Swahili for an 'outrigger' is *tengo*, essentially the same word as the Makassarese *tenko* for the connecting piece between the

Outriggers Designs.
(Makassar after Horridge. All others after Grottanelli)

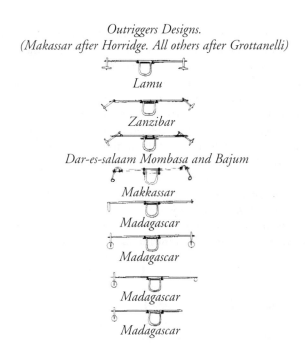

Lamu

Zanzibar

Dar-es-salaam Mombasa and Bajum

Makkassar

Madagascar

Madagascar

Madagascar

Madagascar

outrigger pole and the float. The Makassarese outrigger pole itself is *bara-tang*. In Malagasy *bara-* or *vala-* can mean either a 'stockade' made of vertical poles, or simply a 'pole'. Thus *bara-tengo* – 'the pole that holds the outrigger' - seems also to have crossed the Indian Ocean from Sulawezi. (12) (Interestingly, the word also seems to have gone East. The fishermen of Cape York, in north eastern Australia, one of the regions from which Bugis and Makassarese used to gather *trepang* for the Chinese market, use a double-outrigger canoe that is called a *tango*.)

Another significant feature of the Bajun past that linked them with islands in the Indian ocean, if not actually with Indonesia, was the boat called the *mtepe*. This was the famous sewn and pegged vessel built by the Bajun that was once a regular feature on the East African coast. There is a traditional story (retold by James Hornell) that in some misty period prior to the coming of the Portuguese, a ship-load of people known as the *Wa-diba* were wrecked on the Kenya coast about 35 miles north of Lamu. ('-*diba*, -*dwipa* or *dive*' being Sanskrit suffixes meaning 'islands', the name could refer to the Lacca*dives* or Mal*dives* – or simply, in Africanised form, 'People of the Islands'). The story relates how the Bajun fishing-folk took in the marooned *Wa-diba*, and soon learned how to build the sturdy *mtepe*, which was a large enough boat to carry cargoes long distances (two of these boats carried Livingstone from Zanzibar to the mouth of the Rovuma on the Tanzania/Moçambique border, at the start of his epic journeys of exploration). One feature of the *mtepe* was that it had a square sail, like those of Maldivian boats. Unlike them, however, it had geometric 'oculi' painted on both sides of the bow and stern which aroused the particular interest of James Hornell. "The question of origin," he wrote, "is further complicated by the fact that oculi are not in use either in the Maldives or the Laccadives, whereas in ancient times (referring to the low-relief depictions on the 8th century stupa at Borobudur) Indonesian vessels, hoisting rectangular sails, were provided with oculi on both sides of the stern as on the bows." (13) Every little bit of evidence leaves a fingerprint that points in the same direction – towards the Bajuni being descendants of an ancient Bajo community from Indonesia.

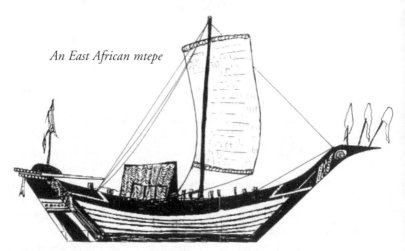

An East African mtepe

If the Bajun were originally linked with the Bajo of Indonesia, the Bugi of Sulawezi have an even greater claim to an African/Madagascan connection.

Under 'M' in the Standard English/Swahili Dictionary one finds:-

"Madagascar, *n.* Buki, Bukini."

There have been numerous attempts to explain how this name came into the Swahili language. Curiously, whilst trying to unravel the 'mystery' of the Bajun, a German ethnographer named Damman once proposed a convoluted linguistic link between 'wa-Bugi or wa-Buki' (as the Malagasy are usually referred to in conversation) with 'Bajun'. Damman's proposal was rejected by Vinigi Grottanelli who said of the term Buki – referring to the *kiswahili* for Madagascar:- "As far as I know this remarkable name has never been explained". And in this the Italian had support from the French expert on Madagascar, Gabriel Ferrand, who said of the term Buki:- "The origins of this denomination remain obscure: the phoneme does not resemble Bantu". (14)

As it is inarguable that Indonesian sailors of some sort crossed the Indian Ocean in the first millennium; and as – from an Indonesian standpoint – it is most likely that they were drawn from *sukus* of Bajo and Bugi, the possibility that their names survive on the African coast simply cannot be discounted. The same arguments can be made, though with less evidence to support it, that the Bajun island of *Manda* derived its name from the boat-building mariners of Mandar in Sulawezi. (15)

And finally, where did the name 'Madagascar' come from?

Marco Polo is generally credited with naming the island at the end of the 13th century, when he referred to it in his writing as *Magastar*. He did not visit it personally; his descriptions were based on hearsay gathered mainly from Arab merchants. He correctly described it as "one of the largest and most fertile" islands in the world. On the other hand he incorrectly claimed that lions and elephants "abound in the country". He also said that "The principal food eaten at all seasons of the year is the flesh of camels." … which conceivably could have arisen from confusion with the island's *zebu* cattle with their large shoulder humps, but which otherwise highlights his ignorance.(16) Because Marco Polo was not always accurate, it is generally assumed – however unlikely it might seem - that he must have muddled the location of the island he described as "one of the largest and most fertile" in the world, with Mogadishu, one of the most arid and barren towns on the entire coast of Africa. Despite the fact that Marco Polo never visited *Magadoxo* (as the Arabs called Mogadishu) and makes no mention of it in his journals, it has nevertheless always been *assumed* that it was from that dust-ridden town of drab mud dwellings that the name 'Madagascar' was derived.

But is this 'assumption' acceptable? In the light of the Bajun/Bajoo, Manda/Mandar parallels, and the curiously unexplained Swahili name for 'The Great Isle', Buki or Bukini, is it not more reasonable to suggest a connection with the other great mariner *suku* of Sulawezi who are commonly linked with the Bugis, Bajo and Manda - the Makassar?

CHAPTER - 11

MORE ABOUT THE MALAGASY

A sailor heading west across the Indian Ocean from the Sunda Strait that divides Java from Sumatra, has favourable winds and currents for most of the year. Sea Nomads sailing from Indonesia to Africa could therefore have easily come directly across the ocean. But if they had done so, surely birds, clouds and the patterns of waves would have indicated when land was nearby, and lured them towards the Seychelle Islands where Mahé's gloriously well-watered and fertile Morne Seychellois rises majestically three thousand feet into the sky.

But it seems that that never happened. The Seychelles, the Amirantes, Aldabra, as well as islands and shoals on the Mascarene Ridge that cuts down across the Indian Ocean to Mauritius and Reunion, all seem to have remained undiscovered and uninhabited until modern times. It is therefore much more likely that the voyagers who eventually landed up in Madagascar took a more northerly route – the one they would have taken for the secretive cinnamon trade in Roman times – either via Ceylon and southern India, or possibly via the Maldive Islands, to the Horn of Africa. Madagascar would not then have been discovered and settled by people sailing directly from Indonesia: it would have been found by people setting out from the coast of Africa.

Sometimes one wonders why so much mystery surrounds Madagascar and its Indonesian connections. Jared Diamond, an American Pulitzer prize-winning author, once described the settlement of Madagascar by Indonesians as "...the single most astonishing fact of human geography for the entire world." (1) His attitude is typical of many. But had he taken the trouble to do half an hour's home-work he would not have written such crass nonsense. Sooner or later, any reasonably competent sailor plying the waters off northern Moçambique would inevitably have spotted Grand Comoro's 7,750 foot Karthala volcano who's huge caldera has spewed out lava and smoke on average every 30 years for thousands of years, less than two hundred miles from the African coast. And from there the other

More about the Malagasy

Comoro islands that lead like stepping-stones to Madagascar, would have quickly been found. So once Indonesian sailors had found their way to Africa, the eventual discovery of Madagascar was inevitable.

In pre-Islamic days, when Arabs were not much in evidence on the African coast, there is no reason to think that there was only one influx of migrants from Indonesia, nor that they were people of only one *suku* or tribe. In fact the indications are the reverse: the Bajo, Bugi, Mandar and Makassarese – if they were the main immigrants - were not necessarily alone. Idrisi's map clearly indicated different Zanj communities who had presumably become established long before he wrote about them, and there is no reason to think they were necessarily friendly to each other. These Zanj had probably been carrying on trade with the 'people of Zabaj' – i.e. Sumatra and Java - for hundreds of years, during which time there would have been a constant flow of new ideas to Africa – with new political and commercial partnerships developing, and new expertise in many different fields (agriculture, mineralogy, music, etc.) being introduced. The early immigrants would inevitably have encountered, and intermarried with, different people in different parts of East Africa; Cushites and Hamites up north; hunter-gatherer San to the south, and Bantu in the process of migrating through Africa from the west. In fact there is every reason to think they would have developed diverse cultural groups who would not necessarily have shared common interests, or even been on good terms with each other. Things must have developed along these lines to account for the introduction of different Indonesian cultural traits in different parts of Africa and Madagascar. For example, outrigger canoes of two or three traditions survived only in specific parts of East Africa and Madagascar, but not everywhere; while Indonesian musical instruments such as xylophones and panpipes were introduced in some places, but not in others (see in a later chapter).

Even archaeologists who are sceptical about the Indonesian legacy agree that the most likely way that 'Kwale' pottery was diffused so rapidly down the Zanj coast early in the first millennium, was by sea. (2) Certainly the 'Tana-ware' pottery found in Madagascar six or seven hundred years later, must have been carried by sea, and it is hard to imagine who else could have been responsible for its spread other than Indonesian or Afro-Indonesian seamen – the people who carried the Austronesian language to the 'Great Isle'.

At the same time there must have been early waves of Indonesian migrants who forsook the sea and probed deep into Africa centuries before the main body of Bantu speaking people migrated into east and central

Africa from the northwest. The 'Zanj' must have spread far and wide into the hinterland; to Lake Victoria - where their canoe and sewn-boat technology, as well as some unusual xylophone features, survived into the twentieth century; to the Mountains of the Moon - as noted years later by Ibn Said; to the highlands of Zimbabwe; and probably to the region known as the 'Upemba Depression' at the headwaters of the river Congo. While those who explored inland readily acquired the languages of the people who's womenfolk bore and brought up their children, it is probable that those who remained on the coast retained their Austronesian language, which survived in Madagascar, but was ultimately displaced on the coast by Arabic and Bantu.

It is possible, even, that liaisons of Zanj sailors and San (Bushmen) might have played a part in the creation of the Hottentots. A number of people have commented on the occasional oriental appearance of some Hottentos; but these are speculative areas; possible, even probable, but only likely to be proved or disproved one day by genetic research.

One can conjecture that the wanderings of the Zanj were not always random; that the people were there at the behest of the powerful rulers of Srivijaya, or other powerful Indonesian rulers of the first millennium. They must have had amongst them experienced miners, metallurgists and prospectors to seek out copper, gold and iron. There can be little doubt that the Zanj penetrated the continent far and wide; only such a scenario can possibly account for the extraordinary mix of people who were eventually to form the foundations of the Malagasy people.

An American social-scientist/historian, Raymond Kent, reached these same conclusions in his book *Early Kingdoms in Madagascar* when he wrote that "...there must have been a vast and fairly gradual human movement from the general direction of Indonesia in the early centuries of the first millennium of our era, a movement one could call by an old Malagasy term *lakato* (or true outrigger people) because they did not belong to a single ethnicity. Moreover, these *lakato* must have spread considerably into the interior of east-central and southeast-central Africa, along the waterways and lakes, *before* the Bantu speakers left their core area Long before the Bantu reached coastal east Africa ... they met the *lakato* in the interior." And in Kent's view it was from fusion with the Khoisan and Bantu whom they encountered that an Afro-Malagasy race eventually developed.

"To put it in the simplest form of statement," he went on, "there *must* have been in the first millennium of our era an *Afro-Malagasy race* inhabiting both sides of the Mozambique channel, which was *then* not a barrier but a duct for the movement of peoples. ... And, this race had its

African and Indonesian extremes with all sorts of admixture in-between."
(3) This mixed race did not survive in Africa because migrating Bantu
absorbed nearly everything in their path. But shielded from Africa by the
Moçambique channel that was impassable to Africans, they did survive in
Madagascar.

As evidence of the extent of 'Africanisation' in Madagascar, language
has played an important role. For example, comparing the Malagasy
language with word-lists of the Bisa (who live in the Luangwa Valley in
Zambia) the Norwegian missionary, Father Emil Birkeli, found 71 Bisa
words closely matched in four Malagasy dialects; Sakalava in the west;
Betsileo of the central highlands; Hova, the Malagasy with the purest
Indonesian blood; and a group of 'aboriginal' Vazimba who are seen as
having been the first wave of newcomers to the island. He then listed a
further 72 words "en apparence communes a Madagascar et a l'Afrique
Central" adding that "Ces examples pourraient etre multipliés..."(4)

Further evidence which amounts to proof of the development of a mixed
Afro-Indonesian, or Afro-Malagasy race came from a group of south African
doctors studying the distribution of the sickle cell (an aberrant, sickle-
shaped, red blood cell that occurs in Africa but not in Indonesia). (5) To
their own surprise they found that, from a test of nearly 1,700 people in
Madagascar and the Comoros, the cattle herding people in the south of the
island had exceptionally high (10%+) percentages of sickling that paralleled
those of short-horn Zebu-herding people in East (and *West*) Africa; while the
independent-minded, agricultural Tsimihety in the north had in excess of
16%. Furthermore, in serological tests they found an identical percentage of
the *cde* chromosome among the three Malagasy tribes mentioned, as among
those in Southeast Africa (15%). From the incidence of the *cDe*
chromosome they could show that the Malagasy were as much as 62%
African – 38% Indonesian. And from the *CDe* chromosome it was even
more pronounced: 67% African to 33% Indonesian. I.e. the Tsimihety in
the north, and the Sakalava and Bara in the south, despite their Austronesian
language, and their definite sense of racial superiority and pride in their
Madagascan ancestry, are in fact two thirds African, a proportion that
cannot conceivably be attributed to the theory, still held in many quarters,
that the African element in Madagascar resulted from the absorption of
'Makua' slaves captured during the well documented Malagasy raids on the
Moçambique coast in more recent years.

The earliest settlers in Madagascar are known to anthropologists as the
tompontany, the 'Masters of the Soil' represented by the *Vazimba*; and the

tompondrano, 'Masters of the Water' represented by the *Vezo* who are mariners and fishermen. (In Malagasy the 'o' is pronounced 'oo' or 'u' and the last letter is practically silent: *tumpuntarn-* ; *tumpundran- u*)

The Vezo are accepted as being 'real' people; but the *Vazimba*, whose name constantly crops up in the literature, are something of a mystery. Arguments abound as to whether they ever really existed, or whether they were ephemeral figments of the imagination. One of the few British academics to do any extensive work in Madagascar, Maurice Bloch, has said bluntly: "There is no reason to believe Vazimba existed"; (6) and a Malagasy academic, M.E. Ralaimihoiatra, suggested the name may have come from Bantu *'bazimu'*, a vague term meaning 'an ancestor', which could be taken to mean 'a ghost'. (7) Others are less sceptical. Robert Drury, an English sailor marooned on the island from 1702 – 1717, wrote in his journal that the "Verzimbers, indeed, by their woolly heads must come from the more southern part of Africa", and gave credence to his view when he added that they were the main producers of pottery for which the Malagasy words are of Bantu origin.(8) More convincingly, a leading French *Malgachisant*, Hubert Deschamps, believed the Vazimba to have been part-African-part-Indonesian as a result of a prolonged period in Africa. Overall the ancestry of the Vazimba and the Vezo is so vague that there is no sure way of telling how long they have been on the island. But a part-African connection seems certain.

The largest and most prominent of Madagascar's inhabitants - roughly a quarter of today's population of around sixteen million - are the Merina, people of mixed ancestry who live in the central highlands around the capital, Tananarive. Soon after the beginning of the 16th century two different sets of people began to migrate from south-eastern Madagascar into the central highlands. First, Anteimoro (*-temuru*) wise men and astrologers, who may originally have come from the southern Ethiopian Highlands (there is an alternative view that they were Muslims from the Persian Gulf or Oman who arrived in the 14th century –could they be made up of both?) established themselves among indigenous Vazimba tribes in the south east. They introduced a more sophisticated astrologically based system of divination than was previously known, and a form of the zodiac, possibly of Indian origin, which governed the layout of their buildings. They are also said to have introduced iron-working – though this may be treated with scepticism as there is no evidence that the Malagasy ever experienced a stone or bronze-age, which would mean they had iron from the time of their arrival in the early or mid- 1st millennium. The

Anteimoro were familiar with Arabic script, which they used for writing the *Malagasy* language. With their ability to write, their reputation as astrologers, their Arabic calendar and their generally superior wisdom, the Anteimoro had an important role to play in the formation of a noble class of people known as the *andriana*, or 'princes'.(9) It was probably the Anteimoro who introduced the name 'Merina' into the language (pronounced something like '*mayern*', meaning 'The Just').

Then, also from the south east, there came others called Hova – pronounced '*Oov*' – who gradually, by conquest and intermarriage with the noble classes, came to dominate the Merina. The Hova were light skinned people, sometimes referred to as *malemy volo* – 'men with supple hair'. Some experts believe they had been on the island for centuries, retaining their racial purity through the strict practice of endogamy, but others believe that they were late arrivals from Indonesia who came to the island around the 10th or 11th century. Either way, in Raymond Kent's opinion:- "There is a very high degree of probability that the Hova represent the only *pure* Indonesian element in Madagascar." The sickle-cell count of the Merina was found to be less than a third that of the Tsimihety in the north, and less than half that of either the Bara or the Sakalava in the south; thus they are, it seems, physically among the least 'Africanised' people on the island. It was the combination of '*Oov*' sophistication and '*Temuru*' wisdom that seems to have provided the Merina with a superior edge over the ancient Vazimba in their future destiny.

But despite these apparent differences, the Merina probably owe their dominance in the island more to the British than to any divine right, or conquest of their own making. (10) Although today they are the leaders intellectually, artistically and administratively, that was not always the case. In a period of Anglo-French rivalry in the Indian Ocean following the Napoleonic wars, the British governor of Mauritius was quick to realise the potential advantages of extending British influence in an island which the French, with several trading posts already established, clearly had their eyes on. Seeing in the numerically strong and intelligent Merina, people whom he felt would best fit his needs as a conduit of British influence, he selected them as partners in a politico-military alliance. In the 1820's a Merina army, trained along European lines and supplied with the most modern British weapons, proceeded to establish its own sub-empire as the major force in the island.

As part of the British deal with the Merina, the London Missionary Society was permitted to work and open schools in Madagascar. The Merina, as a result, became the best educated people on the island, and for a time, Protestantism was the official religion of the Merina state. Later, when Africa was being carved up by the Europeans, an Anglo-French agreement in 1890 once again gave France a free hand in Madagascar, since when the ruling Merina came under strong French catholic influence, leading to a decline in English Protestantism, except around the capital, Tananarive.

On the southern borders of the Merina live the Betsileo, the third most populous group in Madagascar. They grow rice and cultivate terraced gardens even on the steepest slopes of their high plateau in the middle of the island. Predominantly African in origin, they are nevertheless closest to the Merina in customs, beliefs, and tradition.(11) The Betsileo (the name means '*the many unconquered*', though in fact they were conquered by the Merina) had the most pronounced veneration of nobility of anyone in Madagascar, and they provide a dramatic example of how age-old political systems and such concepts as 'divine kingship' which developed on the African mainland, came across with the early Afro-Malagasy.

Links with Africa are everywhere. The universal words for 'God' in monotheistic Madagascar, *Zana-hary*, *Rana-hary* or *Andriana-hary*, directly correspond to the Shona creator, *M'wari*. Malagasy tales of ritual strangulation of a dying monarch to stop the 'king-spirit' passing away are echoed right across Africa. Their custom of burying royal wives with departed kings - which can be extended to the Sakalava, Mahafaly, Antandroy, and even the supposedly more sophisticated Merina – was common in many parts of Africa. And the associated Malagasy cult of *fanany* was paralleled from Zimbabwe to Uganda in the *fangane* cult. Both these customs involved the drying out of the royal corpse, and the collection of maggots that grew in the putrefying flesh. It was said the maggots embodied the spirit of the deceased which, in Madagascar, would reappear from the grave in the form of a *fanany* or *fanano*, a snake, a lizard, or a crocodile; and which, in Central Africa reappeared as *fangane*, a python (or among the Venda of Zimbabwe - *chitebkwe*, a lion). A similar custom was not unknown in Southeast Asia where it may possibly have been ancestral to both the Malagasy and African versions.

"What the Betsileo *fangane* suggests," wrote Raymond Kent, "is the transfer of common belief to royalty in both Africa and Madagascar. Indeed, the *fangane* cult may well have been a cultural link for disparate peoples of the Afro-Malagasy race."

On both sides of the channel a dried corpse was often wrapped in ox-hide. During an excavation of the Great Zimbabwe a skeleton was found wrapped in multiple layers of cloth; while in Madagascar up to 100 woven cotton cloths have been known to envelope a single corpse. In the case of Malagasy royalty 'red cloths' or *lamba-mena* were used, strangely like those that enveloped human remains in the hilltop site of Mapungubwe in the Limpopo valley. Hundreds of cattle were sacrificed at funerals, the horns later erected on the tombs. On both sides of the channel significance was attached to leaping over the animals that had been sacrificed. People shaved their heads in mourning; while feasting and drinking at funerals, leading to orgies of symbolic sex, achieved major proportions in both regions. Some divinatory dice excavated near the Great Zimbabwe might easily have been Sakalava *sila-boa* (charms). Dozens of similar secrets lie hidden in the nooks and crannies of the cultural archives.

"In short", wrote Raymond Kent, "the traditional past of Madagascar makes absolutely no sense without Africa." To which one might add that the traditional past of Zimbabwe is inescapably linked with that of Madagascar...a fact that is all too often ignored by narrowly focused anthropologists, archaeologists and historians working in Africa.

If the Merina had the political and cultural upper-hand in Madagascar, and were the people most closely associated with Europeans in the 18th and 19th century, at the opposite end of the scale were the Bara, cattle-herders living on 40-50,000 square miles of high plateau country to the south of the Betsileo. At the time of the Anglo-French agreement of 1890 only a handful of European explorers and missionaries had ever ventured into '*Ibara*', the country of the staunchly independent-minded Bara, whom the French, even with modern weapons and military organisation, found difficult to administer.

As with so much about pre- and proto-historical Madagascar, views on the early history of the Bara vary from one authority to the next. The 'all-pervading' historian of Madagascar, Alfred Grandidier, thought them to be descended from the passengers of an Indian shipwreck on the south-east coast of the island. The renowned Jaques Faublée saw them as coming from Southeast Asia with iron implements; *Administrateur* Salle, who lived among them, believed they were 'Ethiopians'. The majority view of modern writers is that the Bara came originally came from East-Central Africa. However, though the Bara language contains a large number of 'Bantu' words, it has an Austronesian structure like other Malagasy languages.

It is said that there are seventeen different tribes in Madagascar, although sometimes that number seems to be blurred. Between the Merina and the Betsileo in size are the Betsimisaraka, who inhabit a large part of the north east coast. They were once famous for their elegant sewn *pirogues*, 30' long, 8' in the beam, without ribs or frames, stiffened only by the seat-boards that penetrated the sides, in which they used to travel to Africa via the Comoros to raid for slaves.

Then there are the Mahafaly, cattle-men at heart and cattle-rustlers by nature, who live in sparse conditions in the dry bush country of the far south west. They had an odd custom. If one of their cows was not giving milk, the herdsman blew hard into its vagina to relax it and induce it to give milk more freely. It was a custom the Mahafaly shared with some Hottentots in Southern Africa. (12) The Mahafaly have always been curiously fond of gold, *volamena*, for ornamentation – gold which must have come from Africa, as none was ever produced in Madagascar in ancient times.

The Mahafaly have an artistic streak that traditionally blossomed in the elaborately carved funerary posts, *aloalo*, placed in their rocky family graves. Some of these posts have the same bird and lizard designs that adorn a carved stone column for which the Great Zimbabwe is famous.

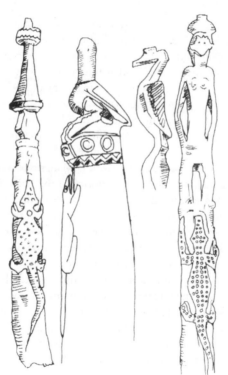

Three Mahafaly Aloalo (wooden grave posts – after Lormian) with (2nd from left) the Zimbabwe soapstone menhir.

The Zimbabwe column in question was carved for posterity in soapstone; but in all likelihood thousands more were carved in wood, as in Madagascar. Some commemorative posts on both sides of the water - for instance those of the Sokoambé - carry birds in different styles; others have arrays of similar geometric designs.

Left: Two carved wooden funerary posts from southern Madagarcar.
Right: carved soapstone shard found at the Great Zimbabwe.
(Not drawn to scale)

Finally there are the Sakalava, who once controlled one of the island's most powerful empires that extended over six hundred miles up the Africa-facing coast. Like the Bara, nothing much was known about the Sakalava until the early 1900's, and confusion reigns (once again!) over their earlier history. Their founding father is said to have been one *Andriamisara* who - depending on which local tradition is held in highest esteem - either came from the sea, or from the sky, or was the son of a previous king in the south; who was white, or who was *not* white. He first appeared on the island in the 14th century (Rusillon), mid-fifteenth century (Flacourt), or around 1650 (Grandidier). Their founder was *Andriamisara 1st*, *Andriamisara 2nd*, or there were several *Andriamisaras*; and according to some he was not even a Sakalava, but a Bara prince. The history of the Sakalava offers a typically Malagasy 'take-your-pick' situation demonstrating the scope for future generations of anthropologists to come up with their own equally debatable versions!

According to Raymond Kent the Sakalava became important only 'from the rule of *Andrian-dahe-fotsy*' (White King), whose ancestors were shipwrecked on the Mahafaly coast in the south-west of the island. "It was Andriandahifotsy who conquered Menabe, known before this time as *Ansakuabé*. He was equally the founder of the *Zafi-voula-mena* (Sons of Gold) branch of the Maroserana dynasty, which ruled Menabe from around 1650." The latter is of particular interest due to the importance of *volamena* (gold) in this part of Madagascar, and the story of how a large quantity of gold is said to have been brought over from the Zimbabwe gold fields soon after the beginning of the 16th century with which the powerful Maroserana dynasty were able to fund the expansion of the Sakalava realm. Quoting Kent again: - "*Maro* means 'many' in Malagasy but the word *Mari* was the term for gold in the Mwene Mutapa's kingdom (in central Africa)." (13)

The Sakalava, like the Mahafaly, are cattle-people through and through. There is a Sakalava sub-group called the *Masikoro* whose name is thought to be derived from a type of scrubby bush in the hinterland of Tanzania called '*mashakoro*'. The Sakalava live in a world of spirits. "The *lolo* are everywhere;" said the missionary, Henry Rusillon, "on the earth, under the earth, in the water, on the water, in the forest, in the river, in the air; they reside in certain trees, and mountains, and nearly always the spirit is an ancestor. ... and after several generations, the ancestor becomes *Zanahary*, the 'Creator'". Their links with Africa seem to have been close and the Sakalava dialect contains more Swahili and Bantu loan words than any other Malagasy dialect. Nevertheless, like all other Malagasy languages, it is Austronesian in structure.

There is one particular feature of Sakalava culture that might give an important clue to the meaning and purpose of the Great Zimbabwe in Africa. It concerns their cult of royal relics known as *dady* which means literally 'grandparent' or 'ancestor'. In material form *dady* is a collection of bits and pieces of the deceased person: the occipital bone, teeth, nails, the right patella, and hair. No Sakalava ruler could assume office without being in possession of the royal *dady*, and he who held the *dady* had power over the Sakalava. Indeed, so powerful was it that when in the nineteenth century Merina forces captured the Sakalava *dady*, they were able to subjugate them, and secure their political obedience. Conversely, when the new French colonial masters returned the *dady* to the Sakalava at the end of the century it was an important tool (despite pockets of resistance and several rebellions) in securing their future support and co-operation.

More about the Malagasy

The *dady* forms a central role in the cult of the *Tromba* through which the people communicate with their ancestors, and, in a trance-like state, seek their help in telling their fortunes and healing their ills. The spirits embodied in the relics of the ancestors, the *dady*, reside in closely guarded repositories (*doany*) in important centres of the *Tromba* throughout the Sakalava country, and are visited by the faithful once a year. The *doany* is to be found in a building within a building in the middle of two compounds, one within another, like Russian dolls, surrounded by (more or less) concentric fences of thick wooden stakes. The name of the building in which the ancestral remains are housed is the *Zomba-bé*, literally "The Great House". Henry Rusillon, who was present at Tromba ceremonies in the early nineteen hundreds made the point that the Zomba-bé was the focal point of the cult. "*Considérons tout d'abord la maison qui est le centre de ralliement...le Zomba-bé*" he said. (14)

Zomba-bé? Is that not the same word as 'Zimbabwe'?

CHAPTER 12

FROM MADAGASCAR TO AFRICA...

Not only does the Zomba-bé of Madagascar sound like 'Zimbabwe'; but the two words seem to have the same meaning: *Zimba-* = house + *-bwé* = great . Although on this point not everyone agrees.

Latter-day academics - contrarians by nature who love to complicate simple things - like to think that 'Zimbabwe' is either a contraction of the Shona *dzimba za mahwe*, 'houses of stone', or *dzimba woye*, 'venerated houses'. Of these, *Dzimba dza mahwe* has won out as the favourite, and is the one that appears in school text-books and tourist brochures.(1) What it does not take into account, however, is that none of the 150 or so 'Zimbabwes' that lie hidden in the bush between the Zambezi and Limpopo rivers ever contained '*Houses* of Stone'- not even the formidable stone enclosures of the Great Zimbabwe itself. (2)

Flying the flag for a simpler alternative meaning of 'Zimbabwe' was Charles Bullock, a Native Commissioner in Rhodesia in the 1920's, fluent in *chi-shona*, and author of the definitive book of its day - "*The Mashona*".

"Zimbahwe," he said, "also called Zimbabwe, Dzimbahwe, Tsimbabgwe, and in Portuguese records, Simbaoe or Symbaoe, is generally interpreted as meaning 'stone-houses'. But if I ask a native to say 'stone-houses', he says *Dzimba dza mahwe* – 'houses of stone'. Portuguese records say the word signifies 'Court', and I have certainly heard it used for the ordinary pole and daga huts where lives the priestess of the mondoro cult; and also for burial places of Chiefs; and also for the miniature huts built at places of sacrifice to the tribal spirit. I hazard (without native confirmation) 'Lo! A great house.'" (3)

The stone walled enclosures within the Elliptical Building of the Great Zimbabwe bear direct comparison with the layout of the Great Compound of the Tromba Cult in Madagascar, the vala-bé. Within the walls of a large compound was a smaller compound in which stood the 'Great House', the *Zomba-bé*, a traditional building stoutly made of timber and thatch which if it had been built in a similar fashion in the Great Zimbabwe, would long since have rotted away.

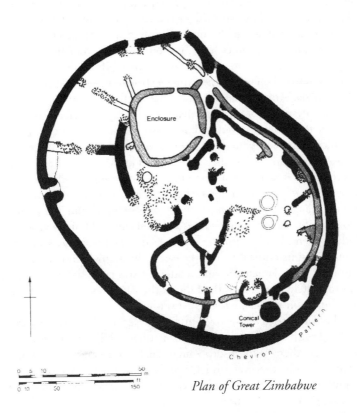

Plan of Great Zimbabwe

It would be difficult to prove that the ceremonies that took place in the *vala-bé* of the Tromba were the same as those that were once performed in an African Zimbabwe; but with every link that strengthens the chain of connections spanning the Moçambique channel, the likelihood of similarities in the worship of the ancestors becomes greater. It is therefore valid to quote, at length, some passages from Henry Rusillon's rare book on the Tromba cult which may well echo the sort of things that went on during feast days at the Great Zimbabwe. The short title of the book is *Un Culte Dynastique avec Evocations des Morts chez les Sakalaves de Madagascasr – Le "Tromba"*. The translation is mine:- (4)

"In the middle of the *Vala-mena* (the 'red', or 'royal' compound) is the large house that is the centre of the rally – the *Zomba-bé*. The

109

outside of the *Zomba-bé* is unprepossessing. It is a rectangular barn-like wooden building, covered in thatch with a row of ribs from raffia fronds tied across the roof to protect it from violent winds. The interior, on the other hand, is a bit gloomy – the building has just two doors and one window – hopefully inducing quiet philosophical thoughts rather than expectations of any unusual phenomena. Around the circumference of the *Vala-mena* are tied the oxen destined for sacrifice, divided in groups by tribes. As, one by one, the order is given to kill them, they are led out into the middle of the compound, near the *Zomba-bé*, and a man comes forward from the tribe they represent. The Malgache never care much about how they kill an animal; but nevertheless what we see now in the royal courtyard is specially savage and cruel. Armed only with an ancient sacred spear, rusty, jagged-edged and blunt, the animal suffers a thousand tortures as it is slaughtered. Its unyielding hide is pierced only with the greatest effort; with its head on the ground and its horns dug into the earth, the animal's throat is sawn through. It is a lamentable and repugnant spectacle."

"Immediately after the death of the ox the sacred spear is taken back to its place in the *Zomba-bé* to be washed in one of several water-filled bowls carried by the royal princesses' servants. The water, dirty and red with blood from the spear, is then avidly drunk by those who hope thereby to absorb some benefit from the spirit of the ancestors. Whatever water is left over is thrown over the crowd that is pushing and jostling outside, trying to get as large a portion of the benediction as they can."

"The floor inside the *Zomba-bé* is covered in mats; and the large room is divided by a huge calico curtain into an ante-chamber and a sacred area. In the north-east corner of the inner sanctum is the *Zomba-faly*, a small hut built on stilts, accessed by a rickety staircase or ladder. Into this sacred area come all the descendants of the ancient kings, while other intruders are brusquely expelled. Also in this area are stored the various royal relics from the past that are now considered sacred … things such as clumsily shaped pitchers, the old rust-covered spears, and other weapons whose shape and weight reek of antiquity. In addition, there are hollowed gourds containing fat, and a series of small dishes which (so they say) held incense to be burnt in the presence of the kings. A sort of Indian bed completes the furniture, all of which is on view just once a year."

"The *Zomba-faly* contains the remains of four great kings, preserved in small silver and wooden boxes. ... Inside the ante-chamber, after the drinking of the sacred water, the women clap their hands and sing a monotonous song, always the same, entreating the spirits to show themselves, to pardon and bless them; but perhaps one can be forgiven having doubts whether the singers understand the dirges they chant! Behind the great curtain the princes and princesses arrange the bed, which has the appearance of a table. It is covered with a mat; then a large white cloth is stretched over it, making one think that the table is going to be laid for a meal. Beneath the bed are placed small cups of burning *emboka*, the Sakalava incense that gives out a strong, disagreeable, acrid smell."

"While this is going on an old man, possessed by an ancestor, comes forward, with difficulty, his body shaking in violent spasms. He slowly climbs the ladder to the *Zomba-faly*, and for no apparent reason his right arm begins to tremble. He remains there for nearly an hour. At last, his head shaking, he speaks ... but the people understand nothing. Whilst he is talking a second individual is possessed also by a spirit and enters into a trance; and there is an altercation over the place at the top of the ladder. The second man is an orator and also wants to address the people. He jerks his head in a strange manner, shaking it violently, and he speaks through his nose as though his mouth is full of water. He launches into a faultless discourse, more comprehensible than the last. He reproaches the people for letting themselves be carried away by modern customs; he tells of the sorrows of the ancestors; entreats the people not to be deceived; to restrain themselves; and to set themselves to shedding warm tears."

"A woman now approaches the ladder and there is discussion between the spirits. They pretend to agree on something, and word goes round:- "The key! The key!" sometimes called for in French, sometimes in Malgache. At last! The door of the *Zomba-faly* is opened. All the Princes range themselves around the base of the hut. An earthenware jug filled with the water in which the sacred spears have been washed is handed over to the old man who is possessed. He splashes it generously over all those who are present, throwing it far and wide. This is the benediction of Andriamisara to all his descendants."

"When the ritual washing is finished, four individuals designated by the ancestors – i.e. 'officials' of the *Tromba* – put on long red shirts and red, pointed, woollen hats (red is the royal colour). The people are told that the ancestor approaches. The rhythmic noise of hand-clapping is redoubled; the chanting grows louder; the drums beat. A man strikes a triangle; another shakes a sort of indigenous tambourine, a *kahiamba*; there is the sound of a large sea-shell being blown; and outside in the compound, guns are fired. All the royal family gather round the 'table', blocking off the view so that only a tall man can see what is going on."

"Then the four 'red men', carrying four little boxes on their shoulders as though they were incredibly heavy, cross, with calculated slowness, from the *Zomba-faly* to the table a few metres away, where they lay down their burdens. The princes bow, then kneel and dance in slow twisting, undulating movements, and raise their hands above their heads as they fling themselves about in various forms of salutation."

Each of the 'red men's' boxes has three or four compartments, like inkwells, in which the *dady* are kept. These are now carefully taken out to be washed - the teeth, hair and fingernails, and other bits and pieces – reminiscent of the ritual bathing of the Merina queen in Tananarive. Then, with tender loving care they are wiped with a cloth soaked in a mixture of honey, castor oil, water, and a fragrant forest herb of some sort, and returned to the *Zomba-faly*. Outside, the women who were not allowed to enter the *Zomba-bé*, gather in groups, elegantly dressed in all the colours of the rainbow. They kneel down, beating their foreheads on the ground and raising their hands above their heads as they reaffirm their vows. Men in the crowd gather noisily, shouting and threatening each other as though drunk, scrambling, according to tradition, to collect their shares of the sacrificed oxen. For the sacrificed animal is more than a victim, it is the deity himself, and as such is essential for a life of harmony. Then, at last, night begins to fall; and soon the Vala-mena is empty, and the *Zomba-bé* falls quiet.

Might the same sort of ceremonies have once been performed within the high stone walls of the Great Zimbabwe?

Within the walls of the Great Zimbabwe there is an anomalous structure known as 'The Conical Tower' that has so far defied explanation, but which, like so much else in Zimbabwe, may find an explanation in Madagascar. The Zimbabwe archaeologist Peter Garlake has described the Conical Tower thus: "...a solid circular tower, 18ft in diameter and 30 ft high, decorated round the top with a dentelle-patterned frieze (now vanished), ... built between the old wall and the new Outer Wall. Its beautifully regular coursing has the usual slight batter, giving the tower the shape of a slightly irregular and truncated cone, hence its name: the Conical Tower. Visually and technically, it forms the most important single feature and the architectural focus of the building in its final form."(5)

The Tower has been poked and probed by archaeologists since doomsday and found to consist of nothing but large flat stones. No skeletons or treasure have been found beneath it; only virgin soil and rock. Many functions have been attributed to it by various 'experts' over the years. Garlake himself surmised that it might be a 'symbolic grain-bin'; the Rev Dornan thought it was 'a grave super-structure; Schlicter, 'a gnomon'; Randall MacIver, 'a symbol of a chief's power'; Leo Frobenius, 'an emblem of a sacrificial ant-hill'; Schofield, 'a tribal initiation structure'; two early Rhodesian enthusiasts, J.T. Bent and R.N. Hall said respectively that it was for 'phallic worship'; or that it was simply a 'a giant phallus.' (6)

In archaeological circles there is a marked reluctance to call anything a 'phallus' unless it is incontrovertibly obvious. Therefore the mere fact that this 30-foot 'thing' sticks straight up in the air, and once had a sort of *dentelle* 'glans' around the top is not considered sufficient evidence that it ever had sexual connotation. Bent and Hall's salacious suggestions have therefore been consigned to the bin by the establishment.

But might Bent and Hall have been right?

Hundreds of small cylindrical clay and soapstone objects have been found in numerous locations around the Great Zimbabwe. Dozens of these have been unearthed near the Conical Tower, and dozens more (together with small clay models of horned cattle identical to the widespread *sanatry* connected with the Tromba cult in Madagascar) found randomly buried elsewhere in the vicinity. To the layman most of these objects, would be considered "phallic"; but they have been dismissively described by Garlake as "small cylinders carved from soapstone and *formerly described* as 'phalli'".

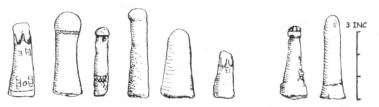

Small phalli found in Zimbabwe

Certainly 'phallic' worship has never been a big thing for the majority of Bantu people. But elsewhere in Africa that has not always been the case. In the late 1920's, during five years of research in Gala and Konso country not far from lakes Abaya and Chamo in Ethiopia, two French archaeologists counted over 10,000 grave markers, stelae, monoliths and menhirs that were blatantly, undeniably, 'phallic'.(7) In fact the non-secular artwork of the Konso is the most brazenly phallic of any people in Africa. Their large wooden funerary monuments have exaggerated male organs on their foreheads; the priests wear similarly phallic regalia; and (coincidentally?) in their stone walled cult-sites where phallicism is all-pervasive, they erect ritually significant dry-stone conical towers, smaller, but in many respects similar to the conical tower of Zimbabwe.

Equally interesting are the vast numbers of granite monoliths scattered over hills and valleys in Gamu Gofa and Sidamo in Ethiopia's southern

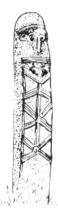

A phallic stone from Sidamo, c 6' (1.8 m) high.

highlands. They vary in height from a few feet to as much as 20 feet above ground, and though their meaning is lost on today's people, the procreative power they exude as they thrust out of the earth is inescapable.

The normally cautious ethnographer, G.W.B. Huntingford, when discussing possible sources of these 'phalli', pointed out that:- "…it has long been recognised that Indonesian influence has been at work from quite early times on the eastern coast of Africa and in South Arabia. Moreover, parallels between hagioliths in Abyssinia and Assam, suggest something more than coincidence, and Neuville has in fact suggested that the Abyssinian hagioliths might be due to influence from South-east Asia which made itself felt, at an unspecified time (but *before* the establishment of the Kingdom of Aksum) … Such an origin is not impossible…. In Madagascar are found stone tombs, together with monoliths surmounted by ox-horns and squared wooden posts surmounted by human figures of wood. That Madagascar was colonised by Indonesians is an accepted fact. It is not therefore by any means impossible for Indonesian influence to have reached Abyssinia by way of Arabia, since Aden was probably an established Indonesian port of call." (8) Huntingford's grounds for looking to Southeast Asia as the womb that nurtured the monolithic cultures fits well with Kent's contention that the Anteimoro (-*temur*) astrologers and scribes in Madagascar dwelt for a long period in Ethiopia.

There is a distinct thread of evidence running down the ancient Zanj coast linking the phallic menhirs of Ethiopia to areas as far south as Kilwa.

Pillar tombs. Kenya.

It takes the form of square or rectangular Islamic tombs with tall pillars rising from them, many of which, like some of the minarets of the oldest mosques, are plainly 'phallic', reflecting a fusion of latter-day Islam with pre-Islamic (Zanj?) culture. (9)

Across the water in Madagascar, menhirs and monoliths - sometimes cut in one huge piece from the granite hills - abound in many places, Betsileo and Antandroy particularly. *Orimbato, vato mitsangana, tsangambato, tehezana,* and *fahatsiarovana*: all are 'upright stones' that may have been erected in honour of dead parents; to commemorate people killed in war; to mark private agreements between individuals or clans; or simply for some event worthy of being remembered for future generations. Then there are *vatolahy*, literally 'male stones.'(10) Though more often than not *vatolahy* serve the same purpose as other 'upright stones' and no longer have any sexual connotation, there is no doubt that sometimes they have real phallic significance, as dramatically noted in 1939 by a well known *Malgachisant*, Charles Poirier, when he chanced on two phallic cults in the Betsileo countryside, one of which he described in romantic terms thus (my translation):- (11)

"In the beauty of dawn, the melancholy of dusk, and the dazzling light of a warm noon", wrote Poirier, "... in the crystal-clear night sky, caressed by the breezes filtering through the scattered bush and the murmuring of the Ranovao river; on the slopes of a gentle hill, two hours walk to the west of Alakamisy, near the village of Ampasampirafy, is the *vatolahy* celebrating the exploits of the sorcerer Rafirokana, son of the sorcerer Rafahitra...

"Rafirokana's soul, incarnated in this monolith which is dedicated solely to sexual union and the strength of the male organ, receives the wishes – though rarely granting them – of those seeking renewal of their diminishing and faltering carnal urges; of the small and puny who are looking for enhancement of their senses, sharpening of their minds, and expansion of their horizons, in the hope of satisfying their unfulfilled aspirations.

"The conflict between make-belief and nature may occasionally be settled to the advantage of nature; but influenced by its great fame, fate brings to this shrine a large number of Betsileo and Merina men - and women - who, despite frequent disillusionment, continue, undiscouraged, to make the pilgrimage. Early in the 19th century Rafahitra used to prescribe a drink made from the powder of certain twigs, which was supposed to strengthen the sexual organs. When

Rafahitra died, Rafirokana continued administering this concoction and became even more famous than his father. Rafirokana, nicknamed 'King of the Assegais', was a man of enormous stature, and before dying he wished to commemorate his 'memories' and his 'triumphs'. Thus he came to erect his *vatolahy*.

"'I erect this stone', he proclaimed, according to oral sources, 'for the personification of my soul. If you wish to obtain from me or my ancestors a healthy and strong body, come and pray at the base of this stone. Coat my *vatolahy* with fat from the skin of a vigourous bull, and ask of it the powers you wish to acquire. I will bless you, and your plans will be accomplished according to your desires.'

"Before the ceremony, a male supplicant will have made a life-sized wooden 'maquette' of the organ to which he would aspire. Similarly, a lady will have prepared, in cow-dung, the 'feminine sexual charms' she would enjoy offering. The 'thought' having thus become a reality, it is left at the bottom of the north-facing *vatolahy*. 'Here I am at the bottom of your *vatolahy*, Rafirokana, to ask you to make me better developed. I beg you to allow me a *mahalehi-lahy* (or in the case of the lady a *mahavehi-vavy*) similar to the example I am placing at your feet.'"

The modelled phalli were left as 'food' for the *vatolahy*. The women were allowed to take theirs' home, or protect them from the rain beneath a

stone. Charles Poirier counted about 30 phalli at Rafirokana's *vatolahy*, some ten of which "gave testimony to recent pilgrimages."

In view of there being so many connections between Madagascar and Zimbabwe, it is not mere prurience to suggest that the hundreds of small penis-shaped cylinders '*formerly described as phalli*' found in many parts of Zimbabwe - around the Conical Tower in particular - were offerings to a procreative cult common to both Madagascar and Central Africa, which had its origins on the other side of the Indian Ocean. Was not the Conical Tower – as suggested years ago by Bent and Hall – nothing more than a truly monumental phallus, the *vatolahy* of all *vatolahy*, the central symbol of once widespread fertility worship?

Two hundred miles northeast of the Great Zimbabwe, in the hills that form Zimbabwe's border with Moçambique, are the remnants of another enigmatic culture that once covered a huge area in the uplands around Nyanga. This ancient complex is less well known than the Great Zimbabwe, but covering, as it does, some 2,500 to 3,000 square miles (7,000 or 8,000 sq kms) of dramatic mountain countryside rising to over 8,500 feet, it encompasses one of the most extensive areas of ruins anywhere in Africa. For sixty miles the hillsides are traversed by literally thousands of miles of stone-faced terraces, interspersed with hill-top forts and stone enclosures, punctuated by occasional ditches, drains and water furrows, stone cairns, monoliths, and – particularly curious - hundreds of well constructed stone-lined pits that are unique to this area, and a mystery both to archaeologists and today's local inhabitants. (12)

Many fanciful suggestions have been put forward as to the purpose of the Nyanga pits: 'slave pits'; water tanks; places for washing gold; 'leopard's cages'; children's play pens; grain silos modelled on Astarte's womb, are among the most bazaar. But the current archaeological opinion is that they were for the safe-keeping of *miniature cattle* within the heart of the homestead, protected by the depth of the pit from the cold winds of winter. But does this make sense? Isn't this another case where the experts have got it horribly wrong? (13)

On average the 'mystery' pits are about 6 metres in diameter, varying in depth from about 2 metres to a maximum of 3m. Typically they are set in the middle of a circular ring of rock and rubble that creates a level platform around the pit from 2 to 9 metres wide on which, at one time, circular huts were built. In most cases entry to the pits was through a 20 – 30 feet long passage dug out on the uphill side and covered to form a tunnel (*Why a tunnel? Would not an open passageway have been more convenient for cattle?*) and almost always curving (*why?*) gently to the left, leading down to a stone-lintelled doorway into the pit. The tunnels were lined with dry-stone walling (*Which showed no sign of damage or abrasion from horns*) and were astonishingly standardised in size, invariably within a centimetre or two of

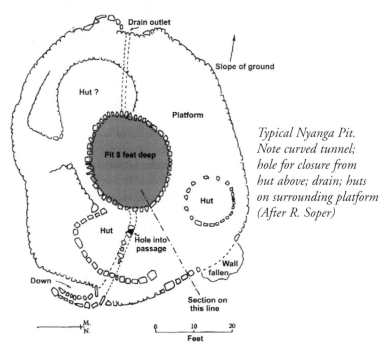

Typical Nyanga Pit. Note curved tunnel; hole for closure from hut above; drain; huts on surrounding platform (After R. Soper)

120 cm high and 60 cm wide. About 10 feet from the pit there was usually a hole in the tunnel roof and a carefully made shaft leading from the platform above. In many cases there were signs that a small hut had once been built above the shaft, from which a post or some sort of security 'door' could be dropped down to close the tunnel. Sometimes, in the same platform, there were two pits, each with its own entrance tunnel which converged (but never joined) at the point where the vertical shafts were located, so that both shafts were controlled from the same hut on the platform above. (14)

The pits themselves were lined with large stones, smooth sides facing inwards to present a more or less flat wall. Although floors were paved with flat stones and appear to have been kept clean, they usually sloped downwards to a narrow drain leading out beneath the wide rocky platform. Sometimes the angle of the floor was steep. In one example an elliptical pit 8.6 x 7.3 metres had a fall of one metre from the entrance to the drain (*surely not comfortable for cattle?*).

In the lowlands, on less steep hills, the pits, which, in the main, had similar tunnel entrances and other features to those of the uplands, were frequently constructed *within* a substantial stone walled compound which could, if need be, have served as a perfectly adequate cattle kraal on its own. Some of the lowland 'pits' were built above ground level, with a wooden bolt that could be pushed horizontally across the tunnel to close it. Lowland pits averaged only 10'-11' in diameter – some as little as 6'6".

A huge amount of effort went into the construction of all the Nyanga pits. They were clearly of great importance to the people who lived around them. And one has to ask why so much effort and unusual design was needed to provide shelter for cows?

The 'cattle' theory was originally floated by a well-respected archaeologist, John Sutton, and later taken up by Robert Soper as a central feature in his definitive, 2003 monograph on 'Nyanga'. By Soper's own admission the evidence for his cattle theory is sparse. In the late 1990's he found remnants of a breed of very small cattle in an atypical site at Muozi, on a precipitous spur in the Nyanga hills. There were very few bone fragments, and he was only able to estimate the horn-spans of two of the cattle. In the absence of any complete long bones it was not possible to give an absolute estimate of their height; but he reckoned they were on average 20 – 30% smaller than the modern Nguni cattle commonly used elsewhere, small enough in most cases to pass through the tunnel entrances into the pits.

But in Soper's own words: "The width of the horn-span could have

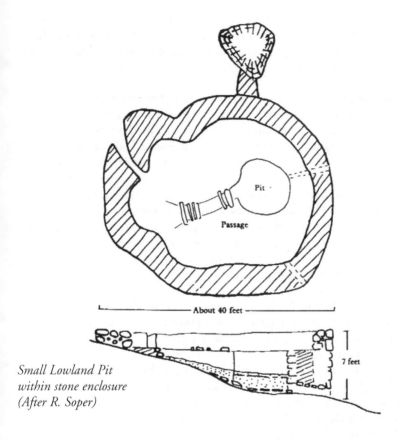

Small Lowland Pit
within stone enclosure
(After R. Soper)

posed a problem for animals with large horns. Horns could have been polled … but there was no evidence for this. A pregnant cow may also have found the width a tight squeeze…"(15)

With refreshing openness for one who had to some extent hung his reputation on the case for 'cattle pits', Robert Soper admitted that: "The relationship of the atypical Muozi site to the more typical pit structures and enclosures is not entirely clear" and that … "Given the special nature of the Muozi site, it would be inadvisable to draw any conclusions on the wider animal economy…of the Nyanga terrace complex." To this he added, in a personal letter to the author: "I agree that the pits are far more elaborate and labour demanding than necessary for purely functional needs and am convinced that they have a strong symbolic significance – I'm not quite sure what, but wombs and fertility spring to mind."

The Phantom Voyagers

It would be tempting to respect Robert Soper's views and let the matter lie if it were not for the fact that pits' use as cattle pens seems so unlikely, and because there are good reasons for thinking the pits were for much more profound purposes.

It may be pure coincidence that the Betsileo of Madagascar live on a high plateau that is in many ways reminiscent of the Nyanga mountains in Zimbabwe. The Betsileo hills rise to almost exactly the same height as Mt Nyangane; they are on almost identical latitudes; both of them are the highest points for thousands of miles around; the climates are similar. The Betsileo have been described as "the best farmers and possibly the hardest workers in Madagascar."(16) They keep cattle which are used for drawing carts and sleds, trampling rice fields, ploughing, harrowing and winnowing the rice. They live in some of the most picturesque countryside anywhere on the island – range upon range of hills and valleys with scarcely any flat land, the outlines softened by growths of eucalyptus and other trees, the beauty enhanced by mile upon mile of skilfully terraced fields on all but the steepest slopes.

Could it possibly be that there was once a Betsileo-type culture in the geographically similar highlands of Zimbabwe? And if so, might that provide clues as to the purpose of the 'pits'?

Could the pits, for instance, have been *tombs*?

Whilst not expecting to find any exact parallels, Malagasy tombs may well shed a ray of light on the problem. Throughout most of Madagascar tombs, which are at the heart of peoples' lives, vary enormously, particularly those of the Betsileo, Merina, and Tanala. Nothing is more important than a fine tomb. Alfred Grandidier, author of the multi-volumed *Histoire de Madagascar* quoted an old Merina adage: "*haren-kita fasana*" -"un tombeau est le vraie richesse, une richesse que tout le monde voit". Or as the 18th century Merina ruler, Andrianampoinimerina, put it: 'dwelling on earth is no more than a voyage, but dwelling in a tomb is for eternity.'

Sometimes a rich individual will make sure he has his own personal tomb; more usually they are built for the whole family. People always live near them; sometimes, even, the tombs are built within the village. Rich people used to entrust a favoured slave or *ko-drazana* - nicknamed *valala fiandry fasana*, 'the guardian locusts' - to guard the family tomb. (17) Maurice Bloch commented: "All travellers unacquainted with Merina culture cannot but be struck with (the tombs') solidity and importance which contrasts with the impermanence of the houses of the living". (18) Since the coming of concrete there has been a tendency for the rich to build more and more elaborate tombs, decorated with expensive arches and fancy finials.

Across the landscape of the Merina, Betsileo, and their eastern neighbours the Tanala, visitors have been struck by the variety of tombs. There is a picture in one the Rev James Sibrée's books, written at the end of the 19th century, of old Merina pit-tombs built on the edge of a village with walls that rise just above the surrounding ground. Like all Malagasy buildings these tombs are rectangular not round, and instead of a tunnel entrance, they have steps, or ramps, leading down to a lintelled doorway and a hugely heavy stone door. The tombs are roofed with a shallow dome and appear to be covered with earth or turf. Water must inevitably have got into the tombs in heavy rain; but as they are on high ground above the village in the background, one assumes there must have been drains of some sort leading out on the lower side. If a Nyanga pit was roofed with a similar dome it would have looked very similar.

Traditional Merina tombs.(10)

Consider Sibree's description of Betsileo burials:- "… the tombs (near Fianarantsoa) which here-abouts were very numerous, were the plain square or cube of undressed flat stones … it was clear that the chamber in which the corpses are deposited does not project at all above ground, as it does in the Hova tombs; and I afterwards ascertained that this chamber is excavated at considerable depth beneath the square pile of stones, which is therefore not a grave, but only marks the place of one far below the surface. I noticed also that there was a long low mound of earth extending from one side of the tomb to a distance of from thirty or forty to eighty feet and upwards. This, it appears, marks the line *of a long tunnelled passage* gradually descending from the surface to the deeply sunk burial chamber" (19) ... a feature that is directly analogous to tunnels leading down into the Nyanga pits.

John Mack of the British Museum, in a more recent publication, described subterranean Merina tombs with tiered shelving on which to lay the shrouded corpses. "Many Betsileo tombs are constructed in a similar manner...but they lack the structure of shelving which characterises Merina tombs and instead the dead are laid out on matting." Mack discussed various types of Betsileo tombs, some involving an underground cavity, and others built wholly above ground. "These they call simply *trano vato* ('houses of stone'). ... Usually they will be placed outside the village boundary, but in special circumstances they might be *located within the settlement* thus imitating royal tombs which were sited within the palace itself." All their tombs are frequently visited and often opened for the process of regrouping the corpses known as the *famadihana*. (20) "They are 'lived with'; where there is a village or a deme there are always, in the same territory, tombs." (21)

And finally Ralph Linton's description of a Tanala tomb:- "... the 'kibory' (tomb) consists of a large rectangular *pit lined with dry stone masonry* and covered with stone slabs or planks. The earth is heaped above in a mound ... " (22)

So the notion of a Nyanga pit being a tomb – the most careful and elaborate construction in the family compound - is by no means implausible ... sloping tunnel access ... pits lined with dry stone masonry ... timber planks spanning the roofs sealed with earth piled in a shallow dome. Was the hut built over the shaft in the entrance tunnel to the Nyanga pits the residence of the 'guardian locust'? Was the left-hand curve of the entrance tunnel a device to foil the *lolo*, the spirit of the dead, from escaping? Were the Nyanga pits once roofed in the same way as a Tanala tomb?

Flat-roofed houses used to be common in several parts of Africa: in Eritrea; in Upper Volta; among the Burungi and Alawa ... the Gogo ...and their relatives the Gorowa, all of Tanzania; and the Iraqw south of Lake Manyara who built houses either wholly or partially underground. (23) The backs of the Iraqw houses were usually excavated into a hillside, the slightly curved roof was supported by posts every three or four feet, and overlaid with wattle-and-daub – a material that was more fire-proof than thatch. But perhaps most interesting of all, a hut with a 'daga' roof was found at one of the *zimbabwes*, Khami; and some archaeologists believe that many of the houses in the Western Enclosure of the Great Zimbabwe may also have been roofed with shallow 'daga' domes as it was less of a fire hazard than thatch. (24) Such roofs, left to decay over many decades, would leave no clues beyond the thin layer of mould and earth that typifies the deposits found on the floors of the Nyanga pits.

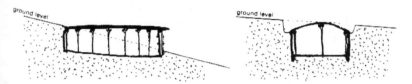

Elevations of Iraqw earth-roofed houses, south of Lake Manyara, Tanzania.

No graveyards or cemeteries to counter the 'pit tomb' hypothesis have been found at Nyanga; in fact apart from one or two atypical burials there is no direct evidence indicating how the dead were disposed of. (25) One could ask: 'If the pits *were* tombs, why have no bodies been found in them?' But the absence of bodies is not entirely surprising. If the people of Nyanga followed the Malagasy model, their dead, wrapped in '*lambas*', would have been laid in the tombs on mats or make-do shelves. And if, when the old culture's day was done, the ancestors were not removed in some sort of final *famadihana* ceremony, they would long since have fallen pray to the scavenging of animals and the destructive powers of the elements.

CHAPTER - 13

"Above all else it was the 18 or 20 Chopi xylophones that tingled the blood in my veins and left unforgettable memories in my mind. Even now I can hear the leader somewhere in their midst hammering out a rapid introduction on his treble xylophone – then a slight pause, followed by the ear-splitting cacophony of all the other instruments, each with its own distinctive part, the two deep drums, the shaken rattles, crashing in with rhythmic precision. But more was to come when twenty or thirty dancers in their skin capes and leggings, spears and cow-hide shields held high, entered the arena swaying rhythmically, bursting suddenly into song in a rich base unison, thrusting the air with their spears, changing pace and speed, leaping high, then BANGING their shields flat on the ground with the sound of a single pistol shot, wheeling and dancing with the exactness of a shoal of fry, turning as one, and turning again, sweeping the spectators along in a torrent of emotion – and then, without warning – an abrupt stop. Stillness and silence, but for the continued tinkling of the treble and alto timbila." (1)

THE MUSIC TRAIL

Early in the 20th century Erich von Hornbostel set out the tunings of four xylophones from Africa and four from Burma and commented on their remarkable similarity. Then in 1935 Jaap Kunst, an ethnomusicologist and curator of the National museum in Djakarta, observed: "Outside the Malay archipelago there is only one region apart from Central America, where instruments of the *gender* type occur. This region…is Africa." Kunst, like Hornbostel before him, compared tunings and scales of African and Indonesian instruments, and found them to be the same. His conclusion was unequivocal:

"…it is from Java that this instrument came to the African continent …" (2)

Xylophones are found with scarcely a break across the sub-Saharan regions from the Gambia to Lake Victoria; and in a dog-leg across the southern Congo down to parts of South Africa and Moçambique. Though most African xylophones are played either individually or in groups of two, or three, there are notable exceptions: both the Ganda of Uganda and the Chopi of Moçambique have – or had - xylophone orchestras comparable to the magnificent *gamelans* of Indonesia.

Some years later than Kunst, the staunchest advocate of the Indonesian-African musical link was the Rev. Dr. A.M. Jones, a Welshman gifted with 'perfect pitch', who started his working life as a missionary in Northern Rhodesia. With his musical background, and his interest in African music, it came as no surprise when, after twenty years in the bush, he left the church to become a full-time ethnomusicologist at the School of Oriental and African Studies in London.

Father Jones liked to tell the story of how one day, early in the 1950's, there was a knock on the door of his room, and in walked a man with a bundle under his arm and introduced himself as Bana Kanuteh. Mr Kanuteh was a Mandinka *griot*, a professional wandering minstrel and storyteller, whose homeland was in Sierra Leone. Untying his parcel, he produced a xylophone which he said he had made himself, and proceeded to give an expert performance of his own West African music. Father Jones listened in astonishment, for in this Mandinka music he immediately recognised many of the same unusual features that had been recorded in the xylophone music of the Chopi four thousand miles away near the mouth of the Limpopo. Being well aware of Kunst and von Hornbostel's work, Father Jones decided to put their theories to the test independently.

"In my room at the university" he wrote, "I placed a Cambodian xylophone (Indonesia) and one from the Mandinka tribe of Sierra Leone (West Africa). Bana Kanuteh … had, of course, never set eyes on an Indonesian xylophone before. He ran his playing sticks up and down its keys and immediately began to play his own African music on it. He told me it was the same as the Mandinka model and asked me if he might buy it! He then started playing, without stopping, first on one instrument and then on the other – and still more remarkable – with one hand playing on one xylophone and the other hand simultaneously playing on the other. Lastly he started singing Mandinka songs accompanying himself on the Cambodian xylophone." Though there is no clear musicological imperative for it to have been so, the fact that the pitch and tuning of xylophones were identical - from Southeast Asia to Southeast Africa, and to the furthest Atlantic coast of West Africa - went beyond the realm of coincidence, and firmly suggested that at some time in history there must have been a direct link between them.

Father Jones was fortunate to have made this experiment when he did.

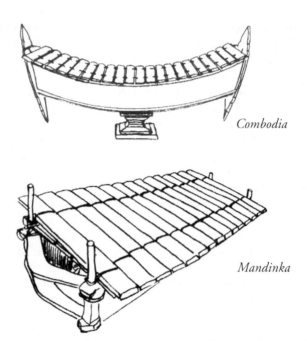

Combodia

Mandinka

Such has been the decline of traditional music over the past fifty years both in Africa and Indonesia that today he would probably have found it impossible. Jaap Kunst lamented the fact that by 1970 there was not a single 'gong-smithy' left in Java or Bali who could make the traditional gongs for a *gamelan*; and in Africa there has been a similar decline. For a time Chopi music was sustained in one or two of the Rand goldmines where policies towards African culture were sometimes surprisingly enlightened even in the days of *apartheid*; but when South Africa cut back on migrant labour, performances of all tribal dance groups were curtailed. On top of this, with Moçambique's 20 year civil war, and the abolition of the chiefs who were once the sponsors of proudly competing village groups, support for the Chopi orchestras became virtually impossible to obtain, and though there may still be one or two aging orchestra-leaders, they have long since given up creating the new routines that always typified their brilliant repertoire.(3)

Five hundred years ago the Chopi must have undergone changes as traumatic as those in recent years, but happily with less dire consequences. According to the late great expert on African music, Hugh Tracey, their oral historians told how at the end of the fifteenth century in a time of war and upheaval in Zimbabwe, their people broke away from the Karanga – a prominent Shona clan - and moved to their present location three hundred and fifty miles away near the southern Moçambique coast. As the Karanga were the traditional custodians of the ancient buildings at the 'Great Zimbabwe' it is extraordinary to think that there must have been a time, long ago, when the towering walls of the Elliptical Temple regularly echoed to the thunderous sounds of some of Africa's most brilliant instrumentalists.(4)

The significance of the Chopi relationship with the Karanga and the Great Zimbabwe is of much more than passing interest. If xylophones and xylophone music were introduced into Africa by Indonesians, as is now generally accepted, it means that their direct descendants must once have lived in the heart of one of Bantu Africa's most renowned ancient culture-zones. It supports contentions already expressed that the *Zanaj* of Indonesia must have been closely involved with the *Zanj* of Africa in the gold mining region of *Ard Sufala*, at the centre of which lay the Great Zimbabwe. The fact that the Chopi separated from the Karanga roughly 500 years ago also brings to mind the story, well authenticated in Madagascar, of how the Maroserana came from 'Mijomby' (Moçambique) to present-day Tulear in Madagascar with a shipload of gold which ultimately enabled them to gain supremacy over the local people and create the huge Sakalava Empire. (5) When the court musicians moved to the coast – perhaps harassed by invading Bantu warriors - were they hoping to escape to Madagascar with Andriamandisoarivo, their new Maroserana king? Were they, for some reason we shall never understand, abandoned and left behind in Africa?

Apart from a very primitive version played in a few parts of the island, the Malagasy have never been xylophone players, an odd omission that clearly supports the view that there was not just one single Indonesian imprint left on Africa, but many different ones from different points of origin, and arriving at different times throughout the thousand years of Zanj dominance on the coast. The contention expressed earlier that different Indonesian *sukus* made up the people of Zanj – the Bugi and the Bajoo, for example; or the Mandar, and the Makassar - suddenly makes greater sense. Each group of Indonesians brought a different facet of their culture; had their own specialisations; and settled in different regions – the Bajoo and the Mandar in the northern islands where they continued to live their traditional life, and became the builders of the *mtepe*; the Bugi and the Makassar who were prominent in the colonisation of *Buki* (Madagascar); others from Sumatra, the 'Island of Gold', to develop the minerals of the hinterland; and yet others whom we shall encounter who sailed on round the Cape of Storms to far away West Africa.

A scenario such as this helps to explain some anomalies in the world of xylophones and other musical instruments. Bana Kanuteh's xylophone, for instance, had a box resonator similar to a Cambodian instrument. Large xylophones in the southern Congo, shaped not unlike half a huge truck-tyre, so that the player could reach all the notes without moving, were very similar in appearance to arrays of tuned metal gongs of Thailand called *khong vong*. Chopi xylophones, and the beautiful *marimbas* of their cousins the Ndau (from where our word '*marimba*' comes) have individual resonators like Javanese instruments. It is very likely that certain instruments were introduced in some areas but not in others.

In the music world the direct comparison of instruments is one thing; but much the strongest evidence of Indonesian or Southeast Asian origins lies not so much in the morphology of the instruments as in the principles behind the music; the type of scales used, how they are tuned, and so on. Suffice to say that on both sides of the Indian Ocean musicians used heptatonic and pentatonic scales with similar intervallic relationships. The same principles do not just apply to xylophones, but to other instruments as well, e.g. such instruments as the 'finger piano', or *mbira*, popular in Central Africa, but which has no precise counterpart in Indonesia. (6)

In our Western world nobody minds if music written, say, for strings, is transposed for the piano or some other instrument; and the same sentiments seem to have been shared in both Indonesia and Africa. Music composed for instruments of one type was often played on instruments of another type. A delightful, if extreme, example of this was on the island of Natuna Besar in eastern Riau, where women once had their wooden mortars 'tuned' to a perfect heptatonic scale so that they could make joyful music as they pounded their rice, thumping their pestles up and down in interlocking rhythms. History does not record what the music was; but one can be fairly sure that it was not written specially to be played on *pestle and mortar*! The fact that finger-pianos and xylophones share the same scales is therefore unremarkable. It is not the instrument that really matters; but the principles behind the music.

The last paper Father Jones wrote before his death was on African panpipes.(7) That 'bible' of everything to do with music, Grove's Dictionary, says – incorrectly - in the current edition (2004) that panpipes are only found in Central Europe or around the Pacific rim. Panpipes were also once an instrument of western Java(8); and they are a very important instrument in parts of South Central Africa where they are found in a large swathe of country roughly between the Limpopo and Zambezi rivers stretching inland to the Upemba depression around the headwaters of the Congo. They are played by the Chopi of Moçambique, and in the mountains of Basutoland:

they are also played by Bushmen and Hottentots, suggesting that panpipes may have been around in southern Africa for a long time – possibly since before the Bantu migrated into the area.

Hugh Tracey's musicologist son, Andrew, recorded his impressions when he heard panpipes played in a Nyungwe village near Tete on the Zambezi: "I will never forget the first time I heard (an ensemble). I was immediately surrounded by about 50 men and women singing and playing the panpipes, and a richly harmonic sound on all sides, something like being in an organ loft among the pipes." (9) Both Tracey and Jones agreed that the scales and pitch of the panpipes is the same as for *mbira* and xylophones: and Jones' contention, once again, was that the scales, pitch and tuning of the African panpipes had their origins in Indonesian music.

Had Father Jones lived longer he might have noticed two other factors that seem to confirm a direct relationship between African and Southeast Asian panpipes: the first - how the Nyungwe panpipes are bound together with strips of palm leaf in an attractive criss-cross plaited knot *identical* to the 'plaited ligature' of panpipes in Vanuatu. The second is how, in order to reduce the size of the opening at the top of large pipes to make them easier to blow, the Nyungwe push several sections of smaller pipe - in diminishing sizes - into the mouthpiece, fastening them with beeswax in exactly the same way as Solomon Islanders. (10)

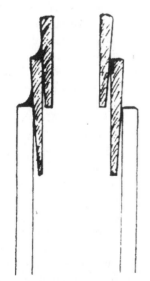

Nyangwe & Solomons

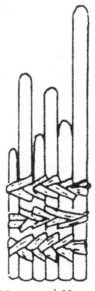

Nyangwe & Vanuatu

131

Did they dream up all these things independently, or do they – as Father Jones wrote – "… force us to admit that there must have been diffusion"?

In January 2004 a 'replica' of one of the outriggers depicted on the walls of Borobudur, having sailed from Java to Africa, passed down the *Ard al Waq-Waq*, rounded the Cape of Good Hope, and set off through the Atlantic swells to Ghana in West Africa. When, in ancient times, our Phantom Voyagers blazed the trail for these latter-day adventurers, music, as much as anything else seems to have marked their progress up the west coast. Other evidence may lack the cogency of that for xylophones and panpipes, because after a thousand years of mingling and merging with indigenous inventiveness it is not always possible to be absolutely certain where the divisions lie between African and Indonesian legacies. But there are numerous patterns in 'African' musical instruments and sounds which, however much they might claim pure African ancestry, display features that are tempting to associate with those of Southeast Asia and Indonesia. Although their provenance may be argued, they make up such a strong body of 'coincidences' that it would be perilous to ignore them.

As the voyagers headed north towards the desolate Skeleton Coast of Namibia it is a near certainty that they would have made landfall at Cape Cross to replenish their larders from the millions of seals that gather there on the beaches. Should they have done so, they would have been able to see the Brandberg Mountain, sixty or seventy miles inland, its head shrouded in cloud 8,400 feet above the surrounding desert. And if lured inland, the voyagers would have found a mountain cut across by deep ravines and huge, chaotically strewn boulders, as well as the only really good water for miles around. Should they also have been looking for minerals they might have found gold, alluvial tin and copper, the last of which has been extensively worked in ancient Namibia by 'persons unknown'. They would not have been the first visitors; the rock-shelters of the Brandberg are rich in stone tools and ancient ash deposits: and many exceptional rock paintings of animals and figures, including a series described by the once famous antiquarian, the Abbé Breuil, as 'musicians'.

The Abbé Breuil's 'musicians' are odd looking people with longish hair who do not look African at all. One of them is carrying a pair of strange leaf-shaped objects that Jaap Kunst, the Dutch musicologist, with support from other ethno-musicians, once firmly identified as *kemanaks*, elegant percussion instruments played in Java. They are, he pointed out, very similar to iron percussion instruments still played in various parts of

West Africa. (11)

Further up the coast it would have been impossible for our voyagers to miss the mouths of the Congo, the Gabon, and other rivers flowing from the uplands of the Cameroons. Throughout this area there are several instruments that are so uncannily twinned with those of southeast Asia that it is hard to deny a relationship. How is it, for instance, that bar-zithers have been collected in the Olombo forests (A) on the north bend of the Congo River that are indistinguishable from bar-zithers collected in Northern Moçambique (Makonde B), Southeast Madagascar (Antaimoro and Sakalava D), and (apart from a couple of minor details) in Sulawezi in Indonesia (C)? (12)

At least four styles of message gongs on either side of the world are identical in concept if not in artistic style – small hand-held 'anthropomorphic' gongs with carved heads from Java and the Congo; 'zoomorphic' gongs specifically with horned buffalo heads at the ends, from Southeast Asia and West Africa; message gongs with single slits from Java and western Africa; and others with double 'mouths' from the Igbo on the

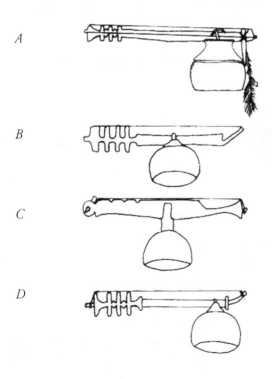

A

B

C

D

Niger river, and New Britain in Oceania. (13)

As we go further north and nose our way into the hidden channels of the Niger delta we find the Igbo playing small wooden kettle-drums called *ekere-mba* - graduated and differently tuned drums arranged progressively in a rack and played like the xylophone. There may be nine or ten kettle-drums in a set, arranged in a semi-circle around the lead player, or on straight wooden racks so that they can be played by two or three players at the same time. (14) In Thailand there is an instrument called a *kong tock* which, apart from the fact that it looks more sophisticated and its resonators are metal while those of the *ekere-mba* are wood or pottery, is essentially the same instrument. (15) Is this, too, pure chance?

It is easy enough to say that these were all invented and developed independently. Maybe beating a hollow tree put the same idea into so-called 'primitive' people's minds thousands of miles apart and the same variety of designs inevitably followed. 'Diffusion' may be an unfashionable word. But if we know that certain people travelled from one area to another (and it will hopefully become clearer that Indonesians must have travelled to West Africa) the balance in favour of 'diffusion' rises as the probability of 'independent invention' falls.

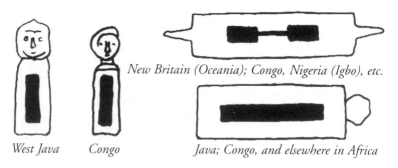

New Britain (Oceania); Congo, Nigeria (Igbo), etc.

West Java   *Congo*   *Java; Congo, and elsewhere in Africa*

(Carrington's Illustrations)

Some years ago when setting up a museum in what was still the British Cameroons I and my band of collectors – museum assistant, interpreter, cook, bearers of camping gear, bearers of empty trophy-boxes, bearers of sacks of cash-money – came into the remote forest village of Bamumbu where we were entertained to a performance of double-gong music that to the best of my knowledge had not until been written about. In the Cameroons the 'double iron gong' (technically these instruments are 'clapperless-bells' not gongs) is the symbol of *Kwifon* – the chief's special society for the maintenance of law and order. Though usually symbolic, they are sometimes played as instruments in small groups: but those in the rain-sodden hills of Bamumbu were something else. In all there were ten pairs – twenty tuned gongs – ranging in size from about ten inches to three feet tall. In addition there were two tall drums and a pair of grass rattles – the same instrumental mix as a standard Chopi orchestra in Moçambique; plus a bunch of single percussion gongs.

The fourteen members of the orchestra stood in a curved line. A player near the middle set the pace, beating his gongs with a soft wooden stick. The man on his right then came in, taking up the rhythm from his neighbour; and this went down the line until all ten double gongs were producing an amazingly complex swirl of sound. At last came the drums, adding a deep throb to the hollow cacophony of the gongs, followed immediately by the brittle rushing-sounds of the wicker rattles; and finally the bunch of single gongs, clashed together, punctuating the whole marvelous din.

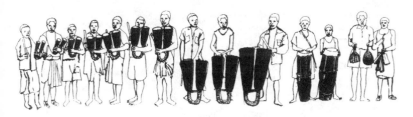

Double 'gong' Orchestra. Bamumbu. Cameroons (1959)

The phenomenal sounds produced that day among ramshackle houses on that rain-sodden spur gnawed at every nerve; but this was no wild-cat jazz. Each player conformed to well-defined and practiced rhythms. Only once had I heard anything like these incredible sounds before - in South Africa, listening to a xylophone orchestra. Every beat of the gongs, every interlocking harmony, every throb of the drums, and susurration of the shakers, brought back vivid memories of the Chopi. I had no recording equipment; so a memory it had to remain - a memory as vivid as Andrew Tracey'smust be of when he first heard an orchestra of panpipes – but the crux of that memory was the similarity of the sounds from two disparate orchestras on different sides of the continent. (16)

Gongs of the type played in Bamumbu are found all over western Africa, and a dozen or so have been unearthed by archaeologists in and around the Great Zimbabwe. When Chopi *timbila* rang out across the

Zimbabwe *veld*, were they alone, or were there double-gong orchestras beating out their raucous, rhythmic, music as well?

There is a low relief on the walls of Borobudur that depicts three instruments: a xylophone, being played by a man sitting at the end of the instrument as Africans sometimes do; a man tapping an Indonesian *ketuk* gong; and a third beating a hand-held clapperless-bell on a curved stem reminiscent of the double bells of Africa.(17) Is he, one wonders, trying to tell us something?

An Anecdote.

When collecting African crafts in the Congo, I once met up with a Baptist Missionary named John Carrington, who lived and worked for years among the Olombo, Mba, and Lokele. John was a renowned expert on the regions gong-languages, and it was he who first pointed out to me the similarities of some of the Congolese instruments to those of Southeast Asia. He was a big man, with the build of a lumberjack, and when preaching, he used his knowledge of the gong-language to full effect. He always kept two sticks in the pulpit, and if he felt his congregation was not paying attention he would pause – pull out his sticks – and rap out his sermon on the edge of the pulpit!

Later I discovered the efficacy of the gong-language myself...

In the village of Bengamisa on the banks of the Lindi river I was taken to a small workshop where they made their famous 'Bengamisa' chairs – originally two pieces cut from old canoe-sides that slot neatly into each other to make a 'seat' and a 'back'. They had forty eight chairs in stock; and to their incredulity I purchased the whole lot.

My fame was instant.

I drove on to the Mission where I was staying, and, having settled in, went for what I thought would be a quiet pre-supper stroll down to the banks of the Lindi to listen to the bull-frogs croaking in the luxuriant undergrowth and watch the blue herons and fish-eagles swooping on their prey. But the peace was broken by the sound of shouting, and the muffled splash of paddles. Several canoes, from upstream and down, emerged from the overhanging jungles and broke out across the current to the point where I was standing. At first there seemed to be nothing strange. But suddenly I became alarmed. All the occupants were carrying enormous spears, with blades two feet long and wider than a hand. Some also carried sickles, large as scythes – desperate looking weapons – and they were heading towards me, shouting. In my alarm I decided to retreat slowly back up to the Mission house. But my way was blocked by a dozen more men, each carrying these enormous sickles and spears. Frankly, I was nervous … until one of them started speaking to me (in Swahili, surprisingly) asking me if I wanted to buy spears!

I had only left Bengamisa an hour or so earlier. But it then dawned on me what all that drumming was that I had heard as I drove the ten miles along the river-road from the village. They had been announcing the arrival of a mad Englishman who would buy *anything*.

It is a long-winded language. To have sent this message in the tonal Mba gong-language would (going by John Carrington's drum-vocabularies) have involved hammering out something like: *tukutukutukutukutukutuku* (- to rouse the neighbours) *kelembangumbangu* (come quickly) *bosongo bolyakuka kulekuka* (a European has arrived) *bosongo swaba akundalibogo* (he says he wants) *ingbilingbili ngoma* (spears). Naturally I obliged, and purchased a large number to accompany the chairs on their long journey to my customer in New York.

A day or two later I was guided through the forests west of the Lindi to see one of their huge canoes being made. I am not sure whether the makers were Mba (Bamanga) or Olombo; but this 60 foot monster was being made for sale to a Lokele trader who had already put down a deposit. It was several miles from the 'sea' as they called the Congo, and would require seventy strong men from the village to haul it to the water down a pre-laid track of slimy poles when finished. As we walked through the forest, the family – men and women – who were making the canoe were forewarned of our coming by my guide *shouting* the gong-language in a falsetto shriek - *ah-u-u-u-ah-u* – warning them of our coming. Another instance of sounds designed for one instrument been 'played' on another!

Left: End of slit-gong. Cameroons. Bamenda Museum.
Right: End of large slit gong. Naga. Assam

CHAPTER - 14

ON THE DARKER SIDE OF LIFE

In 1947, J.H. Hutton, an anthropologist who worked both in Nigeria and Southeast Asia, wrote a paper titled *West Africa and Indonesia: A Problem of Distribution.*(1) It was a slightly rambling paper and, on the whole, too unspecific to be at the cutting edge of any argument. His views were prefaced by a brief discussion of the merits of 'diffusionism' and 'independent invention', and thoughts on 'coincidence' and 'probability'.

"In areas so far apart as Indonesia and West Africa," he wrote "a presumption of independent development must obviously be made unless the wealth of identical features of culture prove to be so great that such a hypothesis can no longer be maintained." The precise point where an accumulation of similar features overwhelms the probability of independent evolution is a matter of individual judgment, and will inevitably vary to some extent the doctrine of mathematical probabilities being inexact. "One can only examine the similarities reported and frame an opinion in the light of one's own experience and one's individual estimate of the probabilities in the case."

His own position soon became clear when he listed around forty culture traits that he saw as being common to Indonesia (and Nagaland – some of whose people came long long ago from Southeast Asia) - and to Nigeria. These ranged from the underlying philosophies behind head-hunting, through cannibalism, to burial customs and the promotion of fertility. They included such things as a man's need to take a head before he could marry; the head as a vehicle of fertility; the wearing of an extra feather in the hair when a head was taken; the licking of blood from the blade which had taken the head; the ceremonial exposure of heads; the significance of the lower jaw; the special significance of large wooden message gongs – their place in society, their frequent decoration with buffalo heads; shaft and tunnel burials allowing the spirit to communicate with the body; the drying out of corpses; wrestling to promote the fertility of crops.

Cannibalism was widespread in West Africa, being occasionally practiced by the Yoruba, and their neighbours the Ibo, or Igbo. The rituals of cannibalism were usually bound up with concepts of fecundity and procreation, evident in the large number of priapic monoliths found in Yorubaland. (2) Though in many respects humane and caring, Yoruba society was often cruel, with powerful secret societies such as the Ogboni society known to have practised ritual human sacrifice. Numerous Ife sculptures show people with gags tied in their mouths - part of the preparation for the execution of criminals and sacrificial victims to stop them cursing the Yoruba gods when they were about to die.

But Hutton's conviction that the rituals shared a common source was as clearly expressed in his general comments as in the specifics. "Perhaps the most striking of Nigerian-Indonesian parallels are the beliefs and practices associated with head-hunting. ... Moreover the parallels apparent between the head-hunting cults of Nigeria and the head-hunting cults of Indonesia and south-east Asia involve not merely matters of doctrine and belief but a regular complex in which the material culture is involved as well as the underlying philosophy which inspires it."

In Hutton's view the possibility of independent development in Nigeria and Indonesia could be considered if there was a more general similarity of beliefs in neighbouring parts of Africa and Asia. "But as it is, the number of independent beliefs and practices common to the two areas and absent elsewhere involves an assumption of coincidence, both in their presence in the two areas and in their absence elsewhere, which goes, as it seems to me, far beyond probability. Coincidence does not account for similarities and contrasts on such a scale. It may account for some of them, but not for the whole complexes."

He goes on to quote a study of blood groups carried out in 1947 by Lattes - *Individuality of the Blood* - which indicates identical distribution patterns for Indonesia and the area of West Africa where the culture parallels are found. He accepts that the coincidence of blood groupings and culture patterns could conceivably be due to environment or some other cause, but maintains that a simpler hypothesis would be that in some remote period in the past there was direct contact between Indonesians and Nigerians. "There is no reason why Indonesian sailors, who could carry their language and culture to Madagascar, should not have gone yet further, have doubled the Cape and sailed up northwards to the Bight of Benin. I suggest that an hypothesis of this kind offers the least difficult explanation of the close analogies to be observed in Nigerian and Indonesian cultures."

Hutton was a well known figure in the anthropological world. His paper is readily available. There is nothing obscure about it. But it is seldom read and even less seldom quoted. Its problem lies in the fact that it was written nearly sixty years ago and – by now fairly obvious – it's message fits nowhere in orthodox teaching. Thus Hutton has always been side-lined and seldom discussed: he is seen as something of an out-of-date eccentric who may lead unwary students into an academic slough. So Africa's historians plodding through the forests along the Fage/Oliver highway have once again steered away from compelling evidence that Indonesians came to Africa.

Hutton's dark world of head-hunting and cannibalism makes an interesting platform from which to explore the swampy regions of the Niger delta. Had he himself cast his net wider, he would have found other Indonesian links, particularly among the Yoruba and the Igbo. They are discernible in lots of ways that we shall discuss: in plantains and yams, the region's staple foods; possibly in the beads with which they adorn themselves; in cowrie shells, an important measure of wealth; in their high arts; in the deepest recesses of their religion and divination systems, and in the loathsome disease - *elephantiasis*.

Yoruba sculptures depict a number of diseases including leprosy, anacephaly, and several that clearly show people with *Wuchereria Bancrofti,* (elephantiasis). The most horrific of these sculptures - found in the grove of Osongongon Obamakin in Ife - is a terracotta of a squatting man with testicles larger than croquet balls. The Yoruba treated this disease with particular awe - presumably on account of its obvious procreative associations - and even today when an elephantiasis victim dies there are rituals in which a priest of the 'Bull-roarer' cult removes the man's scrotum for special ritual treatment to ensure that no other member of his family suffers the same fate.

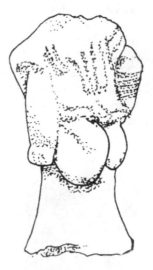

Headless Nok figure representing man with elephantiasis of the testicles.

The fact that elephantiasis was also depicted in some of the ancient Nok terracottas indicates that it must have been around in Nigeria for a very long time.(3) The Nok culture dates back to the 4 - 5 century BC continuing into the first millennium AD, making its terracottas among the oldest fired-earth artworks found anywhere in sub-Saharan Africa.

In 1968 Dr B.R. Laurence of the Department of Entomology, London School of Hygiene and Tropical Medicine, published his researches into the origins and spread of elephantiasis.(4) In the guarded language of a scientist breaking new ground, he wrote: "It seems to me that the origins of Bancroftian filariasis are in S.E. Asia and one has now to account for its distribution through the tropics. We know that there was settlement in Madagascar and we have to account for the presence of the disease on the mainland of Africa. The early Africans were not sea-going people so one then has to assume that the disease was brought to Africa by a sea-going people. The movements of the Bantu were west to east, not the opposite direction, and we have to account for portrayal of elephantiasis and the presence of elephantiasis in early European reports from West Africa. It therefore seems to me possible ... that the Indonesian influence is present in West Africa as well as the accepted presence in Madagascar and East Africa."

It might be supposed that the spread of such a disease, which is transmitted via mosquitoes, would be as easy as that of malaria, and that it could have swept across the African continent from person to person, or mosquito to mosquito. But it is not as simple as that. First of all, quoting Dr Laurence: "Man is the only known definitive host of the nematode, and the microfilariae produced by the adult worms in man are taken in by mosquitoes while sucking blood, undergo development in the mosquito, and are then transmitted to new hosts when the mosquito feeds again. .. Unlike other vector-borne diseases such as malaria, plague and yellow fever, there is no replication of the parasite in the mosquito host." Thus the range of transmission is restricted to that of the limited ambit and brief life of the engorged mosquito.

Dr Laurence goes on: "Casual exposure to the bites of infective mosquitoes rarely produces patent infections of filariasis. To move a disease of this kind, one would have to suppose that a number of individuals in the migrant populations were infected and these would also have to be infective to the mosquitoes in the new environment ..."

In other words, for it to spread over any appreciable distance, it is the actual movement of infected *people* that is essential.

Given the slow rate of spread of Wuchereria bancrofti in a static community, and the unlikelihood of it being carried to Nok or Ife by any movement of people from points of introduction in East Africa 3000 miles from the Jos plateau, by far the most likely manner of its introduction from southeast Asia, as Dr Laurence observed, would have been by sea, up the Niger and Benue rivers and the tributaries of the Benue that flow down from the Jos plateau. No date-analysis of the terracottas depicting elephantiasis has been done, so we have no precise idea when the disease might have been introduced, but Nok's early dates are the first of several indications that Southeast Asian contacts may go back to a time well before the Christian era.

Dr Laurence and Professor Hutton were both convinced of a Southeast Asian connection with Nigeria. Neither of them proposed a time-frame; though the elephantiasis link with Nok would suggest a *terminus a quo* in the latter part of the 1st millennium BC - a date by no means out of line with Hornell's Pre-Dravidian settlement of 'Polynesians' in India, or early spice trading through the Horn of Africa to the Middle East. But is there another hook on which one can tentatively hang some dates?

Iron is a possibility. But that said, the coming of iron-working to Africa is so fraught with uncertainties that any attempt to draw firm conclusions from the evidence currently available would be akin to sticking one's head into a Bessemer furnace.

Some basic guidelines:

In western Africa, the earliest sub-Saharan dates for iron are 4th – 5th century BC at several sites strung out between Taruga (in the Nok culture zone on the Jos Plateau) and the Du Chaillu hills in Gabon, 800 or 900 miles to the south. Two Gabon sites are very near the sea in the Gabon River estuary; others near rivers 200 – 400 miles inland.(5) The most obvious source of iron technology in these parts would be Meroe, the capital of the old Kushitic empire on the Nile just south of Khartoum, roughly 1000 miles east of Taruga. Meroe was in full flower from c. 4th century B.C. to the 1st century A.D. and was a producer of massive amounts of iron. It was known to have had overland links to the Horn of Africa and the Red Sea, and journeying west to the Niger via Darfur should not have been a problem.

However, if iron technology had come from Meroe, the route would also have led directly past Daima, one of the most reliably dated settlements in ancient Nigeria which extends back in time to the Nok period. But iron smelting in Daima did not begin until the 5th or 6th centuries *A.D.* 8 – 900 years *after* the Taruga dates. It is hard to conceive that Daima could possibly have been bypassed and left in the dark for so long if the technology came overland from Meroe.

Roland Oliver has suggested that iron-smelting may have come from Do Dimmi at the south-western end of the Air Plateau 600 miles north of the Jos plateau in the Sahara where dates for iron smelting go back to the 7th century BC. But this presents some of the same problems as the Meroe hypothesis. Why are there no signs of ancient iron-working, for instance, at Kano, which lies *en route* between Air and Jos?

1500 miles to the east of Du Chaillu in Gabon there are numerous Early Iron Age sites in the Great Lakes region. Most of these date from the first and 7th centuries A.D, but some compare in ancient-ness with those of western Africa. Quoting Roland Oliver again: "… there remains a small but obstinate minority of **BC** dates from north-west Tanzania and Rwanda, which, despite re-testing, refuse to go away." (6)

Many historians assume that the sub-Saharan iron story began in eastern Africa, with influences from the Indian Ocean or the Nile valley, and that it spread overland from there … and linguistic evidence supports such a contention. But, with the sort of cussedness that so often bugs Africa, there is at the same time, and in the same region, equally strong linguistic evidence suggesting that iron spread across the Congo forests *from the west*. The problem is exacerbated by the fact that between the Taruga/du Chaillu line in the west, and the Tanzania/Rwanda iron-age sites in the lacustrine region there is a vast area west of the Ruwenzoris that was not occupied by Bantu people until approximately the second or third century A.D, that remained without iron smelting until centuries later. Additionally, archaeological data, however incomplete it may be, suggests that the spread of iron west of the Ruwenzoris was *not* from the east. (7)

In short – discounting the extremely unlikely chance that the necessary pyrotechnology for iron smelting was independently discovered in several parts of Africa – it seems that it must have been introduced separately a) in the eastern part, spreading as far as the lacustrine region, and b) in the west, down the Taruga/Du Chaillu axis.

But did the western stream necessarily come overland from Meroe or from anywhere else in the north, as many people believe? What if it came from the sea?

Two of the major early iron-age sites are located near the sea on either side of the Gabon Estuary; and all the Cameroon/Gabon locations are approachable up river valleys from the Atlantic. Likewise, Taruga and most of the other Nok sites are either on or near Benue tributaries such as the Gurara and the Mada; or the Katsina Ala, that flows from the Bamenda highlands.

The Aryans of India had learnt to smelt iron early in the first millennium B.C.; and it had spread to all the main centres of southern India by Mauryan times. Sri Lanka may have had iron even before southern India. The Sri Lankan archaeologist, S.U. Deraniyagala, interestingly, has pointed out that Sri Lankan chronicles refer to a settlement of the *Nagas* (whom he speculates were "… the Early Iron Age peoples of Sri Lanka") just north of Colombo, about 600-500 BC. (8) If, therefore, Hornell was right in equating the *Nagas* with 'Polynesians' there is therefore the fascinating possibility that iron technology could have been brought to Sri Lanka and southern India from Southeast Asia, and from there carried on by Indonesians to Africa, where we know that the Zanj were workers of iron.

This is speculation. But, at very least, iron technology was established and available in the Indian Ocean by the time Indonesians 'came west' to Africa, so the possibility of its introduction by Indonesian mariners in both East and West Africa as early as, say, 450 B.C., cannot be cast out of the window.

There is one other item that should not really appear in a chapter entitled 'On the Darker side of Life' – rather the reverse - but which does not warrant a chapter of its own: the game known as *mancala* or *wari* in Africa, or *congklak* (the 'cowrie shell') in Indonesia; or simply 'the board game'… the game that is played on boards with two lines of six or more 'pots' from which seeds or other small objects are transferred (usually at tremendous speed and with much noise) to a pot at either end, until one player has acquired the lot. It is an ancient game. The Royal Gaming Board of Ur in Babylonia dates to 2,600 B.C., other evidence suggesting it might have been played even as early as 3,300 B.C. (9). It is a game now played widely throughout the world, and for some reason many people believe that it originated in Africa – possible because so many beautifully carved boards have been found there (some from the Congo, Angola and Ghana thought to date back to the sixth century -?) (10). In Indonesia (where some equally beautifully carved boards can be found) it has also been around for many centuries; though since when precisely is moot. In Indonesia it goes by dozens of different names from Malaya, Sumatra, Java and Sulawezi, to the Philippines, and is connected with a variety of beliefs – in some places reserved to be played only after the death of a relation, in others to be played by farmers to calculate the seasons, or as a system of divination.

So, how did *wari* get to Africa – and how did *congklak* get to Indonesia?

Once again we are in the realm of speculation; but there are some interesting pointers. If the sixth century date for some African boards is correct (and there must be doubts about this (11)), the game was in Africa long before there was any known contact from the Mediterranean either by sea or across the Sahara. Assuming it was introduced, rather than independently invented in parallel with that of Babylonia (!), the only viable alternative would be that Indonesians, who appear to have brought other things to West Africa at a very ancient age (see below), also brought the 'board game' which they could easily have themselves acquired from the Middle East in Roman times, if not even earlier (viz the 'cloves to Babylon - goats to Timor' stories, above). Failing an Indonesian introduction, a

Transaharan introduction down the trade routes of the Middle Ages would have been very possible; but this would not have predated the 8th or 9th century, and it is also unlikely to have brought the game to the Niger delta region where it is strongly in evidence, which lay 1000 kilometres from the nearest major route.

Added to this is another anomaly. The powerful Bushongo tribe of Central Congo (Kasai), who had ancestral links with Equatoria near the upper Nile, claim that they did not know about the game until about 1600 AD when their hero-king Shamba Bolongongo (*Samba Mikepe*), the African 'Confucius', introduced it along with other fine things from the coastal regions where he had been travelling for several years before he came to the throne. Indeed Shamba's emblem (as can be seen on the British Museum's contemporary sculpture) was the *lela* board, the game for which he was famed.(12) So either it arrived in the Congo region very late (1000 years later than the supposed 6th C. date of some boards), or it goes to prove some peoples' belief that things did not spread as rapidly across Africa as others would have us think.

CHAPTER - 15

PLANTAINS AND YAMS

In 1959 an American professor, George Murdock, showed that several of Africa's most important food crops - the water-yam (*Dioscorea alata*), taro or the cocoyam (*Colocasia esculanta*), and bananas and plantains (the *Musaceae*) – came to Africa originally from Southeast Asia. (1) They were introduced into East Africa, he said, by Indonesians *en route* to Madagascar, and in due course carried overland to West Africa via Somalia, southern Ethiopia and the Sudan by people he referred to as 'megalithic Cushites'. No one now seriously questions the Asiatic origins of these plants (probably from the Philippines, Borneo or Sulawesi where all of them grew); but there are a number of reasons why Murdock's views on when they arrived and how they got to West Africa are now questioned. The suspicion is that whilst some varieties may have been introduced on the East Coast, the most important food varieties were introduced directly to West Africa by sea. And here's why opinion has swung away from Murdock....

First: ... a look at bananas and plantains - the *musaceae*.

The *musaceae* found in Africa can be divided into several genetic types, including:
a) the sweet bananas (*musa* AA and AAA), and...
b) the farinaceous cooking bananas, or plantains (musa ABB and AAB, the last of which has two subfamilies in Africa often referred to as 'Horn' and 'French').
c) several hybrid tetraploid types: AABB, ABBB and AAAB The origins of these tetraploids are in the New Guinea/Solomon Islands area. Although they have been recorded in the Bight of Benin, they are not common, and could be later introductions.

Musa AAB – the common plantain – is the one that interests us most, so it would be useful to have some idea of its distribution in Africa.

The 'hybrid triploids' ABB and AAB do occur in East Africa, but the most common *musaceae* to be found there are the 'sweet bananas', AA and AAA. Writing in 1987, banana experts Stover and Simmonds noted the presence of AAB plantains but pointed out that because they are still spreading inland they may "represent a relatively recent addition to the bananas of East Africa." (2) A distribution map drawn by J.C. Flinn and J.M. Hoyoux in 1976 shows that *musa* AAB was virtually absent from the eastern part of Africa (apart from an 'island' in Uganda); and nearly absent also from Madagascar.

Moving west, beyond the Ruwenzoris and the great lakes, into the rainforests of the Congo, Gabon and the Cameroons, and all the way across West Africa to Senegal, *musa* AAB becomes more significant. Here it is still the staple food, as it must have been for many centuries; but precisely how long is open to debate.

An indication of the length of time bananas and plantains have been present in any one area can be approximately gauged in several ways:

- by the number of different varieties, or 'cultivars', that have developed;
- by the extent to which they have become embedded in society as a part of daily life;
- by the various uses to which the plants have been put;
- the language associated with them;
- the rituals that have evolved around them;
- how firmly established the root words for the plant are within the language family;
- or, on the other hand, whether they appear to have 'jumped' linguistic boundaries, suggesting more recent borrowings.

As domesticated *musaceae* are reproduced vegetatively, (i.e. from suckers thrown up by the parent plant) the process of mutation is slow ... very much slower than in the case of plants that reproduce from seed, for which random cross-pollination can lead to rapid mutation. Hence the larger the number of varieties that have developed in any given area, the longer they are likely to have been there.

For instance, in one of the most extreme cases so far studied, the Olombo, in the Congo forests between the Lindi and Aruwimi rivers, recognize - and have names for - no less than 58 different cultivars of the AAB plantain. Such an astonishing number of varieties suggests that *musa* AAB must have been grown in that area for 1500 - 2000 years, or, as we shall see, possibly even longer.

And herein lie the seeds of controversy. How did the Olombo first get their plantains? Were they diffused from the East Coast as Murdock first

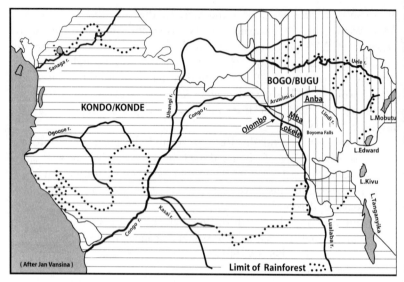

Map showing distribution of root words for banana.
(After J. Vansina.)

suggested … or what? It happens that the Olombo are more or less in the middle of Africa, roughly 1200 air-miles from the mouth of the Tana river in the east, and 1200 river-miles from the mouth of the Congo river in the west. Thus, from a geographical point of view, there is no obvious answer as to how they got their *musa*.

Apart from having the largest number of cultivars so far recorded for any specific area, (implying, in theory, that they have had the AAB plantain for longer than anywhere else in Africa) the Olombo forest stands out in other ways in that it is right at the meeting point of two language-zones in which the names for 'plantain' are different, thereby implying possibly different points of origins for the fruit. Of the two different root-words for plantains and bananas in Central Africa the most widespread is –*ko*, –*konde*, or –*kondo*. But in northeastern Congo there is a large area extending into the Central Sudan and regions around the northern lakes (L.Edward and L.Mobutu) where the generic root word is –*bogo* or –*bugu*. (3)

In his book, *Paths in the Rainforests*, Jan Vansina surmised, along more or less the same lines as Murdock, that the -*bogo* group may represent an early introduction of the 'Horn' variety of AAB which, having been brought across from Indonesia, was diffused from the East Coast, via the upper Nile and Equatoria to the Congo. He admits this would not have been easy, as, being

150

a plant that requires moist conditions, there are not many areas in the east where it would have flourished; and its progress would have been discontinuous from one 'island' of higher rainfall to the next.

Taking a closer look at the meeting point of the –*bogo* and –*kondo* language zones… specifically the region bordered by the Aruwimi in the west and north; the Lindi in the east and the Zaire in the south - in this area live:

a) the Anba, in the higher reaches of the Lindi and Aruwimi. (plantain = *libogo*),

b) the Mba, southern neighbours of the Anba on either side of the Lindi. (plantain = *libogo* in their gong-language, but not in their spoken language).

c) the Olombo, along the north bank of the Zaire. (plantain = *likondo*), and …

d) the Lokele, the famous Congo river fishermen and traders who live for months on their huge canoes travelling hundreds of miles downstream from the nearby Boyoma Falls at Kisingani. (for whom the plantain = *likondo*). (4)

So here we have two '*libogos*' (a. and b.)in the territory stretching away to the northeast towards the upper Nile; and two '*likondos*' (c. and d.) closely associated with the Zaire River that winds like an umbilical cord down to the Atlantic.

This is fascinating. According to Vansina, the Mba (and the Anba) migrated into their present location from the upper reaches of the Ubangi river sometime in the first millennium A.D., after the Western-Bantu-speaking Olombo and Lokele had become established there. I.e. the '*libogos*' came after the '*likondos*'. As can be seen, the –*kondo* group stretches far away to the west, to the Atlantic ocean, and if the -*kondo* root is the one that is associated with the Western Bantu speaking people, who had migrated slowly through the forest from the west, (they did not reach the Ruwenzoris until after the beginning of the 1st millennium AD) it is a fair indication that the AAB plantain was introduced on the West coast, not the East. This proposition is supported by the near absence of AAB in Eastern part of the continent, and the slowness and lateness of its movement westward across Africa, as reported (above) by Stover and Simmonds. Furthermore, with a typically African twist, there is actually a possibility that the *libogos* may also have spread from the West, -*bogo* and –*poku* being terms used for 'banana grove' and 'banana tree' in northwestern Gabon, on the Atlantic coast. So is it not probable that AAB plantains, by whichever name, were both introduced in the west?

Diffusion from the east coast, if it ever occurred, would have been precarious for want of suitable habitats, and would have taken many generations to reach the Congo forests. On the other hand the forest areas along the Gabon and Cameroon coast would have presented a perfect habitat for AAB. From there, up networks of rivers that have always acted as major highways, with short hops between the major river systems, the water-men of the day - the Lokele on the Congo and their brethren elsewhere - could theoretically have diffused the root-stock in a matter of weeks.

At the turn of this millennium, archaeologists working at Nkang, in the Southern Cameroons, about 90 kilometres northwest of Yaoundé found banana phytoliths in levels reliably dated from associated charcoal to about 450 B.C. (5). Phytoliths – literally 'plant stones' – are described as 'siliceous mineral inclusions in plant tissues' whose morphology provides fairly accurate clues as to the type of plant in which it was formed. Although the phytoliths found at Nkang are *musaceae* of some sort, it is impossible to deduce their precise genetic make-up. Though they were definitely some variety of *musa*, whether or not they were the AAB plantains cannot be confirmed..

It would be rash to read too much into so few bits of archaeological data; but, one wonders, is it purely coincidence that the earliest evidence of plantains so far found on the west coast is in the same geographical area as the earliest iron-smelting sites between Taruga in the north and '...Du Chaillu in the south?' Is it also coincidence that the 5th century phytolith dates are contemporaneous both with those of the most ancient iron-workings, *and* the proposed beginnings of the Nok Culture in which the alien Southeast Asian *elephantiasis* was a recognized disease? Can all three be linked to a much earlier (c. 450 BC) Indonesian presence than hitherto realized?

The spread of AAB plantains was not restricted to the Central African forests, for they became one of the main staples of all the forest people of West Africa, from Nigeria, Ghana and Liberia, to Senegal and the Gambia. Over 100 distinct types of AAB have been identified on the Guinea coast, from which it is concluded – as with AAB in the Olombo area – that the plant *must* have been present in the region since very remote times, the middle of the first millennium B.C. being well within the realm of possibility.

Is it really conceivable that AAB plantains were disseminated overland from Africa's East Coast, to the furthest parts of the Atlantic Coast so early on? Aside from the fact that Stover and Simmonds found AAB varieties still spreading inland from the East Coast in the twentieth century, they would, in their westward march, have been contending with large stretches of country fundamentally unsuitable for their propagation; and they would have been traveling against the general migration routes of people. In every respect, as pointed out by Roger Blench(6)... "The evidence seems to support the coastal strip from the mouth of the river Zaire to the Bight of Bonny as the original centre for the dispersal of the plantains (*Musa* AAB) in Africa." It is also worth noting that, despite his previously published scepticism of a West coast introduction, the banana-expert, Simmonds, later came to agree that it was the most likely.(7)

As for Southeast Asian yams and cocoyams, although dozens of cultivars of both have been recorded – fourteen varieties from the coast of the Cameroons, for instance – their story is not so well documented. This is probably because, today, they are not of such economic importance to the outside world as bananas and plantains. But this does not imply that they, along with plantains, did not at some stage become vitally important to virtually all West African people. As Fage and Oliver said in their "Short History of Africa": "The botanical evidence... suggests that the occupation of the forest by anything like its present densities of population (which, from the Cameroons to the eastern Ivory Coast, are today amongst the highest in all Negro Africa) was not feasible before the introduction of the Southeast Asian food-plants." (8)

The importance that these plants acquired was born out vividly in the journals of Richard and John Lander, the first Europeans to travel down the lower Niger through the country of the Igbo, or the 'Eboe' as they called them. (9)

"November 7th1830 ... Plantains, bananas, and yams, are cultivated by these villages to an almost incredible extent."

"November 11th 1830 ... (carried in their huge 50' dugout canoe that drew 4' and sat at least 60 people four abreast, plus numerous boxes and other cargo) two thousand yams for the master of a Spanish slaver..."

"November 14th 1830 ...Plantains and yams are cultivated by them to an extraordinary and almost incredible extent, and for the space of nearly *twenty miles* scarcely anything else but plantations of these shrubs and vegetables are to be seen."

For the Igbo, both yams and coco-yams play a fascinating role in their origin myths. The Igbo have among them a specialised group of 'priest kings' known as the *Nri* who once saw themselves as being at the centre of a ritual system which had powerful religious and political influence over a wide area of Igbo-land on both sides of the lower Niger river. The origin story, which seems to link the Igbo's cannibalistic, hunter-gatherer background, with the advent of a more enlightened agrarian life-style, is as follows:-

"...the first people, Eri and his wife Namaku, lived on *azu igwe* ('back of the sky', or 'sky substance'), but when Eri died this food supply ceased and Nri (Eri's son) complained to the great spirit, Chukwu, that there was nothing to eat. Chukwu told Nri that he would send from the sky to the earth one Dioka who would carve *ichi* [cicatrised] marks on the faces of Nri's son and daughter. Nri was to cut their throats and bury them in separate graves. Nri reluctantly did so, and when shoots appeared he dug up yams from his son's grave and cocoyams from his daughter's grave. ... Accordingly, although a man taking up the post of *eze Nri* (the leader of the *Nri* sect) no longer has to kill his first-born son and daughter, both are still marked with *ichi* in remembrance of the time when the first *eze Nri* thereby brought food among men." (10)

And who was the first *eze Nri*? He seems to have been in some way associated with those who first brought yams and cocoyams to West Africa, both of which we know came originally from Southeast Asia (with bananas and plantains) many many years ago.

CHAPTER - 16

"One of the fascinating things about archaeology is that since it is rarely possible, in a logical sense, to give a watertight proof of anything, the interpretation of archaeological data is always a matter of balancing probabilities."
Thurston Shaw in *"Those Igbo-Ukwu radiocarbon dates: Facts, Fictions and Probabilities"* in *JAR xvi , 4 (1975)*

THE BRONZES OF IGBO UKWU

One day in 1939, just before the outbreak of the second world war, Isaiah Anozie was digging a cistern beside his house in Igbo-Ukwu, a small Ibo town twenty five miles south east of Onitsha, when, no more than eighteen inches below the surface, his hoe hit something hard and metallic. He dug around the object and pulled out an elaborately decorated bronze bowl, green with age except for the bright yellow indentation where the hoe had struck it. Leaning it against the wall of his house, he continued digging, and to his astonishment soon unearthed a variety of other strange bronze objects which his neighbours came in droves to look at. In the belief that 'they would make good medicine' Anozie gave a number of pieces away to his friends.

Twenty years later Bernard Fagg, the head of the Nigerian Department of Antiquities, invited a young archaeologist, Thurston Shaw, to Nigeria to excavate Isaiah's compound, and those of his family neighbours, Richard and Jonah Anozie. The three locations, known as Igbo-Isaiah, Igbo-Richard and Igbo-Jonah were to become one of the most famous archaeological sites in the whole of Africa. Isaiah Anozie had hit upon what can only have been an ancient royal burial of major importance. (1)

Thurston Shaw's subsequent excavations revealed a magnificent assemblage of pottery, textile fragments, items of ivory and wood, about twenty five receptacles in cast bronze, scabbards, knives, and dozens of other small copper and bronze items for personal wear or practical use. The larger pieces included human figures; two beautifully decorated bronze shells about a foot long; a 'ritual calabash' and lid with low-relief geometric patterns; a pot with a strange bronze 'net' floating freely around it; a pectoral plate; strings of beads; a bead-studded head-dress surmounted by a copper crown; a pair of bead wristlets; what is described as a 'bronze alter stand' shaped like a large cotton reel nearly a foot high, elaborately decorated with low relief designs; and bronze bells.

Bronze bell. Igbo Isiah.
5 $^1/_2$ ins x (13.7 cm) high

Some of these displayed very sophisticated technical expertise described by Thurston Shaw thus:-- "There are two castings ... made up from more than one piece that use an adaptation of the casting technique to join the pieces together. Fresh molten metal was poured, or 'burnt in' between two pieces already cast, a technique not in use north of the Sahara." (2)

There was also a truly splendid five-handled ceramic pot 16" high with swirling low- and high-relief designs that included one of the favourite designs of the Igbo; two coiled snakes. (3) This pot bore some interesting similarities to a small *mimbo*-bin (for palm wine) that I had collected for the Bamenda museum in the Southern Cameroons. The Bamenda pot had the same rotund shape and five strong handles in much the same style, and a 'swag' around the top that could easily have been a stylised 'snake'. Though it was much less elaborate than the ancient Igbo pot, other Cameroons bins are sometimes as highly decorated, suggesting the possibility that some of the artistic traditions of Igbo-Ukwu may have continued virtually unchanged for over a thousand years, albeit in the Bamenda highlands rather than the Niger delta.

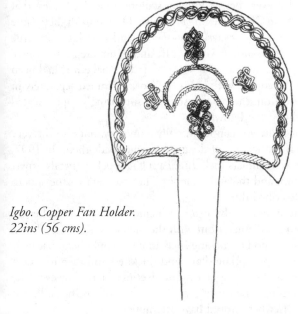

Igbo. Copper Fan Holder.
22ins (56 cms).

Over and above this marvelous horde, Thurston Shaw and his gang unearthed an enormous quantity of glass beads (of which more later), and some of carnelian which he thought could have come from as far away as India. Such exotic material in this obviously important site made him think that it might have had a connection not just with the *Nri*, described in the Igbo origin myth in the previous chapter, but with the burial of an *eze Nri*, one of the most powerful members of the sect.

The origin of these treasures mystified the archaeological fraternity. At the time it was thought that the nearest available sources of copper were either in the mountains of Air, 1000 miles north of Igbo-Ukwu; or in the Congo, even further away to the south. At that time no copper deposits were known anywhere in Nigeria. However it soon transpired that colonial geological surveys had only been interested in metal deposits of 'industrial' proportions. They had disregarded those of 'no apparent commercial value', and it was only later that small deposits of copper were found near the village of Abakaliki, seventy five miles east of Igbo-Ukwu, from where it was subsequently confirmed by isotope analysis that 90% of the copper used in the Igbo bronzes was mined.

The three Igbo sites were reliably radiocarbon dated to ± 900 A.D., some 300-400 years earlier than the more famous 'bronzes' of Ife, and 650 years earlier than the even better known sculptures and plaques that adorned the palace of the Oba of Benin. They also differed from their more famous counterparts in other ways. The metal works of Igbo are true *bronzes*; whereas the better known works of Ife and Benin are mostly brass, containing a fair proportion of zinc. It seems that a special effort had been made to blend the Igbo copper with at least 5% of tin, mined separately in a location far removed from the copper, showing surprisingly sophisticated metallurgical technology and knowledge.

Not only was the source of copper initially a mystery, but also the very high level of technical proficiency of the artisans who made them. In 1997, in a joint paper by seven scholars including Paul Craddock, a metals expert at the British Museum, and the archaeologist Thurston Shaw - the superb workmanship was described thus:-

"To give but one example, the bronzes include several hemispherical bowls of about 30-40 cm diameter but with the metal no more than 1 or 2 mm thick. The usual method of making such an item would be to hammer out sheet bronze to the appropriate shape and thickness and then to attach the separately made handles by soldering or riveting. Here, however, the bowls and handles are just one casting, a *tour de force* of casting skill, but which no craftsman elsewhere would have attempted." (4)

The question inevitably arose: could these amazing objects have been made over a thousand years ago by the Igbo people themselves? A commonly held orthodox view of the Igbo, based on oral histories, language and other evidence, is one of an 'acephalous society' that has remained in its present location unchanged for many centuries. Since their first contact with Europeans, though their skill as iron-smiths has long been recognised, the Igbo were looked by upon by outsiders as being singularly 'un-innovative', and there was general incredulity that earlier generations of their people could have made such treasures as those of Igbo Ukwu. In fact the authors of the paper quoted above wrote:-

"There was a very real, if unarticulated feeling, that the native population must have had outside help to produce work of the quality abundantly displayed in the bronzes".

They then went on to draw up a list of possible origins for the work, considering the following options:-

"a)   The bronzes discovered at Igbo-Ukwu were imports, conceived and made somewhere outside Africa.

b)   The bronzes were of local design but made by foreign craftsmen sing their own supplies of metal.

c)   They were of local design and manufacture, but used imported metal, and probably some outside inspiration, at least for the technique of lost-wax casting.

d)   The bronzes were completely indigenous in design, manufacture, and materials with minimal or no influence from beyond West Africa."

Finally, having delved deeply into every aspect of the Igbo bronzes and satisfactorily established the nearby sources of the copper, lead and tin through radio-isotope analysis, the authors concluded a summary of their findings with the following mind-blowing non-sequitur:-

"These results support arguments previously advanced that the metal used to make the bronzes was local, *thereby confirming their indigenous design and technology*".(My italics)

A curious thing about this extraordinary conclusion is that, in part, it seems to have been justified by the fact that the craftsmen were too clever by half! What the authors of the paper were saying in effect is that no sensible bronze smith, however expert, would consider casting bowls only one or two millimetres thick, in one piece with their handles. Even an experienced caster would have considered it a folly almost bound to fail. Therefore they must have been made by a local novice who had no idea what he was doing ... yet was a natural genius! Charming though it might be, this view is completely untenable. It is no insult to the Igbo of 1000 years ago – if, indeed, it was Igbo people who made these things - to suggest that:-

• to prospect for the tin and copper in two different locations;

• to smelt the ores to such a high level of purity;

• to blend them, in correct proportions to make true bronze;

• to create designs of such sophistication as the bell shown here, with low-relief *repoussé* guilloche decoration;

• to create the moulds and pour castings of such infinite fineness

...that all this cannot possibly have been the result of a sudden burst of 'independent invention' deep in the Niger forests. To say that it must have required some outside help is not an insult. It is common sense.

But who, and from where, might that outside help have come?

CHAPTER - 17

SOURCES OF IGBO GENIUS

Let's look at some of the more obvious possible sources of the 'genius' behind Igbo-Ukwu.....

Thurston Shaw suggested that iron smelting technology might have come to Nok from Carthage in the 1st millennium BC. But elsewhere he pointed out that the unusual 'welding' technique used on the Igbo bowls is unlikely to have come from north of the Sahara. So what is the likelihood that either people – or metal-working technologies - reached the Niger delta from the Mediterranean world all those years ago?

The first person on record to have traveled down the Guinea coast of Africa was the Carthaginian, Hanno, who in the fifth century B.C. was bent on founding colonies on the African coast 'beyond the Pillars of Hercules.' Having established settlements in what is now Morocco and Mauritania he sailed to a place where "...great streams of lava poured down into the sea and the land was unapproachable because of heat." He sailed on when he saw flames leaping above the land, and after observing: "... in the middle ... a high flame taller than the rest, reaching, as it seemed, to the stars. By day it was seen to be a very high mountain called the Chariot of Fire".(1)

There is only one major volcano visible from the sea down the whole of the West African coast, and that is Mount Cameroon which Hanno must have been lucky enough to see in full eruption. He and his men were clearly frightened of the wild natives they encountered on the coast, and made no mention of imparting anything, let alone the complex arts of metallurgy, to anyone.

It is just possible that penetration of the darkest parts of Nigeria from across the deserts could have been by members of an overland expedition described by Herodotus in the 5th century B.C. (2) He related how ... "a group of wild young Nasamonians (from Libya) sons of chieftains in their country, had, on coming to manhood, planned amongst themselves all sorts of extravagant adventures, one of which was to draw lots for five of their number to explore the Libyan desert and try to penetrate further than had ever been done before....After traveling for many days over the sand they saw some trees growing on a level spot; they approached and began to pick the fruit which the trees bore, and while they were doing so were attacked by some little men - of less than middle height - who seized them and carried them off. ... They took their captives through a vast tract of marshy country, and beyond it came to a town, all the inhabitants of which were of the same small stature, and all black. A great river with crocodiles in it flowed past the town from west to east".

Though most scholars seem to think the river would have been the northern bend of the Niger, Herodotus, in line with thinking that persisted for another fifteen hundred years, thought it must have been the Nile. Either way it seems unlikely that a bunch of 'wild young fellows' from Nasamonia - more like year-off students than VSO's by the sound of them - would have been the bearers of first-world technology to the little black people who took them captive. If they had been on such a mission, no doubt that they would have recorded it with pride.

Obviously there may have been other unrecorded expeditions; but in both Herodotus and Hanno's writings there is nothing positive to support the hypothesis that the secrets of iron smelting came to Nok from Carthage. As for bronze, that was still hundreds of years in the future.

When the Romans sacked Carthage in 149 BC, their first preoccupations were with maintaining administrative control of their north African colonies, and containing the troublesome Garamantes warriors whose charioteers were a constant nuisance, impeding Roman exploration in the interior of Tripolitania. In any event, the Romans were not in Africa for conquest or exploration. They were primarily there for whatever trade they could drum up, and - more importantly - to develop the agricultural potential of the fertile North African land in order to feed the citizens of Rome.(3)

In about 100 A.D., in the Emperor Trajan's reign, the Tripolitanian Romans introduced a 'secret weapon' that not only instantly turned the tide in their battles with the Garamantes, but enabled them, for the first time, to explore deeper into the southern Sahara than had hitherto been possible. Until that time the main means of desert transport had been the horse whose range was severely limited by a lack of water. But now, in Trajan's reign, the Romans awakened to the stamina and brilliance of that amazing animal the camel ... the piston engine of the desert that could travel hundreds of miles on a single load of fuel ... and soon the Romans were maintaining regular contact with Tibesti and the Hoggar mountains, eight hundred miles across the sands.

It has been suggested that they were lured south by gold, ivory, and ostrich feathers for Rome's rich, and even wild animals for the Roman games: but as all these items were obtainable far closer to home this seems unlikely. Pliny and Strabo believed that Rome's real interest in the southern parts of the Sahara was as a source of *carbuncles*. "Our only intercourse," Pliny wrote, "is the trade in the precious stone imported from Ethiopia which we call the carbuncle." Strabo had written in a similar fashion a century earlier, referring to the Fezzan as the country carbuncles came from, and to both writers the 'Garamantian Road' stood for the carbuncle trade. E. W. Bovill, in *The Golden Trade of the Moors*, expressed his opinion that: "Tibesti may be regarded as the farthest point in the interior of Africa west of the Nile reached by the Romans."

But by the time Romans had got as far south as Tibesti, the people of Taruga and Nok had already had iron for centuries; and looking ahead in time, still more centuries were to pass before Igbo-Ukwu had its bronze workers. A direct trans-Saharan Roman connection with the Niger communities is therefore extremely unlikely.

There is, however, one unexplained oddity. In 1931 a Roman coin of Constantine's reign was dug up at Buea near the coast of the Cameroons, over one thousand three hundred miles south west of Tibesti. How on earth did it have got there? There is no record of Romans have sailed as far as the Cameroons. Though it must remain a mystery, the answer *could* lie in the fact that Roman coinage was in widespread use in the Indian ocean throughout Rome's trading days with India and the far east; it is therefore possible that the coin found at Buea, and others found in various places around the coast of Africa, were left behind by ancient mariners caught up in the international trade of the times.

All the inhabited country lying between the Sahara and the Gulf of Guinea – a belt varying from 700 to 850 miles wide - was known to the Arabs as the *Bilad al-Sudan* – 'The Land of the Blacks'. If seen as a map of the vegetation this belt might be painted in a range of gradually merging colours, from the scorching yellow of the Sahara sands through pale greens and browns of savannah and woodlands, blending seamlessly with the sultry dark greens of the coastal forest belt, and finally the impenetrable black of the mangrove swamps bordering the ocean. There are few hard boundaries; but in general the people termed 'Sudanic' are those who occupy the grazing areas – the pale greens and browns – to the north of the coastal 'forest zone'. Before one can begin to understand what might have been going on in the first millennium in the Niger delta, or elsewhere in the forest zone, a basic understanding of the Sudanic people is useful.

People with reasonably sophisticated cultures have been living in the savannah-lands between Lake Chad and Africa's west coast for a very long time. In Dafuna, in the far north-east corner of Nigeria, not far from Lake Chad, archaeologists have found remnants of a dugout canoe carbon dated to 6,000 B.C. – not only Africa's oldest, but one of the oldest known boats found anywhere in the world. It is not known who the people of that era were, but they seem to have worked with bone tools, were proficient in basketry and mat-making, and were probably dark skinned. By about 1000 BC – possibly long before - some of them were practicing agriculture, growing bulrush millet (*pennisetum*) and a type of African rice. They also had domesticated cattle and either sheep or goats, both of which would have come originally from the Middle East.(4)

Early in the first millennium A.D. 'white' pastoralists from across the deserts began to infiltrate these savannah-lands, but apparently made no attempt to penetrate the belt of thick coastal forests where by far the largest portion of the *Bilad al-Sudan's* indigenous population lived. The first of these new Sudanic settlers may have been Cyrenaican Jews who, having fallen foul of Rome, are believed to have made their way across the desert to settle among Soninke farmers on the right bank of the Senegal river not far from the Atlantic coast. At roughly the same time, Hamitic Berbers, crossing the continent from north east to the far west, began to encroach on the good Sudanic grazing lands around Adrar, Tagant and Hodh, in lands also drained by the Senegal and upper Niger rivers. (5)

Apart from the fact that they would have been unsuitable for their cattle, the reasons why the newcomers didn't move into the forests seem to be clear: firstly, they rode horses, donkeys, or camels that would not have survived in the forest environment; secondly, staying in the less populated areas meant that there was no competitive threat, and thus no pressing need to build up military strength; and thirdly, if they had tried to penetrate the forests, they would in all probability have been overwhelmed and – if there was truth in later stories - eaten.

Eventually it was the Berbers who were to form the most powerful group of new immigrants; and it was they who, by the eighth century, had gained control over the valuable Saharan salt mines at Taghaza and Taodeni. Worked by Negro slaves, these mines provided one of the main *raisons d'etre* for the Saharan trade routes along which kola nuts, copper, money-cowries, and other commodities soon began to flow between Morocco and the western Sudan.

In early times the presence of mineable rock-salt in the desert, and of gold around the headwaters of the Niger and Senegal rivers; as well as relatively fertile lands watered by streams that flowed down from Mount Nimba and the Guinea Highlands to form the Gambia, Senegal and Niger rivers, must together have made these western savannahs more attractive for settlement and exploitation than most of the country further to the east. Because of these advantages, it was in these regions that the powerful political states for which West Africa became so well known first developed.

The process by which power became centralised was a direct result of the trans-desert traffic. The 'termini' at the southern end of the trade routes that crossed the 'sea of sand' were like 'ports' that became both commercial *entrepots*, and political centres. Those who had authority in these centres controlled the trade. The stronger the political organisation and the greater the security of the trade routes, the more likely became the emergence of powerful states. (6)

From about the fourth century the 'whites' who had settled around Aukur – probably Jews, by now deeply integrated with Mande-speaking Soninke agriculturalists – began to organise settlements that, by the 8th century, were to culminate in one the most stable and long-lasting of all the Sudanese polities, the Empire of Ghana, which survived, despite numerous vicissitudes, as a great Soninke state until the end of the twelfth century. Ghana's strength was built largely on its trade in gold, most of which was produced in the neighbouring region of Wangara and exchanged by 'dumb barter' with Mandingo miners in return for salt, dried fruits, copper and cowrie shells.

In the eighth century pure-blood Soninke ousted the half-caste 'white' rulers of Ghana, who fled west to Tekrur on the lower reaches of the Senegal. "By this time," wrote John Fage "the 'whites' were to all intents and purposes an African people speaking an African language. These were the people today known as Fulani …"(7)

So, from the fourth to the fourteenth centuries, like golden medallions suspended on slender threads of trade from the Mediterranean coast, Ghana, Tekrur, Sosso, Mali, and various other lesser states, became the primary foci of power and wealth in the Western Sudan; while further to the east others slumbered on in less spectacular ways. In the middle of the eleventh century, on the Middle Niger, the hitherto pagan Berber farmers who had created the state of Songhai, adopted Islam; and in the fourteenth century, they became, briefly, the furthest eastern dependency of the rich and powerful Mali empire, by now in its twilight years.

Like all the other Sudanic states, the interests of the Songhai people lay in a north-facing arc, from Ghana and Mali in the west, to Tunisia and Cyrenaica in the north, and Egypt in the east. Thus Songhai remained - until late in the fifteenth century its fanatical ruler, Askar Mohammed 1st, set off on a series of campaigns that resulted in a vastly enlarged Empire stretching from Timbuctu on the northern bend of the Niger, all the way to the ocean in the west.

Nearer Lake Chad, in the 10th century, there came into being the state of Bornu, whose relations were primarily with the north and east rather than the western Sudan. Gaining lasting prominence to the west of Bornu, were the seven Hausa states, the *Hausa Bokwoi*, a mixture of people who have never had much political power, but who practiced – and still practice - a common 'Hausa' way of life and speak a language (of Berber origin) much modified by Arabic. The Hausa became Islamised in the fourteenth century and, though it was never wholly accepted as a religion, Islam greatly influenced their systems of law and administration. (8)

Throughout these early years the Sudanic peoples' main interest in the 'Negro' south was as a source of slaves, gold, and a few products for daily use such as Kola-nuts. This trade must have involved limited contacts with the forest people, never altering the fact that the main concerns of the Hausa lay across the deserts to the north rather than with the black people in the south.

So what conclusions can be drawn from all this that are relevant to Igbo-Ukwu?

One glance at the map (and in this there seems to be general agreement) shows that of all the forest areas throughout West Africa, the Niger Delta was the most remote and the furthest away from any of the major trans-Saharan trade routes in the 9th and 10th centuries. If for this reason alone, of all the people of West Africa least likely to have benefited from, or been influences by, any technological expertise that might have come from across the Sahara were the people of the Niger Delta.

One or two observers have suggested that trade in elephant ivory between the lower Niger and Songhai - which has never been proved - may have been the 'conduit' for the technology. Anything was possible on a navigable river like the Niger; but as there were plentiful supplies of ivory nearer the major northern trade routes, one has to ask why they would have bothered? And if ivory traders were the source of refined bronze technology in the Niger delta, why is there no evidence that they ever had a culture of bronze artistry in their own Sudanic cities? All in all it is an unlikely red-herring.

By the 6th century, Roman control of North Africa, constantly under attack from Berbers, Vandals and disaffected Christians, had fallen into disarray. Towards the end of the 7th century, Arabs, who had by then conquered Egypt, began to display an interest in the vast territories west of the Nile. Spurred by sheer lust for plunder, small groups of horsemen swept across the entire breadth of the Mahgreb, and in 678 Okba ibn Nafi, one of their most courageous leaders, rode his horse triumphantly into the Atlantic waves.

These early adventures, however, had the quality of hard-hitting but short-lived S.A.S. incursions. Although Arabs subjugated much of Spain just thirty three years after Okba ibn Nafi's dramatic but short-lived occupation, another four hundred years was to pass before the Beni Hillal and Beni Hassan, with other marauding Bedouin tribes from Arabia, completed the Moors' earlier desert conquests, and brought the whole of north Africa under their control.

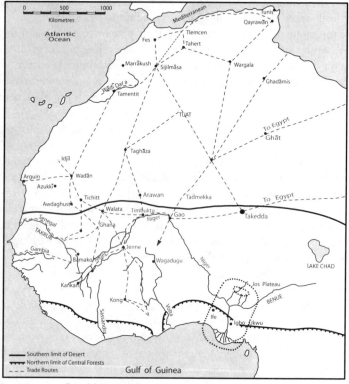

Trans-Saharan Trade Routes c.1000 -1500 (After Levtzion and Hopkins)
Note how far removed from the routes are the Jos Plateau , Igbo Ukwu and Ife,
yet how closely associated they are with the Niger Delta

166

Sources of Igbo Genius

Always on the lookout for new opportunities for trade and new sources of wealth, one of the major tasks of Arab explorers and geographers, from the moment they became involved in North Africa, was to learn more about the *Bilad al-Sudan*, the Land of the Blacks, south of the desert. For a long time stories had been heard of great rivers beyond the sands and it was rumoured that amongst these might be found one of the long-sought sources of the Nile. But locating the sources of the Nile and unraveling the mysteries of the Niger proved hard nuts to crack.

From the mid-9th to the mid-14th century at least fifty Arab chroniclers wrote about the regions south of the Sahara. Many of them simply parroted the accounts of earlier travellers, and none of them – except Ibn Battutah in the 14th century - ever actually set eyes on the Niger! In fact Ibn Battutah was the only one who ever took a boat and traveled down the river. (9)

The main focus of interest for the Arabs was in the West where they sought information about the rich goldfields of Bundu, Bambuk and Wangara between the Senegal and Gambia rivers. Al Bakri, writing in the 11th century (though possibly of an earlier period) told how the gold fields lay within the powerful empire of Ghana, whose king could "put more than 200,000 warriors in the field, more than 40,000 of them being armed with bow and arrow." But Al-Bakri's informants were still 1,500 crow-miles from the Niger delta and it is hardly conceivable that Ghana's iron-workers and goldsmiths could have had a hand in imparting their skills to the people of Igbo-Ukwu buried deep in the coastal forest. In any event, nearly two hundred years had already passed since the craftsmen of Igbo-Ukwu had produced their master-works in bronze.

It is quite clear from the records that the Arabs did not relish the idea of penetrating too far into the *bilad al-Sudan*. Ibn Battutah related how: "A group of these Sudan who eat humankind came with an emir of theirs to the sultan Mansa Sulayman. ... The sultan did them honour and gave them a slave girl as part of his reception-gift. They slaughtered her and ate her and smeared their faces and hands with her blood and came in gratitude to the sultan. I was informed that their custom whenever they come in deputation to him is to do that, and I was told of them that they say that the tastiest part of woman's flesh is the palms and the breast." And when Mansa Musa, the powerful ruler of Mali, was deceived by his *qadi* who claimed, falsely, that he had had some money stolen: "He was enraged with the qadi and banished him to the land of the infidels who eat mankind. He stayed among them for four years, then he returned to his own country. The infidels refrained from eating him simply because he was white, for they say that the eating of a white man is harmful because he is not matured. In their opinion the black man is the matured one." (10) This may seem to contradict an earlier statement of Arab fears, but regardless of who had the best flavour one can understand the Arab's reluctance to take unnecessary risks!

Throughout the centuries of Arab contact the source, the destination, even the direction of flow of the Niger River remained constant mysteries. No one had ever been quite sure of where it came from or where it went since it was first rumoured to exist in Roman times. Pliny had said that the 'Nil', as the Niger became known, flowed 'under the desert sands'. Mela said it flowed west to east, but he knew not where. Ptolemy was vague. Al-Bakri had it emptying into the Atlantic. Al-Dimashqi had part of it emptying into the Indian Ocean near Mogadishu. El Edrisi had two branches, one of which flowed firmly east to west; with which Abelfida agreed. Several others had it flowing into Lake Chad. Ibn Battutah correctly reported it as flowing from west to east, but believed it was the Nile. He described it thus:-

"Then the Nil descends from Zagha to Tunbuktu, then to Kawkaw (Gao - as far down as Ibn Battuta went), then to the village of Muli, then to the land of the Limiyyun, then to Yufi. Yufi is one of the biggest countries of the Sudan, and their sultan is one of their greatest sultans. No white man enters this country because they kill him before he reaches it." (11)

The last sentence is of great significance. The generally accepted view among academics is that 'Yufe' was 'Nupe'. But Nupe, in the bend of the Niger across from northern Yorubaland, was one of the minor Hausa states. In Ibn Batutta's day, the Hausa people of Nupe, downstream from Gao, were already accepting Islamic ways, and are thus unlikely to have been antagonistic to 'Whites'... certainly not to the extent that 'Whites' would be killed on sight. By 'Yufi' it is therefore more likely that Ibn Batutta was referring to 'Ife', one of the main centres of the Yoruba, the largest and most powerful state in that part of the *Bilad al-Sudan*, who had their own complex religion, and who steadfastly rejected any Islamic culture until the end of the nineteenth century. (12)

A hundred years before Ibn Battutah traveled on the Niger, Ibn Said had described the area south of Lake Chad as "... jungles and deserts inhabited by savage beings like ogres which are harmful to men and which a horseman cannot overtake. They are the nearest of animals to human form". He may not have been referring directly to the Yoruba or the Igbo; but his derisory attitude towards the black infidels of the forest zone was probably shared by most Arabs, who were not in West Africa in the guise of British Council do-gooders.

Postscript on the Niger:

After Ibn Batutta's time, the story of the Niger as recorded through Arab eyes and ears, seemed to be closed. But in 1518 along came a brilliant young Arab from Fez called El-Hassan ibn Wezaz who had spent years traveling in remote parts in Africa. On his way to Italy after one such expedition he was captured by Christian corsairs who found in his possession the draft manuscript of a most remarkable work, written in Italian, entitled "*The History and Description of Africa and the Notable Things therein Contained*". Realizing they had come by an exceptional prize, and in hope of rewards greater than they might have received selling their captive into slavery, the corsairs made a present of ibn Wezaz to Pope Leo X.

Until that time the Vatican had relied for their information on Africa on the out-of-date writings of AI-Edrisi and Al-Bakri. Now, providing more detailed, and probably more accurate information, ibn Wezaz was found to be a man of considerable value. Established in the Vatican and converted to Christianity, ibn Wezaz acquired a new name, Giovanni Leone, the name from which he came to be known to the world as 'Leo Africanus'. In addition to being granted his freedom, Pope Leo arranged for him to be endowed by the Vatican with a handsome pension to enable him to complete his work.

Leo Africanus had a greater knowledge of the Niger river than any writer up to that time. He had traveled to Timbuktu, and from there, by boat, for at least five hundred miles downstream in a southern and easterly direction from Timbuktu. And yet - and this must surely be one of the most curious cartographical mysteries of all time - when in 1526 he completed his work for publication, Leo Africanus wrote that: -"The Niger flows *westward* into the ocean ...we navigated it *with the current* from Timbuktu to Jenne and Mali."

Because Leo Africanus was by then such a respected traveler and writer, Portuguese cartographers, accepted that the Gambia and the Senegal were in fact the mouths of the Niger, thus perpetuating earlier errors. As late as 1700 the French geographer De Lisle published a map showing the same mistake - though this was corrected in 1714 when he published another correctly showing it flowing to the east. D'Anville in 1749 had it flowing east; but in his map it joined up with another river flowing west at a place he called Wangara; and in the same map he showed a distinct river which he named the 'Nile of the Negroes' flowing northwest into the 'Lake of Bornu'!

In the second half of the eighteenth century a whole succession of

European explorers, many of whom were British, were sent out to try and resolve the problem of the Niger once and for all. In 1795 a young Scottish doctor named Mungo Park was able to confirm that the Niger did, indeed, flow from West to East. He and his companions died trying to negotiate rapids on the middle Niger, but not before he had sent most of his journals back to England. Although it was by now suspected that the river disgorged into the Gulf of Guinea, its precise final destination remained a mystery as it had no obvious estuary debouching into the sea.

Other explorers from Europe followed Mungo Park, most of whom died of fever and tropical diseases, or were murdered by 'unfriendly natives'. In 1821 the British Government sent an expedition consisting of Major Denham, Dr Oudney and the naval Lieutenant Hugh Clapperton; but this, too, failed to find the outflow of the great river. Undeterred, they sent Clapperton back once again, with his faithful servant Richard Lander.

Clapperton died. But having buried his master's remains, the twenty six year old Richard Lander, son of an inn-keeper in Truro, was determined to complete his work He returned to England, and after much argument and discussion persuaded the British Government to send him back to Nigeria. As part of their agreement the government offered him a gratuity of £100 on his return and agreed to pay Richard's wife the princely sum of £25 per quarter for one year. Richard Lander's twenty three year old brother, John, despite being refused either salary or the promise of any reward, volunteered to accompany him on his explorations.

The brothers left England in January 1830. Later in that year - traveling on a shoestring with only a simple hand compass and a handful of faithful Africans to help - one of the greatest of Africa's geographic mysteries was finally solved by a couple of underpaid, underprivileged, British working class lads in their twenties. As they headed for the Niger delta through mile after mile of yam and plantain fields, surrounded by some of the most uncouth and unpleasant people they encountered on their entire journey, the Lander brothers would have passed within twenty five miles of the homesteads of Igbo-Ukwu, beneath which were hidden some of Africa's most remarkable works of craftsmanship more than a thousand years old. Reading their journals today, there is nothing they encountered on their extraordinary journey to suggest that northerners of any sort - European, Arab, Berber, Jew, Roman, Carthaginian, or any others - had passed that way before them.(13)

If the technology behind the metal-work of Igbo Ukwu had come from outside, it can only have come from the south – from across the sea.

CHAPTER - 18

THE MYSTERIES OF MAIZE

There is very strong evidence that maize, a Central American plant, reached Yorubaland long before Columbus discovered the Americas... a proposition that has caused much mystified head-scratching in academic circles. How could it possibly have got there? Can it really be true?

Old Yoruba buildings were made of puddled mud surmounted by fine thatched roofs. In a Chieftain's compound the best houses were large, forty feet or more from ground to finial, built with at least one inner courtyard known as an 'impluvium' where large earthenware pots could be placed to catch the rain. Characteristic of the 'impluvia' of the grandest Yoruba houses were the beautiful paved floors made from pieces of broken potsherd buried 'on edge' in all sorts of interesting patterns, frequently with white quartz pebbles filling the spaces between them.

Such floors had long since fallen out of use by the time Europeans arrived. But some that were subsequently excavated by archaeologists in Old Oyo aroused special interest as many of the broken potsherds bore designs made, unmistakably, from the imprint of old corn-cobs. One or two of these floors were buried beneath ten or twelve feet of earth and debris seemingly accumulated over centuries. They were dated, by thermoluminescence, to a period between the twelfth and fourteenth centuries, meaning that maize must have been grown in Yorubaland long before the Portuguese arrived on the scene. (1)

Maize has never existed in a commercially viable *wild* form. The plant, as we know it, was deliberately hybridised from a type of Mexican grass (*zea mays*); hence it has been described as 'a thoroughly cultural artefact ... truly a human invention' that can only survive 'if sown and protected by humans'.(2) Although first cultivated in Central Mexico around 2,700 BC it was not until the middle of the second millennium BC that it had spread to both the east and west coasts of modern Mexico. Its domestication and gradual improvement is considered to have been an important factor in the rise of the high civilizations of pre-Hispanic Meso-America. So how and when could it have reached Africa?

Years ago, a District Officer in the Cameroons, M.D.W. Jeffreys, wrote an article suggesting that maize was introduced by 'Arab sailors' returning from expeditions to South America in pre-Columbian times. (3) At the time there was growing evidence that the Atlantic had been crossed long before Columbus. There were well authenticated reports, for instance, that quantities of classic Graeco-Roman oil lamps had been found in Northern Peru; that a 2nd century AD Roman terracotta head was excavated in a 12th century Mexican grave; of the depiction of three apparently 'Caribbean' plants in a mural at Pompeii; of the discovery of eastern Mediterranean axe types in Ecuador; of the preparation of 'Phoenician purple' in the Caribbean; of Mediterranean-style burials in Louisiana ... and so on. (4) Jeffreys' curious hypothesis must have been encouraged by these; but his maize 'route' was odd. He maintained that the Arab sailors returning from South America introduced the plant along the banks of the Senegal River from where it spread to the upper tributaries of the Niger, and from there down to the forest zones and - via Timbuktu and Chad - to the Nile, the Middle East, Persia and Turkey; and finally to western Europe. From there, he said... "Other evidence upholds the claim of an early introduction of maize from the orient into Europe". He mentioned various names - *milho marroco* in Portugal; *grano turko* in Italy; *arabosite* in Greece; *turetski khleb* in Russia; *turkse tarwe* in Holland; *turkey corn* in England – all of which were names by which maize used to be known, and which, in his view, pointed to an introduction by Arabs in 'the Orient':

Jeffreys' view was eccentric, but not entirely unconvincing. He pointed out, for instance, that along the Guinea Coast of Africa there was already a surplus of 'corn' available to European ships by 1501, only a few years after its earliest possible introduction by the Portuguese. And in 1505, on the other side of Africa, the first Portuguese Viceroy of India noted that Kilwa had 'plenty of *milho* like that of Guinea'. Critics suggested that the '*milho*' must have been native *sorghum* which looks not unlike corn; but as Jeffreys said, *sorghum* was already well known in Portugal by then, and an educated man like D'Almeida, the Viceroy, is unlikely to have confused the two. An alternative view is that maize was – at some time, by persons un-known - brought across the Pacific from Central America to Southeast Asia, and thence to Europe – and Africa.

When Sir Joseph Hooker went on a plant collecting trip to Sikkim in 1848, long before the cinema age, he wrote in his "Himalayan Journals" that in North Sikkim he was given some 'popcorn'. This, he said, was "prepared by roasting the maize in an iron vessel, when it splits and turns partly inside out, exposing a snowy-white spongy mass of farina. It looks very handsome, and would make a beautiful dish for dessert."

Exactly a century later, this 'popcorn' maize attracted the attention of two American agronomists, C.R. Stonor and Edgar Anderson, who - working independently - were both struck by the same curious fact – that the type of maize in question was a much rarer and more ancient variety than they would have expected to find in the mountainous regions of north eastern India if it had been introduced by Europeans. It was not a type of maize that the Spaniards or Portuguese would have been likely to bring to Asia in the 16th century. It was a small, relatively poor variety found in modern times only in a few scattered and remote parts of the Americas.

"Since it is this early, relatively poor, maize that appears first in Asia," they said, "the assumption of an American origin for maize leads to a hypothesis of early transpacific carriage of such maize and a long history of spreading through the interior of Asia toward the eastern Mediterranean."(5)

This assumption of antiquity was born out by the Assamese hill people Stonor and Anderson were working amongst, who insisted that they had maize long before they had rice. "We know now that rice was extremely late in entering equatorial Asia, e.g. about A.D.1000 in Borneo ... Thus maize could possibly have been carried to South-east Asia and the Assam area centuries before rice arrived. Thus the Assamese legends could be factual."

The view that maize was unknown beyond the Americas until the post-Columbian era seems therefore to be untenable. There in Assam, for all to see, were people growing primitive popcorns, brewing-corns, and green-corns (eaten as a fresh vegetable), of the same varieties as those grown in Peru and Chile in very ancient pre-Columbian times. How did they get hold of them?

A curious fact was that without exception, these primitive maizes were more common among aboriginal people than among their more civilized and sophisticated neighbours. A hundred years ago B.C.Henry, writing about maize, said: "it is now very extensively cultivated by the Chinese, but especially by the aboriginal peoples, among whom it seems to be almost as great a favourite as among the American Indians."

A Siamese authority, Dr Khambanonda, testified that in his country maize was almost exclusively cultivated by the aborigines. A Burmese scholar, Ko Ko Lay, produced similar testimony. Stonor said the same applied to various tribes in the Naga hills: and when he was later transferred from Assam to Papua New Guinea, he noted that corn was grown also by the primitive people of the island's interior. Many of the aboriginal people looked upon corn as having been their 'original' food, grown long before they ever knew about rice.

"That maize could in post–Columbian times have spread to each of these various hinterlands without entering into the economies of the more civilized people who would have handed it on, almost passes belief," … mused Edgar Anderson. And while accepting that bigger and better varieties of maize had been introduced throughout the region in *post*-Columbian times, both he and Stonor agreed:- "To the authors the conclusion seems inescapable, that there are at least two races of maize in Asia and that one of these must have crossed the Pacific in pre-Columbian times."

There seem to be just two likely ways in which maize could have been brought from South America to the highlands of Assam and Burma:-

- By the Chinese. There is extensive evidence that the Chinese 'discovered' Central America centuries before Columbus. However if Chinese sailors had brought back maize, it would have been introduced among the 'sophisticated' peoples of the east coast of China, and would not have first appeared among aboriginal tribes in the south and west. (6)
- By Polynesians. It now seems certain that when Polynesians first colonised Easter Island around the 4th Century A.D. their 'master mariners' went further and landed on the mainland of South America. Evidence of this lies in several South American plants apparently brought back to Polynesia and New Zealand in pre-Columbian times:– the gourd; the sweet-potato; and the sword bean (*canavalia*). (7) Maize seed would have travelled well, and there is no reason why it should not have been carried along with the other plants.

As the American geographer/archaeologist, G.F.Carter, pointed out:- "The evidence of trans-Pacific transfer of plants and animals and arts and sciences is massive, and the literature is extensive… It would be surprising if corn was not among the plants carried."(8) From Southeast Asia it would have been carried to India leaving plenty of time for Arabs to introduce it to the Mediterranean world long before the end of the fifteenth century. This could explain the various European maize names mentioned by Jeffreys; and also its presence in Africa.

At first glance it may seem odd that maize is commonly grown high in the jungles of Assam, Sikkim and Burma, but apparently not in the Indonesian islands. As Stonor's explanation of how it got there has a bearing on other things concerning SEA and Africa – e.g. similar design features on the message gongs of the Ao Naga and those found in western Africa - this is a problem worth looking at.

The mountainous popcorn-growing Naga Hills that Stonor studied cover about 30,000 square miles of remote country inhabited by numerous related and not-so related tribes. He lists fourteen different Naga tribes on his map, many of which, he says, display sharp differences in culture, language, traditions, temperament, and physical characters. "It is well established" he says, "that they have elements in their culture complexes indicating wide diversity of origin. There are well-established links with Indonesia, Burma (including the Burma-China border, the Pacific, and India.) The dominant element today is widely different from any of the main cultures of India, and far more bound up with tribal peoples of Indonesia and Southeastern Asia." Of the neighbouring Lushai, Chin and Kuki, who are closely related to the Karens of Burma, he says:- "There are undoubted kinships with Indonesia." And of the largely Mon-Khmer Khasi tribes of Shillong: "It is quite possible that there is an ancient strain in the population akin to the aboriginal stocks of Peninsular India…"(9)

If this line of connections is valid it brings us back to Hornell's assertion that the Naga of southern India were 'Polynesians' creating the interesting possibility that there was once a web of 'Naga' people from insular Indonesia, up the rivers of Southeast Asia to the hills of Assam, and across to Southern India. There is good ethnographical evidence – e.g. 'canoe' burials and 'canoe-like' slit-drums of the *Ao* people - to support the belief that some of the Naga tribes were once people of the rivers and seas rather than mountain dwellers.

Inevitably the Stonor/Anderson views on maize have not been given a free ride by the Africanist establishment and have been criticised by, among others, Frank Willett, the archaeologist who excavated the Yoruba floors that gave rise to the debate in the first place. Despite the confirmed pre-Columbian dates for the corn-cob tiles in the Old Oyo floors, Willett, for reasons best known to himself, managed to turn the article around to support his belief in the *post*-Columbian introduction of maize to Africa.

"Before considering how and when maize reached Africa," he said, "it is necessary to review briefly the latest evidence on the botanical plant since Stonor and Anderson *cast serious doubt on its American origin* [my italics – D-R] suggesting that there was either an indigenous or a pre-Columbian maize in Asia. This paper met with a considerable *succes de scandale*, and is still quoted, in spite of the fact that the conclusions were refuted by Mangelsdorf and Oliver…" (10)

Fine. Except that Mangelsdorf is actually on record as having no doubts at all about the American origins of maize; and when Roland Oliver read the manuscript of this book he did not question the assertion that maize originated in the Americas. While Stonor and Anderson might have been a little clearer and ironed out one or two ambiguities in their text, repeated readings of their article make it ringingly clear that they believed maize to have been carried *from* America *to* Asia rather than the reverse. And once maize had reached China, Assam, and Southeast Asia there is no reason why it should not have been carried to Africa along with the plantains, yams, coconuts, chickens, and other things that we know to have come from that part of the world.

CHAPTER - 19

THE YORUBA - AND THEIR BEADS

When the first Europeans arrived in Yorubaland in southern Nigeria early in the 19th century they found a remarkably sophisticated empire centred around Oyo, and - the oldest and most important cultural city of Yorubaland - Ile Ife. The latter was no mean place. The outer walls of the near-circular metropolis were nineteen miles long, inside which was a walled inner 'compound' a mile and a half in diameter containing the palace of the king, and other buildings from which the complex Yoruba city-state was run.

There was nothing exceptional, or modern, about these defences. Even Ife's huge perimeter walls paled in comparison to those of Eredo a few miles inland from the lagoons near Lagos. Little is known about the ancient Eredo complex whose massive outer ramparts are 100 miles long, and, in places, from the bottom of the surrounding ditches to the top of its walls nearly 70 feet high. It dates back to a period between 700 and 1000 A.D., roughly contemporary with Igbo Ukwu where Nigeria's earliest bronzes (so far) were buried. Obviously something 'big' was going on in the forest regions down near the sea in those days; and in years to come, maybe, more discoveries will be made that will shine yet brighter light on southern Nigeria's past.(1) But in the meantime…

"From almost every point of view," wrote the historian, J.D. Fage, in his classic work on West Africa, "the greatest of the four great forest states was the Yoruba state … It was the earliest to emerge, and it lasted longer than the others. At its peak, it probably covered a greater area and encompassed more people than did Benin, Dahomey and Ashanti. It seems to have reached a higher level of material prosperity and of culture than the other states…." (2)

If you type 'Yoruba Origins' into Google, over 20,000 sites pop up. Serious Nigerian professors lambaste one another with wildly differing views, vouching both for the sensitivity of the subject, and the lack of any certain answers. Like a number of other people in West Africa, Yoruba traditions claim that their ruling classes are people of a different stock, who came originally from some unspecified place in the 'East'. Some say - without any real foundation - they came from 'Mecca'; others that they were from Upper Egypt, citing the similarity of their burial customs, and the manner (also essentially the same as in Madagascar) in which they bind their dead in cloth. (3) Visiting Ile Ife in 1910, the German explorer Leo Frobenius was impressed, commenting that the upper-class Yoruba are "men of finer stature, extraordinary slenderness and delicacy of limb, narrow heads and fairer skins" compared with the lower classes, who possessed the "usual Negro characteristics." John Fage considered that the original Yoruba ruling classes were "*possibly* part-Hamite", and that they migrated to their present location "between about 600 and 1000 A.D." But as myths, legends and traditions are fragmentary and often conflicting, historians agree that their origins are vague. In his "History of Nigeria", some years ago, Sir Alan Burns summed up by saying: "Whatever their origin, it is probable that the Yorubas were not originally of Negro blood, although, in the centuries during which they have occupied their present territories, they have so intermarried with Negro slaves as to have lost their early characteristics."

The Yoruba religion is complex and polytheistic. They believe in one supreme god, Olorun, 'the owner of the sky'. In addition they have a pantheon of 401 lesser gods and goddesses; and they inhabit a world full of fascinating myths and legends. It is never easy to know how much store to put in quasi-fantastic stories that have probably been tweeked and changed in the telling over the centuries; but, taken together, many myths may be pertinent to the Yoruba past, and some are thus worthy of re-telling: (4)

In the beginning, so they say, the High God sent 16 lesser gods to create the world, giving one of them, Obatala, a calabash of sand and a five-toed chicken from which to make the earth. On the way from heaven Obatala got intoxicated on palm wine, whereupon another god, Oduduwa, seized both the calabash of sand and the chicken and descended to the primordial ocean, where the chicken proceeded to spread the sand across the face of the deep, causing land to appear. Obatala, in his drunkenness, having lost his chance to make the earth, was allowed the privilege of making man; but alas! ... once again he overdid the booze, and succeeded only in making dwarfs, hunchbacks, cripples and albinos, the protection of whom thereafter became his special responsibility. By and by the two gods went to war. Oduduwa triumphed, thus becoming the first ruler of Ile Ife: and all seemed well.

But, surprisingly, it turned out that the earth Oduduwa and his five-toed chicken had created from the ocean was not the first earth after all! For alongside this myth there are legendary tales of other people already inhabiting the new world created by the ancestral gods. The autochthonous people whom they encountered were known to the Yoruba as 'Igbo', and they obviously resented the appearance of these new people with the 'five-toed chicken'. One legend tells how the Igbos regularly defeated the Ifes in battle, until a beautiful young Ife lady named Moremi offered to make any sacrifice demanded by the spirit of the stream, Esinmirin, if he would help her discover the secrets of Igbo power and thus enable her people to defeat them.

Moremi was told that she should act as a sort of undercover agent, and marry the Igbo king. This she did; and soon came up with a piece of prime intelligence - that the raffia fibre clothes worn by the Igbo in battle were highly inflammable. Moremi duly engineered her escape, and returned to Ife to impart this important information to the king, who thenceforth ordered all Ife soldiers to go into battle bearing firebrands to set the Igbo skirts ablaze. Thus the Igbo were eventually defeated – an event re-enacted annually at the Edi Festival. But, alas! This only happened after the lovely Moremi had honoured her promise to Esinmirin to sacrifice anything he decreed. Brutally and inexplicitly, he ordered her to sacrifice her only son.

The salient points here are that Oduduwa came down into the *ocean* to create the earth with the help of a *chicken*, a creature that was introduced into sub-Saharan Africa from India or Indonesia ± two thousand years ago; and that when he emerged onto the newly created land it was found to be already occupied by *Igbo*. Now, if Oduduwa had come from the deserts of the north, or been, as some of the legends would have us believe, a 'white man' who came overland from the east, one might expect that he would have arrived in a fiery chariot from the sun or the moon, or something of that sort; but not from the *ocean* with an alien *chicken*.

A legend related in more modern times by the King of Ibokun tells how the Yoruba ancestors only managed to subdue the Igbo aborigines 'because they had the advantage of having iron weapons'. In other words, the newcomers brought iron into a country that had hitherto been without it, (but iron was being smelted in Nigeria, on the Jos Plateau, since about 400 B.C.). Yet another legend is that of Ore, the hunter, who is said to have lived in the old world *before* Oduduwa arrived. Frank Willett, in his splendid and informative book about Ife art and the Yoruba, suggested that Ore being remembered as a hunter may mean this legend harks back to days before agriculture was introduced ... i.e. to the days when the Yoruba were still gathering wild indigenous West African yams, before the arrival of the cultivated Southeast Asian yam, cocoyam and plantain that enabled the populations of Yoruba and Igboland to burgeon beyond belief.

Although the Yoruba are mainly an inland people, they have a close affinity with the sea, and it is noteworthy that Olokun, one of their most powerful gods, is both god of the sea, and god of *wealth*. Willett believed this dual responsibility may have come about: "… because wealth came from over the sea". Though he may have been referring to the arrival of 'wealth' in the form of the cultivated yams and plantains that came originally from Southeast Asia, Willett may also have had in mind the 'wealth of Europe', which arrived with the Portuguese, and subsequent other white folk in their sailing ships.

But as the peak of Yoruba power and culture, and all their greatest art, pre-dated the arrival of Europeans, Olokun's responsibilities for wealth and the sea must surely have dated back long before the late 15th century. So if not the 'wealth of Europe', or the food crops that arrived from across the seas, what other 'wealth' might the legends have referred to? It could have taken several forms, one of which might have been glass beads, which had long been prized items among the Yoruba.

In 1830, on his exploration of the Niger river, Richard Lander purchased, in the market at Katunga (Old Oyo), a "very curious and singular kind of stone" which, he was told, had come from Ife "four moons journey from Katunga". He described it consisting of "a variety of little transparent stones, white, green, and every shade of blue…". Though neither he nor his brother realized it, this was a chunk of fused glass beads which may have been in the process of being re-melted in a crucible. He was told that the piece "was dug from earth in a country called Iffe [sic]" where according to traditions the first Yoruba parents were created and "from whence all Africa has been peopled."(5) Eighty years later, in a grove outside Ife dedicated to the god Olokun, the German ethnographer, Leo Frobenius, found crucibles for melting glass, plus a huge number of glass beads in a rich variety of colours, all of which seem to have been made in Yorubaland and which dated back long before the Portuguese arrived.

About 150 miles northeast of Ife lies the tenth century Hausa town of Bida which, with an abundance of quartz in the neighbourhood and soda imported from Lake Chad, claims to have been the only place in Africa apart from Egypt where glass for bead-making was actually produced from local raw materials. But when and from where the technology came is not clear. Thurston Shaw felt it likely that bead-making had come to Nigeria via the Islamic world. But, checking through Nehemia Levtzion's book on early Arabic sources, of the 65 Arab travellers who wrote about West Africa between the 9th and 17th centuries only 6 of them made any mention of glass 'beads'; in all cases in connection with people living on the edges of the desert far to the north of Yorubaland. As neither Ife nor Bida were on, nor anywhere near, any of the major trans-Saharan trade routes, Islamic origins for bead-making cannot be taken for granted.

Writing of 9th century Igbo-Ukwu, Thurston Shaw noted that "Many of the glass and cornelian beads looked like imports ... perhaps deriving ultimately from India or Arabia." So is it possible that the art of bead-making came to West Africa from India - perhaps at the same time as yams, coconuts, plantains, and bronze casting skills? (6)

Sonja Magnavita, a German archaeologist working at the turn of the 2000's in Songhai, within the Niger bend in the far north-east of Burkina Faso, found glass beads dating to 1st – 3rd c.; 'drawn cylinder' beads of the 5th – 7th century; and others resembling those of Igbo Ukwu. She, like Thurston Shaw, believes they may have been Middle Eastern, imported from some unknown point of origin across the deserts, by the Garamantes. But archaeologists have found no evidence of a bead trade in the Garamantian capital, Germa, through which the caravans would surely have passed. In fact, other than 'guesswork' and 'surmise' there is no convincing evidence at all that either glass beads, or the means of making them, were brought to the lower Niger overland from the north.

And it should not be overlooked that Songhai - where live the mysterious 'Zanj' people who made 'sewn' canoes until very recently - could, as has been suggested in an earlier chapter, have been reached as easily, or even more easily, up the Niger river from the sea, as from across the deserts in the north.

Drawing glass into cylinders for the purpose of making beads is a technique that was developed originally in the great Asian centre of glass bead-making at Arikamedu in southern India, whose history goes back 2000 years. Arikamedu was in close contact with Southeast Asia: in fact, many bead-makers went from there to Kuala Selinsing on the west coast of Malaya, and Oc-eo in the Mekong Delta; and when the State of Funan collapsed early in the first millennium the craftsmen either moved to, or came under the control of, Srivijaya. Only after many productive centuries, when Palembang fell to the Cola navy early in the 11th century, and the Srivijayan capital moved over the hills to Jambi, did glass bead-making come to an end in that part of the world. Could Sonja Magnavita's 'drawn' beads have come from India?

Although they are potentially a hugely useful archaeological tool for tracing dates and patterns of trade, the vast and complex subject of glass and glass beads is fraught with contradictions and controversy, and it is entered into with trepidation. The know-how for making solid glass (as opposed to thin pottery glazes, which had already been known for centuries) has probably only ever been 'discovered' once, and that was by Jewish craftsmen living in the well-wooded hills around the head-waters of the Tigris, some 4,500 years ago.(7) Vitrification of the basic raw materials required levels of sophisticated pyrotechnology previously unknown as well as a knowledge of how to build fuel-greedy furnaces capable of maintaining temperatures as high as 2000° for several days. It also required sufficient curiosity in chemistry to discover the need for alkaline fluxes to give the silicate sands fluidity and clarity. Another important secret the early glassmakers discovered was that once it was made from the basic ingredients, glass can be re-melted at much lower temperatures, and that the addition of broken glass, or 'cullet' as it is called, to the furnace acts as a catalyst that speeds up vitrification.

For thousands of years the glassmakers kept their technology a closely guarded secret within the Jewish diaspora, disseminating it only through the migration of the craftsmen themselves. Thus, when one hears talk of 'Roman glass' the odds are that no Roman ever actually made glass or glassware: it was made by Jewish craftsmen for the Roman market. Similarly, the glass from which Egyptian-ware was produced was not originally *made* in Egypt, because without forests there would have been insufficient fuel to sustain the necessary high temperature furnaces. This inability of Egyptians to make their own raw glass was demonstrated when numerous balks of glass were found in the hold of a ship that had sunk *en* route to Egypt from Canaan – where the glass had been made – to glass-workers on the Nile.

Theoretically, by analysing the chemical make-up of glass and glass beads it should be possible to tell exactly where they came from. But this, too, has its problems. Casting ones eyes over analysis charts, it is obvious that there is huge variation of chemical make-up within the same locality. For instance, at Kuala Selinsing, a seafaring settlement on the Malay coast from the 3rd to the 11th century, and a major glass-bead producer for Srivijaya, the amount of aluminium oxide present in just 14 glass specimens tested, varied from 16.4 to 4.1% with an average of 8.7%. High aluminium?... or medium-low? Certainly the highest in that part of Southeast Asia; but from which of the samples does one make the judgment? Various authorities have pointed out that high alumina glass is, in the words of one: "evidence of contact with the Indian subcontinent".

Indian contacts with Malaya, and even cullett imported from India, may well account for the high-alumina glass beads made at Kuala Selinsing in Srivijayan days. Peter Robertshaw has identified beads in Nigeria that have a very high aluminium oxide content. At the time of writing they are a mystery to him; but might they not have come from the 'high alumina' bead factories of India – or even Malaya?

As mentioned above, the problem is compounded when chemical composition varies within the same locality and even from one bead to another, even though, to the eye, the beads may appear to be identical. The reason for this may lie in the fact - for which there is strong evidence - that from the latter part of the first millennium there was substantial export of cullet (glass scrap) from the Middle East to bead-making centres in the Far East, with the result that the monochrome beads of Malaya (which formed the vast bulk of the production in that region), being thus adulterated, were frequently indistinguishable from Middle Eastern beads. Alastair Lamb, who noticed this oddity, pointed out that: "If this conclusion is correct, then it should come as no surprise that so many South-Eastern glass beads have an essentially Middle-Eastern composition."(8)

These sort of problems have to be taken into account when considering bead analysis. For example, regarding the huge hoard of beads found at Igbo Ukwu, research being done by Peter Robertshaw in 2004 indicated that: "The Igbo Ukwu glass (as well as that from Kissi and Gao in Songhai – D-R) compares well chemically and macroscopically with our 8th to 10th century samples from eastern and southern Africa", which are thought to have a Middle Eastern origin. Does this necessarily mean the huge quantity of monochrome beads found in Africa were *made* in the Middle East? Or could they have been, as Alastair Lamb suggested, made in Southeast Asia from Middle Eastern glass – or glass heavily adulterated with Middle Eastern cullet? There is no easy answer.

But in many ways it doesn't matter. The big question is: How did the beads get to Africa, and who brought them?

If, as Professor Robertshaw has pointed out, the Nigerian beads turn out to be the same as – or close matches with - beads in South and East Africa, it is unrealistic to suggest that they were brought to West Africa across the Sahara and disseminated all the way to South Africa from there. Likewise it would be a remarkable coincidence if, from the same Middle Eastern source, they reached the two regions separately by different routes – one overland to West Africa; another by sea to southern Africa. Might they not therefore have been carried to all areas by sea rather than overland?

If that were the case, it is certain that Arab sailors could not have been the carriers to West Africa, because in the 8th century (Igbo's date) they were unable to round the Cape of Good Hope in their *dhows*. On the other hand, Indonesian sailors – who could have acquired the beads in Aden or Opone - OR brought them directly from the Srivijaya glass bead-making centres – would have had no problem carrying them round the Cape of Storms and up to the Bight of Benin. [This has been shown decisively by the ease with which Philip Beale sailed his traditionally built, wooden dowelled, no iron nails, 'replica' of a double-outrigger depicted on the 9th century walls of Borobudur, round the Cape and up to West Africa in 2004.]

So far, the weight of evidence emerging from the colourful world of beads points strongly to their introduction to West Africa *round* rather than *across* the continent. If that was the case an Indonesian introduction is far more likely than an Arab introduction ... but until on-going research is completed, perhaps it would be fairer to say that the jury is still deliberating.

CHAPTER - 20

SHEKELS AND SHELLS

When Mungo Park and his army of followers set off of on their exploration of the Niger in 1797 the currency they were using in local markets on the west coast was known as a *bar*, based on 'bars' of different commodities ...lengths of iron, bunches of tobacco, bottles of rum, etc. But when they reached the Bambara region, roughly midway between the Gambian coast and Yorubaland, the local currency suddenly changed to cowrie shells.

Cowrie shells, *Cypraea annulus* or *Cypraea moneta*, must have been a popular trade item for thousands of years. They have surfaced in Egyptian tombs; in Tuscan graves; in Pompeii; in Anglo-Saxon and Punic graves; in Transcaucasia; Crete, Turkistan and Scandinavia(1); even in 5th century levels at Broederstroom in South Africa.(2) What they were used for isn't always clear; but we know that in some places - presumably because they themselves look a bit like half closed eyes - they were used as charms against the 'evil eye'; and in other places, because they are supposed, also, to look like a woman's vulva, as charms against infertility. The French used to refer to them as *les pudenda magiques*, whilst more straight-laced Romans called them *porci* or *porculi*, 'piglets'. It is from this word that the Italian 'porcellana' and the English 'porcelain' come ... from the smooth, gleaming polished surface in the fold of the shell. (3)

It is thought that Cowries were first used as money in Shang dynasty China (1766 – 1050 BC), where a basic currency unit was a *p'eng* - - a string of 10 shells. Later, they were important in the development of the Indian money system: 4 *kauri* = 1 *ganda*: 20 *ganda* = 1 *pan* or 80 *kauri*: 4 *pan* = 1 *ana*: 4 *ana* = 1 *kahan*, or $^1/_4$ of a rupee; i.e. 5,120 *kauris* to a *rupee*. But the Indians made no claims to have invented the idea. Sylvain Levi, and other scholars of pre-Dravidian India, believed it was developed by a maritime civilisation "on the shores of the Indian Ocean and the China Sea, i.e. the region where the people speaking the Austro-Asiatic languages were disseminated".(4)

185

Curiously, Mungo Park noted that "… in counting the cowries, they call eighty a hundred; whilst in all other things they calculate by the common hundred." Could this have had something to do with the Indian system of counting 80 cowries to a *pan*?

The most prolific source of *Cypraea moneta*, the type of cowrie generally found widely in West Africa, was the Maldive Islands, in the middle of the Indian ocean. They were described there by al-Tajir – 'Sulaiman the Merchant' – in the 9th century; and a hundred years later by Al-Masudi. "The treasure of this queen is cowries," wrote Masudi of the Queen of the Maldives. "Now the cowrie is alive, a sort of animal. When her treasure diminishes she orders the people of the islands to cut branches of the coco-nut palm with the foliage, and spread them on the surface of the sea. Then the creatures climb up on them and are collected and spread out on the sea-shore. The sun dries out the creatures inside, and the cowrie remains empty and the treasuries are filled with them." (5)

When Ibn Batutta visited the Maldives in the 14th century he told a slightly different, but more enlightening story. "The inhabitants of these islands use cowrie shells as money," he wrote. "This is an animal which they gather in the sea and put into pits there where its flesh disappears, leaving a white shell. They buy and sell with these at the rate of 400,000 for a gold dinar, but they often fall in value to 1,000,000 for a dinar. They sell them in exchange for rice to the people of Bengal, who also use them as money, as well as to the Yemenites, who use them instead of sand as ballast in their ships. These cowries are used also by the negroes in their lands; I saw them being sold at Malli and Gawgaw at the rate of 1,150 for a dinar." (6) Thus there was a tidy little profit for the Yemeni dhow captains if they sold their ballast on to merchants in the North African trade, who took them on across the Sahara … a little matter of a 35,000% to 85,000% mark up from source to end-user!

Al Masudi (10th century) was also the first of the Arab writers to mention cowries in the western Sudan. He related how people "… adorn their women with copper rings, and put cowrie shells in their hair"; but he made no mention of them being used as 'treasure' or money. In fact there was no reference to cowries as a West African currency until the mid-14th century when they were used in Mali and - as an 'alternative' currency - in Kanem, northeast of Lake Chad. (7)

Since pre-Islamic time, Arabs had used cowries as charms to ward off the evil eye; but they never themselves used them either as 'treasure' or currency – a fact that makes one wonder why Arabs should have been responsible for introducing cowries as currency in West Africa, as many people would have us believe.

Mungo Park had previously come across money-cowries when he was in Sumatra four years before going to Africa. There is a footnote in his journal referring to: "…these little shells which pass current as money, in many parts of the East Indies, as well as in Africa." In a small market he set up in Bambaraland to sell his English trinkets for local currency, Mungo Park marveled at the huge quantities of shells required for transactions: "… such was my run of business, that I was sometimes forced to employ three tellers at once to count my cash. I turned one market day twenty five thousand seven hundred and fifty-six pieces (cowries)."(8)

Indeed, everyone who came across them mentioned the enormous numbers involved. The 19th century Anglo-German explorer, Heinrich Barth, noted that cowries, strung together in twenties, were stored in rush sacks called *takrufa*, each of which contained 20,000 shells. Hiskett quoted a Kano manuscript allocating a wealthy man's legacy of 599 sacks of cowries to his 2 male and 3 female heirs. Assuming the sacks were the same as Barth's *takrufa*; 599 x 20,000 = roughly 12,000,000 shells!. If this represented the inheritance of just one Kano family, the number in circulation throughout the land can scarcely be imagined. (Kano did not use cowries as money until early in the 18th century when they were introduced to northern Hausaland from Nupe in the south). Purchasing powers quoted by Clapperton and the Landers throughout their journals create a picture of mind-boggling quantities of cowries being in circulation in the 19th century. Hundreds of examples of 'values' could be cited, but take just one: In 1841 the British Government purchased 16 miles of land on the right bank of the Niger for £45, or 700,000 cowries. (9)

Some interesting rates of exchange have been calculated. Assuming a zero rate of inflation, a *mithqal* or a *dinar* (which in 1800 equalled about ten English shillings) would have purchased 1,150 cowries in the 14thc ; 1,725 – 2000 in the 15th.; only 400 hundred in the 16thc.; about 500 in the 17th .; 2,500 in the 18th; and 3,500 in the 19th. These figures suggest a severe shortage of cowrie shells in the 16th and 17th centuries, suddenly pushing their value way up. There is no reason why the fall-off should be attributed to a fall-off in the trans-Saharan trade, which was still in good shape throughout that period. So what might have been the cause of the sudden increase in value? Might it have been that shells normally came to West Africa via some other route, which suffered disruptions of one sort or another? In which case, what might that other route have been?

One possible alternative was across Africa from the East Coast via the central forest zone.

Traditions of the Bushongo people in the Kasai region of the Congo say that "Cowries came from the south", i.e. from their neighbours the Luba who would, in turn, have received them from the East coast. (10) Is it possible they might have reached Nigeria from the east also? There may well have been contacts in the past between the Kasai/Congo basin and the Shari River that flows north to Lake Chad - and these contacts may have extended into Southern Nigeria. *Bushongo* literally means 'The people of Lightening' - a name they share with their fearsome multi-bladed throwing-knife, the *shongo*, which they originally acquired from people living in the Ubangi-Shari region. In Nigeria, the Yoruba god of Thunder and Lightening is *Shango* which also refers to the East on the Yoruba compass, pointing to the Shari basin. The similarities between, *Shango* = 'the god of lightening' and the Bushongo *shongo* = 'lightening' speak for themselves.

But is an overland route across Africa really likely? Unlike the deserts in the north, there were no old-established trade-routes crossing sub-Saharan Africa from east to west. And even if there were, the quantities of cowries involved, with thousands upon thousands of sacks having to be head-portered and canoed all that way, would have made a remarkable impression, and memories of them would surely have survived.

The only other alternative is that money cowries had first been introduced by Indonesians directly to West Africa by sea and that this had remained the main route of the cowrie trade. If that were the case, rather than being the 'introducers' of the new currency, Arabs bringing cowries overland from the north were simply cashing in on an existing and enormously profitable trade. Historic changes taking place on Africa's east coast in the late 15th and early 16th centuries where the Swahili had recently eclipsed the Zanj; combined with increasing Bantu pressure on ancient Zimbabwe; and Portuguese explorers gradually extending their arms into the Indian Ocean - all severely disrupted the maritime flow round the Cape causing the value of cowries in West Africa to rise.

There is possible linguistic support for a hypothesis involving direct contact with the Maldives. In Igboland the money 'cowrie' is *ayolo*, in Yoruba *owo-*, in Nupe *wo-ni*, and in Hausa *wuri*. None of the terms along the lower Niger have any connection with Arabic; but all could claim a relationship with the Maldivian: *boly*. This is conjectural; but it is eminently possible.

There is one remaining question: When were cowries introduced as money? No money cowries were found in the 9th century Igbo sites. In the middle of Africa, around the Upemba depression, most of the cowrie finds are 12th or 13th century. Ife bronze and terracotta figures dated to around the 13th or 14th century show people with lots of bead jewellery, but only very rarely with cowries. So maybe use of cowries as *currency* in Africa only dates from the 13th or 14th century when it was first recorded in the Sudan. The total absence of records from the lower Niger prior to the late 15th century make the history of cowries in West Africa a problem that may remain insoluble. But one thing is certain: the Indonesian connection with the Maldives, the main source of cowries, and their proven ability to sail round the coast of Africa, means that they cannot be discounted as the primary suppliers of money to Olokun, the god of wealth and the god of the sea.

From Angola to Senegal, West African seamen have, for a long time, had a knowledge of the stars; notable among these is the Yoruba *Irawa-oko*, the 'Sirius Canoe-star'. Rudolph Vilaverde even argued that "the star-maps of Micronesian fishermen were matched in turn by West African navigators using the Pleiades". In the 16th century, Gomes Zurara mentioned birds and stars being used in West African navigation, just as they were in the Pacific. Despite the mainly inland nature of Yorubaland, there were some Yoruba who had an intimacy with the sea that was unusual for Africans. They had a fine reputation – along with other coastal West Africans - for handling canoes far out to sea. Trips lasting several months, even as long as a year, from the Bight of Benin, down the coast as far as Angola, were not unknown. (11) Against the prevailing winds and currents these journeys required considerable seamanship, possibly involving the use of sail. In the 17th century the Dutchman Pieter de Marees reported seeing as many as 700 – 800 canoes fishing off the West African coast, and illustrated some with masts; but in the main, the Yoruba paddled their canoes when in the open sea. (James Hornell noted the distinct similarity between the elongated, pointed paddles of West Africa and those used in parts of the Pacific – particularly surprising in his view, as they are not all that efficient!). Their fearlessness may have been due to their faith in Olokun, the sea-god; but it may also have had its roots in something more - that in the distant past, in days that have been remembered only in myths, the Yoruba rulers came from lands far away over the oceans, and that their skills as mariners have been passed down through the generations.

CHAPTER - 21

THE ARTS OF IFE

The arts for which the Ife people are best known are the superb terracotta and bronze portrait figures made seven or eight hundred to a thousand years ago. Though none of the 'bronzes' (they are technically 'brass' not bronze) are quite so daringly fine as the *cire perdue* castings from Igbo-Ukwu, they are superbly made by any standards, getting high marks from present-day bronze-casters with modern equipment to help them.

Nigeria's art traditions are usually divided into several distinct periods – Nok – Igbo Ukwu – Tada - Ife (Yoruba) – Benin, and so on. But as more becomes known about them the more they merge into a single family with a common lineage … and not just the famous bronzes. Several distinct features are now recognised which point to an ancestry connecting Ife terracottas with the Nok sculptures made at least a thousand years earlier. One such piece is the Ife portrait of the man with a horrifying case of the testicular elephantiasis (see Chapter 14), a subject rarely depicted in African art, but portrayed in both Ife and Nok sculptures. In addition, there are terracotta heads from both periods with identical, and pronounced, low relief 'rings' high on their foreheads, which one feels must have had a common symbolism in both cultures despite the huge gap in years.

Terracotta head found at Nok

Terracotta head from Ife

The Arts of Ife

In an earlier chapter, the connection between the Yoruba and the Igbo has cropped up in relation to the Yoruba creation myths. They are also linked by a joint association with the Iwinrin and Osongon Obamakin sacred groves where most of the famous Ife terracottas have been found. Though there are no obvious stylistic parallels in the arts of *Ife* and *Igbo Ukwu* - apart from the common use of bronze and the shared 'lost wax' casting process - the deeply cicatrised furrows on some Ife sculptures are – or were until recently - sometimes echoed in real-life *itchi* facial markings of the Igbo.

As for Benin, it is a well established fact that their craftsmen learned the art of *cire perdue* casting from the people of Ife, thus continuing an artistic tradition spanning a thousand years of bronze casting and at least two thousand years of terracotta sculpting since its early beginnings on the Jos plateau. Even though, stylistically, the Ife sculptures are essentially African – i.e. their proportions are typical of all traditional African art, with heads unrealistically large for their bodies – the same question arises that cropped up with the Igbo Ukwu bronze hoard:- Is the lost wax technology 'home grown' African technology, or was it introduced by outsiders?

In his preface to Frank Willett's book "Ife", Sir Mortimer Wheeler wrote that "…. it is more than likely that some part of the complex make-up of the art of Ife came from the east or north by or through the savannah zone. When the new Africa finds the moment and the mood for the discovery of its own past, here are matters which, properly understood, will provide a new chapter to world-history."

Frank Willett himself was more specific than Sir Mortimer. "There seems," he wrote, "to be only one element of the Ife culture which must have been introduced from outside, namely the knowledge of bronze-casting, which could have been introduced by a single craftsman traveling one of the trade-routes along the Sudan to the south of the Sahara, or across the Sahara from the Mediterranean."(1)

The notion of 'a single craftsman traveling one of the trade routes' into the heart of the non-Islamic Yoruba country is actually extremely unlikely. It raises all sorts of questions: If he had such expertise, why did he not impart it to people further north, particularly in areas where copper was in super-abundance? Why should he have chosen to attempt a journey into such inhospitable country so far from home? How did he manage to survive amongst people known to have been inhospitable to northern strangers even in the 19th century, let alone the 9th when they would have been more likely to have killed and eaten him? The odds must be heavily against the 'lone craftsman' theory: in fact the wholly one-sided emphasis that academics put on pre-16th century sub-Saharan West Africa's links with 'the north' is so absurdly Caucaso-centric that it must, in due course, be reviewed.

Everything we know from Arab records suggests that 'White people' from the north were not at all welcome in the forest zones, and would probably have been killed; secondly, none of the major trade routes went anywhere near Ife; thirdly, if a craftsman with such talent had come all the way from Egypt or one of the Mediterranean countries, would he not, as already suggested, have imparted his skills to others in one of the major centres *en route*? and fourthly, though many day-to-day objects such as cast bronze 'door furniture' were still being produced in small workshops, there were no strong traditions of *cire perdue* 'art' casting in any European or Middle Eastern country between 500 and 1500 AD.

But once again, an introduction from Indonesia is not just a possibility, but - given the fact that that their sailors almost certainly rounded the Cape and voyaged up the west African coast - it is the most probable answer, for the following set of reasons:-

- *Cire Perdue* casting is as old in South Asia and Southeast Asia as in the Middle East. Bronzes were being cast in Mohendro Daro in the 3rd millennium BC.; and *cire perdue* casting continued throughout history to be an important technique in Indian art. A Sanskrit text, thought to be of the Gupta period, i.e. 4th – 6th centuries AD, set out in detail all the processes to be used – the composition of different alloys, methods of preparing the wax, how to make the moulds, and so on – techniques that are still used in India today. In later years lost wax casting became a speciality of southern India. Tamilnadu become a centre for the casting of solid icons; Mannar in Kerala become famous for such items as bells and bowls. A particularly interesting feature of the Mannar dishes is that they were cast in one piece, along similar lines to the single-piece castings of Igbo Ukwu that Paul Craddock of the British Museum found incomprehensible.

- Early in the first millennium A.D. fine kettle-drums – the famous Dong-Son drums originally imported from mainland Southeast Asia - were being cast by the *cire perdue* technique in the Indonesian islands. The metal used in Sumatra was true bronze (c. 85% copper, 11% tin, 4% lead) indicating a high level of metallurgical knowledge (as at Igbo Ukwu). As noted in an earlier chapter, copper was extremely scarce in Southeast Asia and the Islands, and along with gold might have been an attractive import from Africa where it was mined in abundance.(2)

- In both mainland Southeast Asia and the Indonesian islands in the 8th century bronze icons were certainly being produced, the style and technology having been brought from India. In Indonesia, particularly in Srivijaya, bronzes most commonly represented the Boddhisatva Avalokitesvara, the 'Lord of Compassion.' Avalokitesvara could be recognised by the tiny sitting Buddha nestling in the sculpture's head-dress. Lots of these small images, only six or seven inches tall and probably mass-produced in bronze moulds, have been found in Java and Sumatra in 8th and 9th century contexts. Sometime

Khmer bronze.
8th – 14th century

Avalokitesvara had two arms, sometimes multiple arms like many Indian statues; he was either seated or standing, and generally he bore a lotus flower in one hand. In the front of his tiered head-dress there was always a plume, often showing an 8-pettalled flower similar to many low reliefs of people depicted on sculptures at Borobudur.

These Boddhisatvas were used as votive images, or icons, and were generally not housed in shrines. They were, in fact, just the sort of talismanic items that might be carried by those traveling on long journeys, emblems of good fortune, and reminders of their faith; just as modern-day Christians might carry a cross around their neck, or perhaps a rosary. August Rodin once described the bronze icons of southern India which were essentially the same as those of Indonesia as "the most perfect representation of rhythmic movement in art".

In his book, *Africa and Indonesia*, Father Jones (of xylophone fame) showed a Khmer bronze icon from Cambodia dated somewhere between the 8th and 14th centuries, similar to those described above.(3) In this particular case it does not appear to represent Avalokitesvara; it may be the Hindu god Siva; but Hinduism and Buddhism walked hand-in-hand in that part of the world.

Beside this small sculpture Jones juxtaposed pictures of two well known bronzes of Ife chieftains, or 'Oni's. Apart from the Khmer sculpture obviously being oriental, and the other two – from their proportions – obviously African, the similarities are remarkable. In all three cases they wear tiered (knitted?) headdresses with a 'lotus' plume, or 'aigrette', above the forehead. On one of the Ife sculptures the 'lotus' is in bud, as it is on the Khmer piece; on the other the plume is an eight-petalled flower virtually the same as the plumes on a large number of headdresses on the 9th century Borobudur reliefs. All three figures wear necklaces of beads – more on the Africans than on the Khmer piece – from which hangs a medallion of one sort or another. In the case of the two full length figurines, one African and the Khmer, they are naked to the waste, below which they wear a belted 'skirt' lapping right-over-left where it is folded in the front. Both wear anklets.

But the most striking feature of all is the stance. In all three cases the figure stands with arms bent at the elbow, holding a banana-shaped object in each hand. In the case of the Ife sculptures, the item held in the right hand may have been the handle of a fly whisk, a symbol of authority, and that in the left, a horn: those held by the Khmer figurine look similar, but their identity is not clear.

Two bronzes depicting the Oni of Ife. Note the 8-petalled flower on the plume of the figure on the left

Panel 1.b 113, Borobudur **Part of the Story of Maitrakanyaka**
Note the tiered hats and 8-petalled flower plumes

Father Jones' book was treated with considerable suspicion by an academic world that refused (and still prefer to refuse!) to believe that Indonesians could have reached West Africa. Although Father Jones may not have helped himself by including a number of 'borderline' comparisons, much of the criticism was very unfair, and except among the small group of *aficionados* who are convinced of Indonesia's legacy to Africa, it goes largely ignored. (For example, among the approximately 700 bibliographic entries in Graham Connah's widely read *African Civilisations*, there is not one mention of A.M.Jones).(4) But with an ever expanding body of evidence linking Indonesia and Africa, it would be bordering on irresponsible not to point out the striking similarities of the sculptures he illustrated.

Finally, there is a delightful story depicted on the walls of Borobudur, told in several panels that also incorporate the famous representations of the 'Borobudur ships' (see photograph). It is obviously not history; and no profound inferences can be drawn from it. But inasmuch as it is tied in with the magnificent ocean-going outriggers of the day; reflects contemporary attitudes to travel; and the mode of life in the times of Borobudur, it could help to explain those early days of adventure and exploration. There are a number of similar interpretations of the story, but the version I reproduce here (with his kind permission) appeared in John Miksic's book "Borobudur". Like all such picture-narratives of long ago one cannot be sure of its origins or precisely what it refers to. Anyway, it is charming, and it goes like this:-

The Story of Maitrakanyaka. (After N.J. Krom)

Maitrakanyaka was the son of a Benares merchant who died on a trading voyage at sea. When the boy grew up and asked what work his father used to do, his mother – fearful that he, too, would choose a perilous life at sea - told him he had been a shopkeeper. So, anxious to follow in his father's footsteps he established a business, giving his earnings to his mother to spend on charity.

When someone told him his father had actually been a perfume merchant, he closed his shop and set himself up as a perfume dealer, doubling the money he gave to his mother. Then, having been told by yet others that his father was a goldsmith, he too became a goldsmith, earning even greater sums for his mother's charities.

Jealous of his success and anxious to rid themselves of their rival, other merchants told him that, in truth, his father had been a great merchant and caravan leader who travelled far and wide – a fact his mother could not deny. So when Maitrakanyaka laid plans for a lengthy trading voyage with many other merchants his mother threw herself at his feet, pleading with him not to go.

Furious at her opposition he rudely kicked his mother in the head and departed.

Alas! A sea-monster sank his vessel; but clambering aboard a raft he was washed up on an island called Nandana where four beautiful nymphs greeted him. Despite the pleasure of life, the urge to travel soon returned, and embarking on another vessel he set off in a southerly direction to the city of Sadamatta where eight nymphs welcomed him at the gate.

Yet again the urge to travel overcame him, and he set off southward to Nandana where sixteen ladies greeted him; and then yet further south, to the palace of Brahmottara and into the welcoming arms of no less than thirty two lovely nymphs.

Hoping for yet greater fortune he travelled on to the city of Ayomaya. But here his luck failed. Instead of nymphs he encountered a terrifying tall man with a flaming iron wheel that spun on his head and tore into his skull, causing blood to drip into his mouth. On enquiring who the wretched person was, Maitrakanyaka was told that he was "a man who has ill-treated his mother".

Then, from nowhere, a voice declaimed : "Those who are bound are free, and those who are free are now bound" whereupon the wheel swiftly and mysteriously transferred to Maitrakanyaka's head.

Stricken with remorse for the way he had treated his mother Maitrakanyaka declared: "I am willing to wear this wheel for ever on my head for the sake of my fellow creatures." No sooner had he uttered these words in repentance for his deeds than the wheel was lifted from his head, and at the same moment the Bodhisattva Maitrakanyaka died and was born again into the heaven of the Tusita gods.

Maitrakanyaka's ships are the only large vessels depicted in the reliefs of Borobudur, implying that such ships were those used for the longest voyages undertaken at the time ... for example voyages to distant Madagascar and Africa. It is possible to discern a number of tempting links between Maitrakanyaka's skills and why he might have gone to Africa. As a perfume dealer he would have been tempted by frankincense and other aromatics that came from the Horn of Africa. As a goldsmith and merchant the precious metals from the Zimbabwe mines would have been a huge lure. Benares, from where his father came, was one of Asia's greatest metallurgical centres, suggesting that Maitrakanyaka or some of cohorts may have had the necessary knowledge of brass-working to impart to the people of the Niger delta. Were the fetid swamps of the Guinea coast Maitrakanyaka's Ayomaya from which he never returned? One can only fantasize! But sometimes these ancient stories contain tiny elements of truth.

From one of the panels at Borobudur that depict
the journeys of the merchant Maitrakanyaka.
(Drawing by Aragorn Dick-Read)

CHAPTER - 22

LOOKING INTO THE FUTURE

The desire to look into the future, to know the unknowable, is as old as humankind, and Man has devised a fistful of ways of achieving these ends: by studying the stars, or the entrails of chickens; by gazing into crystal balls, shaking dice, shuffling *tarot* cards; from the creases in the palms of his hands; and hundreds of other ways. But some complex divinatory systems practiced in remote places, thousands of miles apart, are so oddly similar that one has to wonder why and how this could have come about.

In the old days, if the people of the Caroline and Marshall islands in Micronesia wanted to know what to do if someone was ill, or whether it was propitious to set out on a long sea voyage, or to find out why their crops were dying; they would turn to their system of divination they called *Bwe* or *Bei* for answers.

William Lessa studied their secrets early in the nineteen fifties and described *Bwe's* origins thus: "Various myths, basically similar, tell of the coming of the art of *Bwe* to man. The following, from Namoluk in the east central Carolines, is an excellent example: 'Supunemen was a god, who understood the art of divination. On his body he bore the signs of destiny, the *mesanepwe*. Then he took them all and put them on the floor, and they grew to be as large as human beings; there were sixteen of them. Supunamen said to them, Go into the forest, chop wood, and make a canoe! They did so, and in two days they had completed a canoe without a keel. On this boat they came down to earth, and sat in ...." - he gives their designated order. (1)

Lessa then explained the mechanics of *Bwe*. He described how combinations of numbers derived from knots tied at random in palm fronds represented the names of each of the mythical boatmen, and how these combinations were arrived at. In the selection of the numbers, the diviner cut a frond from a young coconut tree – a young tree being "like the mouth of a child – without lies". He split it into thin shafts, and tied several knots in each. It was important that the knots were tied at random

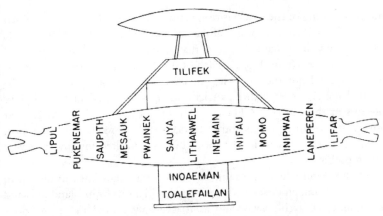

The Seating Plan for the Spirits of Bwe

with no attention paid to the number on each strip, "for that would be meddling with fate." Although only four were needed, the diviner usually made knots in more strips than were necessary, eventually selecting his four, arbitrarily, from the pile.

Having selected four knotted strips the diviner set them aside in pairs – two and two. The knots on each strip were counted out in fours, the number in excess of four being noted down. Thus, if there were seven knots in one strip, the number 3 was noted; if there were eight in the strip paired with it, the number 4 was noted, thus making a pair: 3 + 4.

From the knotted palm strips it was thus possible to obtain a total of 16 pairs of numbers, each of which were associated with one of the 16 named spirit boatmen. These were set down in the correct order as follows:

Ilifar	Laneperen	Inipwai	Momo	Inifau	Pwainek	Sauya	Toalefailan
o o o o	o o o	o o	o o o	o o o o	o o o o	o o o o	o o o
o	o	o	o o	o o	o o o	o o o o	o o o

Tilifek	Lithanwel	Inemain	Mesauk	Lipul	Pukenemar	Inoaeman	Saupith
o	o o o	o o	o o	o	o	o o	o
o	o o o o	o o o o	o o o	o o o	o o o o	o o	o o

Lessa takes up the explanation: "Up to this point we merely have the names of sixteen various possible combinations resulting from knots tied in a single pair of leaves. By themselves these mean nothing. The next step is to take the names for the second pair of strips and juxtapose it to the first, and the meaning of the oracle is read from this. Thus, *Ilifar* and *Laneperen* (4 + 1 and 3 + 1) form a meaningful combination, whereas each alone does not yield any information. The actual number of combinations is, of course, 16 times 16, or 256. ... Each of the 256 combinations has a name entirely apart from the 16 basic pairs ... [*Bwe*] must by no means be regarded merely as superstitious tricks .... *Bwe* is rooted in the religious concepts of the people..." There are various degrees of *Bwe*: the highest form *girot* involving prayers and sacrificial rituals, is reserved for the most serious matters; a much simpler form, *Tib*, is consulted for any and every trifling problem.

Just how and when *Bwe* came to Micronesia is not known; but as, in the course of time, it developed many small variations from island to island throughout the archipelago, and as it is deeply rooted in the religious concepts of the people, it is unlikely to have been a recent introduction. It's 4 x 4 x 4 structure is undoubtedly derived from the Chinese book of changes, 'I-Ching', a product of Taoist and Confucian philosophy dating back to the 12th century B.C.; but the Micronesian procedure has taken it to the extreme, to 4 x 4 x 4 x 4 = 256 named variations.

From its philosophical origins in China, I Ching influenced thinking throughout Southeast Asia. It is therefore unsurprising, in view of Indonesian settlement in Madagascar, to find a method not unlike that of Micronesia, cropping up in 'The Great Isle' in the form of their most important divination system - *sikidy-bé*. In common with the hexagrams of I Ching *Sikidy-bé's* sixteen patterns are divided into 4 'houses', or *trano*, named – in Arabic, for reasons that we shall come to - after the points of the compass. The sixteen names vary from region to region, but as an example, those of a Merina diviner may be as follows:

Taraiky	Jama	Asoravavy	Asoralahy	Aditsima	Alokola	Milahidy	Mikiarija
o	o o	o o	o	o o	o	o o	o
o	o o	o o	o	o	o o	o	o o
o	o o	o	o o	o	o o	o o	o
o	o o	o	o o	o o	o	o	o o

Alehiamora	Alibijado	Alehiazana	Adinkisy	Kiso	Adikiasajy	Vontsira	Sakao
o o	o o	o	o o	o	o	o	o o
o	o o	o o	o o	o o	o	o	o
o o	o	o o	o o	o	o o	o	o
o o	o o	o o	o	o	o o	o	o o

Looking into the Future

There are a variety of ways in which the Malagasy diviner arrives at these combinations; but a common method involves laying out small piles of beans, pebbles, maize, or similar objects, in lines of four.(2) Following long and elaborate blessings he takes away pairs of beans from each pile, until only two, or one, are left – thus arriving at one or other of the sixteen possible patterns shown above. Though *sikidy* may not have quite the same religious significance as *Bwe*; and the procedures to arrive at the all-important patterns are not the same as those in Micronesia, the basic similarities and the essential elements of randomness are obvious.

What seems like a clear connection between *sikidy-bé* in Madagascar, *Bwe* in Micronesia, and *I Ching* in Southeast Asia (all springing ultimately from China) is confused by the fact that in the course of voyages to China towards the end of the first millennium, Arabs must have acquired the same I Ching-based know-how, as a result of which an Arab version known as *derb al-raml*, literally 'sand-divination', became widely popular in the Middle East.

Al-raml is frequently put forward as being a purely Arab invention; but the views of two supreme experts leave little doubt of its Far Eastern origins. The late Professor A.N. Beeston, one of our great Arabists, wrote in a letter to this author: (3)

"I have no idea whether any research has been done on what its (*al-raml's*) ultimate origins are; though I think it could be asserted with certainty that they do not lie in Arabia. In pre-Islamic and early Islamic Arabia, the only physical means of divination (as opposed to the physical ones of dreams and 'second-sight' phenomena) that are recorded are lot-casting and haruspication. I can't think of any parallel which is common in the Islamic world for the special significance attaching to 16, or 4 x 4. The nearest thing (and that is somewhat remote) is the old Semitic practice of using 40 as a conventional round number (as in the Israelites 40 years in the wilderness) which has been taken over into Islam; this however is a different system, in that when it is desired to develop it into higher powers, the result is not 40 x 40, but 40 x 10 = 400. I would think therefore that the predominance of 16 in divination comes from some non-Islamic (and probably non-Semitic) source. For my own part I have sometimes been tempted to wonder whether a link might be traced with the Far East ..."

The second comment is from one of America's best known sinologists, the late Professor Hellmut Wilhelm, who agreed that Malagasy divination showed affinities with Chinese usage "so distinctive that they let one think of diffusion", and that "... any such diffusion has been brought about by the Arabs ... (who) have acted as kind of middle-men for the transmission of knowledge and ideas between east and west in many fields, science as well as literature and folklore." (4)

Long after the first arrivals in Madagascar there came people known collectively as *Antalaotra*, from the Malay *antay-laut*, 'sea people', meaning here 'people from overseas' (although obviously the earliest inhabitants, the *Tompontany*, must also have come by sea!). Some of the *Antalaotra* came from the Middle East. An Arabic tomb-inscription of about the 12th century in north-east Madagascar is the earliest evidence of an Arab *Antalaotra* settlement on the island. By the 14th century they had spread down the east coast; and sometime late in the 15th century the people known as the *Anteimoro* were established in the south-east. They were the last known immigrants who came to the island as a group, and in many ways they were the most unusual people, as we have already seen in Chapter 12.

Raymond Kent wrote of the Anteimoro: "They built no mosques, unlike the Swahili influenced Antalaotra of northwestern Madagascar and the Comoro islands. Although Anteimoro Islam allows for the same sort of syncretism observed on the east African littoral, merging the intrusive and traditional religions, it is nowhere nearly as evolved as Islam of Swahili urban centers." The Anteimoro don't refer to Allah; don't pray as true Muslims do; don't give alms; or make pilgrimages to Mecca. And if Mohammed is remembered as a prophet, so is *Ra-issa*, or Jesus, who is usually considered greater. "They employ an African Age-group system; they use Islamic titles such as *solitani*, not used elsewhere in Madagascar; and *mohadjer* which has 'been reported as common only to one area of north-eastern Africa, namely eastern Ethiopia." The Anteimoro made their own paper, a craft unknown elsewhere in Madagascar or on the Swahili coast of Africa. (5) Their *kitabi* - 'men of books' - writing the Malagasy language in Arabic script, were responsible for hundreds of volumes of local history, the *sora-bé*, sometimes controversial mines of Anteimoro history over the past three or four hundred years. Among the important things introduced by the Anteimoro was a knowledge of that singularly Middle Eastern science, zodiacal astrology. Within a short time of their arrival they had become the pre-eminent '*ombiasses*' - magico-religious specialists - on the island, a status they achieved by combining their astrological expertise with the I-Ching-based form of divination that was probably already in use on the island when they first arrived. The ways in which they used their persuasive powers as diviner-astrologers to make and break kingdoms across the island have been mentioned already in an earlier chapter.

It is the addition of the Middle Eastern astrological element to the traditional 4 x 4 x 4 system which makes *sikidy* so important to the Malagasy and probably accounts for the commonly held *assumption* that the divinatory system as a whole was first introduced by Arabs. (6) But the chances are that this is a misplaced assumption. When we look at 4 x 4 x 4 systems across the water on mainland Africa we will see that they were not tainted with Arab astrology, and probably therefore had nothing to do with the 'Arab' system.

In Madagascar, the Tanala, a tribe of mixed Indonesian/African blood and one of the oldest *tompontany* cultures in the south-east, living on the forested escarpments immediately to the west of the Anteimoro claim that a form of *sikidy* existed long before the *Antalaotra* came to the island. Ralph Linton, in his study of the Tanala, wrote that "The Menabe say that only divination by seeds is native and very few of their 'ombiasy' know any other form. ... There are two forms, one relatively simple, which the Tanala claim is aboriginal, and one complex. The latter is unquestionably of Arab origin. It is commonly used by the Ikongo, but few Menabe ombiasy are familiar with it." (7) The form of divination, known to the Tanala of Menabe by the Malagasy name *Alanana*, employs only Malagasy words, e.g. 'wife', 'old woman', 'ancestors', 'food', 'God', and so on, for the sixteen patterns; and it seems to pre-date the more complex Anteimoro form, with its Arabic terminology. Furthermore, the Tanala system involves the creation of eight piles of *three* nuts, and in this respect seems to be based more closely on the Chinese system of 'trigrams' which limit the number of derivatives to 64, further differentiating it from the Anteimoro form which can potentially be extended to 64 x 4.

There are differing opinions on the origins of the Anteimoro. Pierre Vérin and Narivolo Rajaonarimanana voiced what is currently the orthodox view, which is that: "evidence is now sufficient to assert that the Muslims who came to Madagascar were from the Persian Gulf and southward along the Gulf of Oman to the northwest corner of India." The less orthodox view is that the Anteimoro may be descended from dissenting, heretical Imams who fled Mecca and crossed the Red Sea to take refuge in Somalia and southern Ethiopia before coming to Madagascar. Their name (pronounced '*teimur* in Malagasy where 'o' becomes 'u' and the final vowel is barely audible) has been connected with the 'vanished' tribe named the *Temur*, (see also chapter on the Malagasy) who, according to Enrico Cerulli, were still remembered in the mid-twentieth century by the people of Harar in Ethiopia. "It is certainly the vast Somali hinterland and part of eastern Ethiopia, with their deserts and semi-arid environment, that suggest themselves as repositories of zealotic and fossilised Muslim communities, one or more of which ultimately sired the Anteimoro." (8)

Somewhere in their history they either devised or encountered people with strong pagan ways, which is another reason why some people suspect the Anteimoro came via Ethiopia. The reverence attached to stone funerary monuments in Madagascar – especially in the southeast - many of which are *vatolahy*, 'male stones', or *vatovavy*, 'female stones', led Kent to propose a direct connection between the Anteimoro and the 10,000 or so huge 'phallic' *menhirs* found in Sidamo in southern Ethiopia; and the thousands of phallic funerary monuments of Konso. (9) Equally well they may have had something to do with the 'phallic' pillar-tombs found in the Bajun islands and elsewhere down the Swahili coast that have already been discussed. (10)

Comparing the Arabic terms used in *sikidy-bé* with those of Arab systems in Arabia and north Africa, Alfred Grandidier, the grandfather of *Malgachisants*, found that the terminology used in Madagascar most closely resembled that used in the *al-raml* of Arabs in the Darfur region of the Sudan. If that was the case, it would strongly support the contention that the Anteimoro came from the Horn of Africa, not directly from Arabia. Its also forms a link in the chain connecting what might be called the 'I Ching Diaspora', with West Africa, which we shall come to later.

Not altogether surprisingly in view of Madagascar's close and ancient relationship with Central Africa, similarly based divination systems are found across the Moçambique channel from Losotho in the far south, to Zambia in the north and Botswana in the west – i.e. covering much the same area over which the beautiful, eerie, sounds of the panpipes could once be heard. Though the techniques are different, and they are in many respects less sophisticated, the African systems work on the same 4 x 4 x 4 base as that of *sikidy-bé* .

In his book about the Tromba cult, Rusillon showed a picture of a bone talisman drilled with a familiar *sikidy* pattern, to be hung round the neck. Similarly patterned dice have been found in Africa, but the common African examples come in sets of four, cut in squares, or oblongs, of bone, ivory, or wood, varying in size and design. Their use is ancient. They were mentioned in 1609 by dos Santos; and examples of dice were dug up by Gertrude Caton Thomson when she was excavating the ruins of the Zimbabwe culture. Divining dice were used by the powerful Matabele, who were relative newcomers to the area; but they say it was their neighbours, the Makaranga, the 'people of the Great Zimbabwe', who "influenced them, and who have a more highly organised cult of magic". (11) So it seems likely that the system was disseminated from the Zimbabwe region.

All the dice are named and have some sort of identifying decoration on one side. A typical example might be that of the Venda in the northern Transvaal. The names of the dice of one clan, representing the equivalent of the four '*trano*' of the Malagasy, were:- *Lekholo Lekhuamen* - the Headman or 'king' of the set; *Chuadima* - Lekholo's wife; *Selumi* - the male in the second pair; *Lengwana* - Selumi's wife. (12) When in action, the diviner threw them randomly down onto the ground. If both sides of the dice were observed, 16 combinations were obtainable, and just as with *sikidy* in Madagascar, or *bwe* in Micronesia, each combination had its name which, for the clan in question, were: *Matlakolo, Lekhuami, Matloma-Boni, Salumi, Lengwana-Latangwa, Mogoluwe, Mabhue, Setlaku Marupi, Marekue, Tlapadiwe, Magoelela, Moraru, Mabhiana, Mararuane, and Mphiri–phiri*. None of these names had anything to do with astrology, nor anything else 'Arabic', to connect them directly with Arabised *sikidy* or the Arab's own *al-raml*. This strongly suggests that the system had become embedded in Africa before the Anteimoro arrival in Madagascar and the subsequent Arabisation of their own *sikidy*.

But when one sees how a similar system was engrained in the lives of Bushmen and Hottentots who had minimal contact with the coastal people, the doubts that it was an Arab introduction in Central Africa grow even stronger. Eighty years ago the Rev Dornan, working in Bechuanaland, commented:- "The great factor in the life of the Bushmen is their divining bones, commonly, but wrongly called dice." "Every Bushman carries his set. ... Among the Bushmen these divining bones are magical things and form part of their lives. No Bushman would willingly be without his bones. They are always carried in a small bag on his person, and if he loses them he is very much concerned and will not go any further until he has made every effort to find them. The Bushman's bones ... are usually four in number ... roughly oblong or triangular in shape, and sometimes nicked at one end with or without holes in them. ... They are designated male and female. ..." They have bushman names meaning 'man' or 'manhood'; 'youth or young manhood'; 'young girl, girlhood, joy or pleasure'; 'woman, motherhood or hospitality' once again untainted by Arabic.

The procedures and means of interpretation are almost identical to those of the Venda in the northern Transvaal, and the Rev. Dornan asked: "What is the relation of the Bantu divining bones to those of the Bushmen, seeing that they have substantially the same names, are thrown in the same manner, and indicate similar things? Did the Bushmen get their knowledge

... from the Bantu, or vice versa?" As the Bushmen are far older inhabitants of southern Africa than the Bantu, he preferred ... "to think that the latter got their knowledge from the former." (13)

This seems a logical possibility, particularly as the system is confined to a well defined group of South and South Central Bantu which suggests that it was not 'brought down' through Africa when the Bantu migrated from the north. But right or wrong, the Bushmen and Hottentots had even less contact with the coast than the Bantu, and are thus proportionally less likely to have acquired their 4 x 4 x 4 system from Arabs than the Bantu.

If, on the other hand, divination systems had been part of the culture of the Zanj, *before* middle-eastern influences grew strong on the coast, then the system is far more likely to have been introduced by Indonesians than Arabs.

And so to Nigeria ... half way round the world from the Carolines ... to the Yoruba and their famous divining system, *Ifa*.

"*Ifa* is a system of divination based on sixteen basic and 256 derivative figures (*odu*) obtained either by the manipulation of sixteen palm nuts (*ikin*), or by the toss of a chain (*opele*) of eight half seed shells", wrote William Bascom, the authority on the subject. (14) Like *Bwe*, there are various degrees of *Ifa*, for more, or less serious matters.

Shades of Micronesia?

In the early 18th century systems stemming from the Yoruba *Ifa* were in use as far afield as Ghana and the Ivory Coast; from the Ewe of Togoland to the Igbo on the Niger; and deep down in the Niger Delta among the Urhobo, and others. For a long time Ifa and its derivatives have been, and still are, a powerful and important part of the culture of those who use the system. Descendants of Yoruba slaves practice *Ifa* in Cuba and Brazil, and it still surfaces among West African communities in New York, Los Angeles and London.

Though it appears to be more complex than the Central African systems, *Ifa* procedure is essentially the same. Rather than piles of stones, or sets of dice, the diviner, or *babalawo*, (literally: 'father of the secrets') has lengths of cord to which are attached split seed pods, or half-shells, four on each length like the four knots on each of the Carolineans' palm fronds. Just as the Micronesian diviner selects 4strips knotted with 4 knots, so the Urhobo diviner in the Niger Delta selects 4 strings of 4 split *agbragha* shells, or the Yoruba *babalawo* makes 2 'chains' each linking 4 + 4 palm nuts or seed shells. When divining, the *babalawo* grasps each chain in the middle and lays it randomly on a large divining bag so that the eight half shells fall either open side *up* (o) or open side *down* (x):

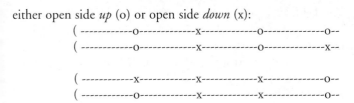

If 'o' represents 1, and 'x' is 2, one finishes up with the same possible number of combinations as in the Carolinean *Bwe*: 16 on one side of the chain and 16 on the other which, when paired off, produce a maximum of 256 combinations. In this respect *Ifa* goes further than the Central African or Malagasy systems which do not seem to recognise so many combinations.

As with *Bwe* each of the Yoruba patterns has a specific name, and they come in a special order, thus:-

Ogbe	Oyeku	Iwori	Edi	Obara	Okanran	Irosun	Oworin
o	x	x	o	o	x	o	x
o	x	o	x	x	x	o	x
o	x	o	x	x	x	x	o
o	x	x	o	x	o	x	o

Ogunda	Osa	Irete	Otura	Oturupon	Ika	Ose	Ofun
o	x	o	o	x	x	o	x
o	o	o	x	x	o	x	o
o	o	x	o	o	x	o	x
x	o	o	o	x	x	x	o

Quoting Bascom: "The real core of Ifa divination lies in the thousands of memorised verses by means of which the 256 figures are interpreted … As for the working of the system of divination, these verses are of far greater importance than either the figures themselves or the manipulations from which they are derived. The verses form an important corpus of verbal art, including myths, folktales, praise names, incantations, songs, proverbs, and even riddles; but to the Yoruba their 'literary' or aesthetic merit is secondary to their religious significance. In effect these verses constitute their unwritten scriptures." Elsewhere he notes: "As an indication of the importance of Ifa to the religious system as a whole is the fact that the most striking religious syncretisms resulting from European contact are to be found in a church established in Lagos in 1934, the Ijo Orunmila Adulawo, which was founded on the premise that the teachings of Ifa constitute the Yoruba Bible."

The mathematics, the deeply religious significance, and the details of *Ifa*-type divination in West Africa, and *Bwe* in Micronesia, are truly remarkable.

So where did Ifa come from?

As there is with *sikidy-bé* in Madagascar, there is a general assumption – yet again – that it was the Arabs 'wot did it'. So much has been written about '*Derb el raml*' or '*Al-raml*' that, in some circles, it is difficult to imagine that there could have been an alternative origin. *Al-raml* has long been practised in northern Nigeria; and a version of it has become popular among Yoruba Muslims in the south where it is called '*Atimi*' – a system that differs from *Ifa*.

William Bascom accepted that... " ... there can be no question of a historical relationship of *Atimi* with Islamic geomancy, (i.e. with *Al-raml*) but," he added, "it is probably a recent introduction among the Yoruba." He pointedly singled out the many fundamental differences between *Atimi* and *Ifa* that suggest different ancestry. None of the *Ifa* based systems use a language that bears any relationship to Arabic. Like the Urhobo *Epha* they mostly employ a special, mysterious, language of their own, which only the diviner understands. In fact the Yoruba's Ifa cult (like its spin-offs) is so deeply embedded in their religion and culture; so complex; so important to their artistic tradition; so dependent on the enormous amount of detailed knowledge required by their *babalawo,* and so altogether unusual that there are major difficulties in accepting that Ifa sprang from the shallower roots of Arabic *al-raml*.

Anyway, if the Yoruba's richness of religion, art, architecture, and so much else had emanated from the Muslim desert and Sudanic people of the north, one has to ask: why is it that Yorubaland did not, long ago, become an Islamic State?

Perhaps it is not surprising. As we have seen time and again, there were no established trade routes into the forests of southern Nigeria. As Ibn Batutta, in mid-14th century, said of the Ife, or 'Yufe' as he called them: "*No white man enters this country because they kill him before he reaches it.*" That alone would have been good enough reason to steer clear of them. And if there had been trade connections, surely at least one of the 63 Arab traveller/historians who wrote about West Africa would have mentioned the extraordinary artistic accomplishments in bronze at Igbo Ukwu, Tada, Ife, and elsewhere.(15) As it was, the great Yoruba culture and their 'high arts' remained unknown to the outside world, and the lower Niger remained a no-go area for the northerners for centuries – for as long as the course of the river remained a 'mystery'.

Bascom obviously did not think Ifa came from the north. Nevertheless he skated around the problem of Ifa's origins: "The purpose here" he said in his Introduction to *Ifa Divination* "is neither to deny a historic relation between the many modes of divination employing sixteen basic figures, nor to attempt to determine the ultimate origin of Ifa."

In a letter to this author in 1975 a few years before he died, Bascom commented that: "Ifa divination is regarded as autochthonous". Autochthonous is a strong word meaning *'originating where found; indigenous'*, synonymous with *native*. Bascom had previously noted the similarities between *Bwe* and *Ifa*, and it is difficult to accept that he felt as strongly about *Ife's* Nigerian origins as Craddock and Co had been about the "indigenous design and technology" employed in the making of the Igbo Ukwu bronzes. One suspects that in the 1960's, when he was writing his monumental work on Ifa, he was wary of being ridiculed if he suggested a connection - direct or indirect - between people in the Pacific, and the Yoruba in Nigeria. By implication he seemed to be distancing himself from such a view, at the same time not wanting to be drawn willy-nilly into the 'politically correct' camp.

As we have seen, *Ifa* is only one of many facets of African culture with strong connections to the East; and however hard it will be for some Africanists to swallow the notion, one day they will have to accept that migrants from the Indonesian Islands did far more than just settle in Madagascar. They will have to look more generously on the view that our Phantom Voyagers penetrated deeply into the African continent from the east coast; that they rounded the Cape of Storms; and that they spread significant elements of their culture throughout a very large part of sub-Saharan Africa.

FOOTNOTES

Chapter 1. Ancient Mariners.

1   Peter Bellwood. *Prehistory of the Indo-Malaysian Archipelago.*University of Hawaii Press. Revised edition 1997. P.187, plus earlier article *The Peopling of the Pacific.* by same author in 'Scientific America'. (date or issue no. not on copy sent me) . Unless otherwise stated I took Bellwood as the authority on the early movements of people in the region.

2   James Hornell. '*The Origins and the Ethnographic Significance of the Indian Boat'.* In the Memoirs of the Asiatic Society of Bengal, Vol 7 1920. Prof. Das Gupta wrote (In the Journal of the Asiatic Society of Bengal Vol XX11 1926.) of the striking similarity of a number of ancient sedentary games played in the   central provinces of India, and those of Sumatra. (Bagchi. *Pre-Aryan and Pre-Dravidian in India.*)

3   Hornell is not alone in his Polynesian/Indian hypothesis. See: G. Coedes *The Indianised States of Southeast Asia.* Notes to page 8. Coedes cites Peter V. van Stein Callenfels ; Heine Gelden; and Nicholas J. Krom.)

4   Pierre-Yves Manguin. *Pre-modern Southeast Asian Shipping in the Indian Ocean: The Maldives Connection.* New Directions in Maritime History Conference. Fremantle, Dec. 1993. Hornell had indirect support for this supposition from Manguin who wrote: "As far as I can ascertain there are two possible explanations for such close similarities between South-East Asia and Maldivian traditions:

a)   The Maldivian techniques could have been introduced by Austronesian speaking shippers of insular South-East Asia that were still regular visitors to the archipelago in the 16th century, either on a trade circuit to and from the Maldives or on their way to the western half o=f the Indian Ocean, and specifically to Masdagascar.

b)   Both the Maldivian tradition and that of Insular South East Asia could belong to one broader tradition that would earlier have encompassed all the eastern part of the Indian Ocean, including possibly the East coast of India. I have discussed elsewhere this hypothesis, basing myself mostly on a shared thesaurus of nautical terms on both sides of the Bay of Bengal.".

Footnotes

Chapter 2. India, Rome and the Mediterranean World.

1 I have followed the orthodox 'Mortimer Wheeler' route down the Indus Valley. Current archaeological view seems to be that the Indus Valley civilisation did not come to a sudden end with Aryans sweeping down from the north in a devastating onrush; but rather a) it might be very much older (3300 B.C.) than we are inclined to think, and b) that the Veda might have been written by the Indus people not by the 'newcomers'. See R. Meadow and M. Kenoyer. National Geographic Mag. June 2000 as a starter reference.

2 Radha Kumud Mookerji. *Indian Shipping: A History Of The Sea-Borne Trade And Maritime Activity Of The Indians From The Earliest Times.* Longmans. 1912

3 V Kanakasabhai,.. *The Tamils Eighteen Hundred Years Ago.* 1904

4 A.L Basham,. *The Wonder that was India* 1954. Sidgwick & Jackson.

5 John Keay,. *A History of India.* Harper Collins. 2000. A useful general history.

6 In correspondence, Professor S.U. Deraniyagala wrote: "Sri Lankans (Sinhalese) were never known as sea-farers. They probably used intermediaries to travel abroad (Tamil, Arabs), eg. to the court of Claudius." But Prof. Deraniyagala seems not to have considered the more likely probability that these 'intermediaries' might have been Indonesians.

7 G.R. Tibbetts, *Pre-Islamic Arabia and South East Asia* in The Journal of the Royal Asiatic Society, Malayan Branch. Vol XX1X, Pt 3 1956. P. 192.

8 "Drawings by Garth Denning after B.Landström, Ship of the Pharaohs, 1970, from The Boat Beneath the Pyramid by Nancy Jenkins, Thames and Hudson Ltd, London"

9 Giorgio Buccellati, in an E-mail to me dated 11th April 2002.

10 Julian Reade, in the introduction of *The Indian Ocean in Antiquity* 1996. And in conversation with Dr Finkel at the British Museum.

11 Lionel Casson. *Ancient Naval Technology and the Route to India* in Rome and India – The Ancient Sea Trade U. of Wisc. 1991. Casson notes that the southwest monsoon, according to the U.S. Hydrographic Centre, "may well be the strongest and most persistent winds over any water area of the globe". He goes on, "Marine insurance rates, which vary between 1 and 1.75 percent during the northeast monsoon, rise to 20 percent by the end of May when the southwest monsoon has set in, and, during the next three months, insurance is not available at any

Footnotes For Page 15-26

price. By September, when the winds have begun to quiet down, it again offered at about the same rate as in May." "Arab ships in that age used a different schedule for getting to India. They prudently delayed departure until the end of August and did their sailing over open water in September when the northwest monsoon has lost a good deal of its bite." See also: G.R. Tibbetts *Pre-Islamic Arabia and South East Asia*. "…most scholars would agree that (the monsoons) were used by the countries of the East centuries before the Greeks entered into competition with them", and therefore before Hippalus' supposed 'discovery' of them sometime in the first century.

12 R, Sewell quoted in Mookerji. P.82

13 Kenneth R Hall ,.. *Maritime and State Development in Early Southeast Asia* p. 29 U. of Hawaii. 1985

14 C. Glover., *Recent Archaeological Evidence for Early Maritime Contacts between India and Southeast Asia* . (Article sent to me without dates or other information. I think it is 1993)

15 R.K Mookerji. *Indian Shipping…* : and Himanshu Prabha Ray. *'Early Coastal Trade in the Bay of Bengal'* from The Indian Ocean in Antiquity 1996.

16 C. Glover, *'Recent Archaeological Evidence …..*

Chapter 3 Cinnamon and Cassia.

1 The best general account of the spice trade in this period is still J. Innes Miller's. *The Spice Trade of the Roman Empire* . Oxford, Clarendon Press. 1969. P. 48

2 The Tanzanian archaeologist, Felix Chami, has written several articles mentioning early off-shore settlements: *Graeco-Roman Trade Link and the Bantu Migration Theory* in 'Anthropos' [Freiburg] Vol 94 Part 1-3 1999 p 205-215: *The Graeco-Romans and Paanchea'Azania: sailing in the Erythraean Sea* in 'Red Sea Trade and Travel', The British Museum Oct 2002.: and an article in the African Archaeological Review, Vol 20, No 2 June 2003.

3 In Papua New Guinea there is a vessel known as a *lakatoi* which is made up of anything from 3 to 14 large, closely spaced, dugout canoes lashed together and secured by heavy beams passing through gunwale holes (See: *A Dictionary of the World's Watercraft*. The Mariners Museum. Newport News.). These maybe 65 feet long and fifty feet wide, usually with two mast set for 'crab-claw' sails or rectangular sprit-sails, steered by a heavy central steering paddle, and one on the quarter. Heavy

Footnotes

matting formed a stable floor across the raft, and there were shelters for the crew. When they reached their destination they were often taken apart and the canoes used individually for fishing, etc, then re-assembled for the journey home.

4 L Casson.. Trans. *The Periplus Maris Erythraei*…: Princeton. 1989 44:15.4-5..and 60: 20.7-10 The three ports lay beyond the very shallow waters that divide Ceylon from India. Roman and Greek vessels would not have been able to negotiate this channel, and would have had to sail round Ceylon to reach them. Goods from the Med. were therefore transhipped on the west coast and carried up the Coromandel coast in shallow draft boats such as the *sangara*.. The fact that the author of the Periplus mentions no large ocean- going boats in the northern ports of the west coast is of considerable significance. One feels that if they existed, he would have said something about them.

5 E.H Warmington. *Commerce between the Roman Empire and India* 1928. It was revised in 1974; but it is probable that his passages on Indian shipping were unchanged.

Allied to the story of cinnamon and cassia, but with some interesting differences, is the story of cloves which, perhaps because they came from even further away than cinnamon, retained an air of mystery and excitement for a period spanning thousands of years.

Until late in the 18th century A.D., cloves were *only* grown in some of the tiny islands of the Moluccas in the furthermost eastern parts of Indonesia. They are the unopened flower buds of a type of myrtle, *Eugenia aromatica* ,a tree that grows to about twenty five or thirty feet in height. Though not recorded in the Periplus, Pliny mentions them as being available in Rome in his time. As to how they got to Rome, Innes Miller, in *The Spice Trade of the Roman Empire*, (Oxford. Clarendon Press. 1969) had this to say about them:-

"The Malay language, which is native to the Malay Peninsular and Sumatra and from an early age has covered the coastwise trading districts of the entire Archipelago, has two names for cloves which point to the history of the trade. The one is chengkeh, probably of Chinese origin, the other lawang, which is related to the Sanskrit lavanga. Some authorities hold that lavanga (like karpura for camphor) is more likely to be derived from the Malay than vice versa. These names suggest a dual direction of the early Indonesian trade – to China via the Philippines, and to India and Ceylon via some port in Sumatra or on the west coast of the Malay Peninsular.

There was also, it appears, a direct route from Java, across the southern Indian Ocean, to East Africa via Madagascar, used for the shipment of cinnamon and other far eastern spices ..."

Innes Miller's suggestion that the 'southern route' was via Madagascar is clearly wrong for reasons that will emerge. On the other hand his view that there might have been a direct route from Indonesia to the Horn of Africa, and that cloves came with, or along the same route as cinnamon, makes eminently good sense, despite the fact that Pliny made no mention of cloves as cargo on his 'rafts'. One can only ponder the possibility that Indonesians may have been trading in the Indian ocean since far, far earlier times than we are generally aware of. But is there any other evidence?

Chapter 4. China and the Kun-lun-po.

1 J. Needham. *Science and Civilisation in China*. Cambridge 1954. Unless otherwise mentioned, Needham was the source of all references to China.

2 Oliver W. Wolters. *Early Indonesian Commerce: a study of the origins of Srivijaya*. Cornell U. Press. 1967. A mine of information about Southeast Asia.

3 O.W. Wolters. *Early Indonesian Commerce.....*

4 O.W. Wolters. *Early Indonesian Commerce.....*

Chapter 5. Jonques and Prahus and other little Ships.

1 Pierre-Yves Manguin. Unless otherwise stated, all marine archaeological references are from various articles by Manguin, including:

   a. *The Southeast Asian Ship: an Historial Approach* in The Journal of South east Asian Studies. Xi/2 1980 p.267

   b. *Southeast Asian Shipping in the Indian Ocean During the First Millennium A..D.* in 'Tradition and Archaeology'. ed. Hamanshu Ray and Jean-Francois Salles. In 'Proceedings of the International Seminar – Seafaring in the Indian Ocean'. New Delhi. 1994. P 184.)

   c. *Pre-modern Southeast Asian Shipping in the Indian Ocean: The Maldives Connection*. New Directions in Maritime History Conference. Fremantle, Dec. 1993

2 This was pointed out to me by Adrian Horridge - an Australian biological scientist with well over two hundred scientific publications to his name; but an abiding secondary interest in Indonesian boats. His

Footnotes

book The Prahu Oxford University Press. 1981, is a standard work on the subject in addition he has published numerous articles and papers on the subject, most of which can be found in the library of the Maritime Museum at Greenwich, England. I am grateful to him also for considerable correspondence over the years. Manguin and Horridge have been my main sources, though there is a wealth of other material available.

Chapter 6 The Early Indonesian States

1   O.W. Wolters *Early Indonesian Commerce*. Cornell University. 1967 p. 37 ff. Wolters has been the primary source of information for this chapter.

2   Kenneth R Hall. *Maritime Trade and State Development in early Southeast Asia*. University of Hawaii. 1985 p. 48. Kenneth Hall's book is also essential reading.

3   J Keays. *India: a history*.... Harper-Collins 2000 p. 194

4   A.L Basham.. *The Wonder that was India* 1985 ed. P. 374

5   G.Coedes *The Indianised States of Southeast Asia* Hawaii. 1968 Indispensable general background in conjunction with Wolters and Hall.

6   David Keys. *Catastrophe*. Arrow Books, 1999. – a well researched, and convincing, account of how a cataclysmic eruption in the Sunda Strait disrupted life, and changed events, around the world in the sixth and seventh centuries. The story of the 'catastrophe' is backed by impressive documentary evidence as well as ice-core and tree-ring evidence from around the world. D.K. was the Science Editor of the Independent newspaper in England.

7   K Hall. *Maritime Trade* p.76

Chapter 7. Srivijaya and the Sea Nomads

1   O.W. Wolters. *Early Indonesian Commerce*. ... p.235

2   K. Hall. *Maritime Trade and State Development in Early Southeast Asia*. p.10

3   O.W. Wolters. *Early Indonesian Commerce*. p. 239

4   David E Sopher. *The Sea Nomads – A study of the Maritime boat people of Southeast Asia*. National Museum of Singapore. 1965 (reprint 1977). Unless otherwise stated my information on the Sea Nomads comes exclusively from this book. See also: Clifford Sather. *The Bajau Laut. Adaptation, History, and Fate in a Maritime Fishing Society of South-*

Footnotes For Page 54-63

eastern Sabah. OUP. Kuala Lumpur. 1998

5 Some observers say that the Bajau, Bugi and Makassarese only moved to their present homeland on the south-west coast of Sulawezi in recent times and that their names might be of recent origin. But at the same time nobody seems to doubt their ancient-ness. In reality there is no way of telling where their 'base' was or what they called themselves two thousand years ago. There is, however, no reason to believe that they are a new flash in history's pan; in fact the number of Bajau toponyms; their wide distribution; and the variations in language and customs that have developed in their various homelands suggests that they must be very ancient.

6 Adrian Horridge, *The Prahu.* Including also the following two paragraphs.

7 Jacqueline Andrew Lineton. Unpublished S.O.A.S. thesis 984 – 356203. *'An Indonesian Society and its Universe: a study of the Bugis of S. Sulawesi.'*

8 A Horridge. *The Prahu.* p.18

9 D Sopher. . *The Sea Nomads....* p 323.

10 George Windsor Earl in 1837. Quoted in Sopher p 323.

11 Pierre-Yves Manguin.

12 K.A. Adelaar. *"Malagasy Culture-History: some Linguistic Evidence".* p.492. in "The Indian Ocean in Antiquity" Ed. J. Reade 1996. . Wolters. *Early Indonesian Commerce..* p.16. also mentions these inscriptions of Palembang and Bangka which date to 682 and 686, neatly spanning the date – 683 – of the great *siddhayatra.*

13 O.W. Wolters. *Early Indonesian Commerce.* p. 348.

14 K. Hall, *Maritime and State Development....* p. 195

15 R.K. Mookerji, *Indian Shipping.* p. 123. One wonders whether Indonesian sailors in the pay of the Indians had a hand in this expedition. A naval battle such as this was so out of character for the Indians!

16 O.W.Wolters . *Early Indonesian Commerce.* pps 250, and 346 and Hall *Maritime and State Development....* p.194.

Part 2

Chapter 8 The Zanj.

1 L.Casson, . *The Periplus Maris Erythraei.* Princeton U. Press. 1989

2 Anthony H. Christie, *Minutes of the African History Seminar,* S.O.A.S.

Footnotes

Nov. 4th 1959

3 Paul Wheatley, . *Analecta Sino-Africana Recensa* in Chittick and Rotberg. East Africa and the Orient. P.104 - 107

4 Paul Wheatley, . *Analecta*..... p 87

5 J Wansborough. . *Africans and the Arab Geographers* in 'Language and History in Africa'. ed. David Dolby. Frank Cass & Co 1970 p. 97 ff.

6 Marina Tolmacheva. *The Zanj Language.* Tanganyika Notes and Records.(?) 1975; *Toward a Definition of the term Zanj.* Azania Vol XX1, 1986 pp 105 - 113; Dictionary of the Middle Ages, vol 12 (1989). Pp 738 -740.
    Also : *The Origin of the Name Swahili.* Tanganyika Notes and Records, No 77, 1976. pp. 27 – 37. In this, Tolmacheva points out the meaning of the name 'Swahili' – derived from the plural form – sawahil- of the Arabic *sahil* or *sahel.* [the word 'Sahel' in West Africa simply means the southern 'coast' or boundary, of the Sahara desert]. The word, referring to the coast of East Africa, first appears in Arab writings in the 9th century when al-Jahiz (d. 869) described Pemba and Zanzibar: "Indeed you have never seen Zanj who are the real kind. What you saw was merely captives from the coasts (sawahil) of Qanbalo (Pemba) ... You have never seen yet a single inhabitant of Lanjuya (Uuguja), either from the coast (sawahil) or from the people of the interior."
    It was not until Ibn Batutta's time (14th century) that the word 'Sawahil' was used as a toponym, i.e. to refer to the 'people of the coast'. Mark Horton and John Middleton, in their definitive book "*The Swahili*", fudge the issue and imply that the Swahili, as a recognised people, date back many centuries before this. But Tolmacheva's meticulous research seems the more reliable.

7 Marina Tolmacheva. *The African Waq Waq: Some Questions regarding the Evidence.* Bulletin d'Information Fontes Historical Africanae. No 11/12 (1987/88) 9. Tolmacheva traced approximately 20 references to the Waq Waq in Arab documents. She points out that much of Idrisi's work derives from al-Masudi (956 A.D.), but not all, whereas all subsequent references seem to be derived from Idrisi. Though proof is lacking, the general consensus that the Waq Waq came from Indonesia seems to be acceptable. Tolmacheva's literal translation of Masudi's *Muruj al-dhabab* includes a passage in which the Zanj and the Waq Waq are linked. "The Zanj settled in this section and their places of habitation adjoin Sofala. The latter is the extremity of the land of the Zanj, and to it reach the

vessels of the Omanis and Sirafis, and she is the farthest of their destinations in the lower parts of the Sea of al-Zanj .... Similarly also the limits of the Sea of al-Zanj and the land of Sofala and the extremes of the country of the Waq Waq; and this is a land abounding in gold, abounding in miracles, and the Zanj have made it the seat of their kingdom." This is of particular interest if there is merit in my contention that the Zanj were of mixed Indonesian/African stock.

The name 'Waq Waq' is interesting, and I have my own theory as to its origins. The dictionary of the World's Watercraft compiled by the Mariners Museum in Newport News, devotes no less than 10 close-typed columns to outrigger canoes from Indonesia to Hawai'i with names similar to Waq Waq. To list a selection starting with: "*vaka. Pacific Ocean.* General term for a single or double-outrigger canoe." Then: single-outriggers of Tuamotu and the Marquesas in the eastern Pacific = *vaka.* Solomons in the western Pacific = *vaka.* Cook and Niue Islands in the central Pacific = *va'a or waka.* Fiji, single-outriggers = *vak.* Gilbert, single-outrigger = *wa.* Carolines, = *wa.* Kapingamarangi, = *waka* (*waka siu,* or 'long waka' for fishing). Papua New Guinea, Bismarck Archipelago, = *wa.* Vanuatu = *wa* or *waka.* Moluccas in Indonesia, = *waa.* Hawai'i the generic term for a single outrigger = *wa'a kaukahi* ... and so on. The double imperative is not an uncommon construction in Austronesian languages, and I believe 'Waq Waq' may be an example simply referring to the 'people of the outrigger-canoes'.

8 J. Spencer Trimmingham, *The Arab Geographers* in Chittick and Rotberg. 'East Africa and the Orient' P.138

Chapter 9. The Golden Days.

1 John N. Miksic *Old Javanese Gold.* Ideation 1989. P. 32 (quoting Groenveldt 1960:60) The quotation at the end of the paragraph is from the same source: page 31.

2 K. Hall. *Maritime Trade and State Development in Early Southeast Asia* ... p. 80

3 John Miksic. *Old Javanese Gold* Quoting van Bremmelen 1944:11, 105

4 Roger Summers,. *Ancient Mining in Rhodesia.* Museum Memoir 3. Salisbury 1969.

5 R.W van Bemmelen. *The Geology of Indonesia* Vol1. Gov. Printing Office, The Hague. 1949 p. 106. On the other side of the Indian Ocean, gold was only discovered in Madagascar at the end of the 19th

century, by the French. Government records state that in 1895 the total production was 8 kilos. By 1913 it had risen to 13 kilos! But not until the end of the first world war did it reach the slightly more significant figure of 260 kilos.

6 Brian Colless. *Were the Gold Mines of Ancient Java in Borneo?* Brunei Museum Journal. Condensed version in SE Asia section of 29th Int. Congress of Orientalists. Paris 1973. Titled '*Gold in Ancient Insulindia*' pp 146-157. See also Tom Harrisson. *Gold and Indian Influences in West Borneo* Journal Malayan Branch [Vol.XX11, Pt 1V 1949] Royal Asiatic Society . And an article by Th. Pigeaud entitled *Javanese Gold*. This was sent to me unmarked, with no mention of when, or in what, it was published.

7 Revil Mason. *Background to Transvaal Iron Age* Journal of the South African Institute of Mining and Metallurgy. Jan 1974 pp 211-216.

8 Eugenia W. Herbert, *Red Gold of Africa* . Wisconsin. 1984. P24/25 b

9 I.R. Phimister, *Pre-Colonial Gold Mining in Southern Zambezia: a Reassessment* in African Social Research, 21 June 1976. Examples of Phimister's views favouring solely African origins: on p. 7, he says "So singularly expert were Shona prospectors that just about(quoting Roger Summers) 'every scrap of visible reef was exploited' in southern Zambezia." Summers in fact was comparing modern Bantu with, quote, "ancient" prospectors who exploited ... every scrap... implying that he believed 'these early prospectors' might not be Bantu. There is no mention, by implication or otherwise, that Summers thought they were Shona. Phimister quotes at least two other similar passages: (p. 9): "..their methods of prospecting" said West in 1965, referring to unspecified 'ancients' "... equalled, or were superior to, our modern ones"; and Fripp in 1911, who wrote:- "Rich gold-bearing quartz outcrops were, by the time of the white occupation, practically non-existent, having all been worked by the ancient miners." (Fripp 1911). Without any evidence Phimister attributed both these to the Shona. This sort of thing makes Phimister's work unreliable.

10 Roger Summers. *Ancient Mining in Rhodesia* All details and descriptions of mining below are from the same work.

11 Herodotus. *The Histories.* The Penguin Classics pp 217/8, or about three fifths the way through Book 3.

12 Roger Summers, *Ancient Mining...*

13 Cyril Hromnik, in his book *Indo –Africa* (Cape Town. 1981) goes to great length to justify his claim that virtually everything exotic in

southern Africa – particularly the ancient gold mines – was the work of Indians. The book contains some interesting points; but his case is fatally flawed by his unwillingness to accept anything other than Indian origins, sometimes based on the flimsiest – sometimes absurd – evidence.

14 Spencer Trimingham. . *The Arab Geographers and the East African Coast* in Chittick and Rotberg. East Africa and the Orient 1975. Africana Publishing, New York. 1975. P. 126 n. Who the 'Zunuj' were is not clear. Levtzion and Hopkins say 'Zunuj' is plural of Zanj. On the other hand Hunwick does not include it as such. See the later chapter on Zanj for more detail.

15 Roger Summers. *Ancient Mining...* Pp. 206-208.

16 Quoted from Basil Davidson *Old Africa Rediscovered.* P.136. David Whitehouse, in his *Sasanian Maritime Activity.* in The Indian Ocean in Antiquity, ed. J. Reade. 1988. Pp 344-347. thought Idrisi might have been referring to Sasanian shipping coming from Uman.

17 Horton and Middleton. *The Swahili.* Blackwell. 2000. Note 35 p.216 Reads in part: "The type site in the south is Matola, close to the Mozambique coast, which has a first-century radiocarbon date, while other sites of the Matola tradition have radiocarbon dates which are contemporary. ... Several of the early sites in the south lie adjacent to the coast (e.g. St Lucia Lake sites, Mzonjani, Enkwazini, Maputo University Campus and Zitundo) and exploited maritime environments, and it is just possible that the eastern component of the Early Iron Age could spread south by boat and not overland as is normally thought." See also: Paul Sinclair. *Chibuene – An Early Trading Site in Southen Mozambique.* In Paideuma 28 1982 pp. 149-164.

18 Brian Colless. *Were the Gold Mines of Ancient Java in Borneo?* Brunei Museum Journal. Condensed version in SE Asia section of 29th Int. Congress of Orientalists. Paris 1973. Titled *Gold in Ancient Insulindia* pp 146-157.

19 *The Travels of Marco Polo* Book 3. Chapter 7

20 www.indonesianheritage.com .and other sites listed under 'Wonoboyo Hoard'. Also ... Professor John N. Miksic on an internet site re Javanese gold: "The almost total silence with regard to old Javanese gold is in stark contrast to its importance in Java and its worldwide fame in ancient times. Thus, Indian and Greek texts dating from the first centuries of our era describe Java as being rich in grain and gold. This is corroborated by the numerous finds of old Javanese gold. In fact, gold

Footnotes

objects by far outnumber any other ancient Javanese remains. They consist of coins, jewellery, ritual objects, and images of gods. Gold items were apparently available to broad layers of society, although Java seems to have imported its gold from elsewhere, probably Sumatra or Kalimantan, for only few deposits of gold and no traces of ancient gold mining have been found on the island.". It is probable that Miksic and others have not considered the possibility of the gold having come from the Zimbabwe mines in the days when there was regular traffic between Sumatra/Java [Srivijaya] and Africa/Madagascar.

Chapter 10. Who are the Malagasy?

1 K.A. Adelaar 'Malagasy Culture-History: some Linguistic Evidence', in The Indian Ocean in Antiquity' J. Reade ed. 1996. P 487.

2 Otto Chr. Dahl. Malgache et Maanjan. Oslo 1951 p27)

3 Christian Gonner . Resource Management in a Dyak Benuaq Village, etc. Eschborn 2000 P3. (6a) and A.B. and Judith M. Hudson 'The Ma'anyan of Paju Epat' in Essays on Borneo Societies . Hull monograms on S.E. Asia 7 1978 .pp 215-232

4 A.B. Hudson, Padju Epat – The Ma'anyan of Indonesian Borneo. Michigan State U. 1972.

5 A.B. Hudson, Padju Epat p 36

6 Otto Dahl. Malgache et Maanjan.... p.372 "Les ressemblances avec le maanjan ne resolvent pourtant pas tous les problemes du malgache. Il y a dans le malgache des elements qui semblent nous orienter vers Celebes. Mais une nation qui a pousse ses expeditions maritime jusqu'en Afrique, a certainement pu, longtemps auparavant, traverser le detroit de Macassar, et a subi l'influence des langues de Celebes."

7 This word is usually mispronounced. It is made up of kisima(the well) and –juu (upper – maybe the most northerly?), with the emphasis on juu as in Jew. *As an indication of the lack of importance of the Bugi, the Bajau, the Ma'anyan, and the Bajun in the eyes of contemporary historians, in nearly 17,000 pages of small text in the Unesco General History of Africa; The Cambridge History of Africa; and the Cambridge History of Southeast Asia, I can find no references to the Buginese, the Bajau or the Maanyan, and no mention of the Bajun people. There are just three very brief mentions of the Bajun Islands!

8 Vinigi L Grottanelli,. Pescatori Dell 'Oceano Indiano. Rome 1955 p.11. "Sarebbe a quel conto piu naturale interpretare il ba- come il noto prefisso plurale bantu: senonche in tuyta l'area bantu nord-orientale il

Footnotes For Page 88-95

prefisso plurale della 1a classe (e quindi dei gentilize) e wa- o va-, non mai ba- . Comunque, il fatto linguistico decisivo che va tenuto presente a questo: qualunque ne sia l'orine etimologica, bajuni, nella lingua locale, parlatta e scritta, non e un plurale composto con il normale prefisso ba-, a cui quindi corrisponderebbe un singulari mujuni, m'juni: forme, queste, inesistenti." Etc.

9 James Kirkman. *'Archaeological Excavations on the Coast of Kenya'*. In Chittick and Rotberg. East Africa and the Orient . 1975 AND Men and Monuments on the East African Coast. London 1964

10 Mark Horton. *'Asiatic Colonisation of the East African Coast: The Manda Evidence.'* Journal of the Royal Asiatic Society of Great Britain and Ireland. 2 (1986) .pp201-213 In East Africa the rectangular Swahili house is considered an instance of 'borrowing' from Indonesia. The Bajun houses differ from others, as described by Horton and Middleton in their book "The Swahili" p. 125/6/7:- "Around virtually every town there are areas of mud and thatched houses, which are spatially distinct from the stone houses. In these live non-patricians, ranging from the families of ex-slaves, to high status masharifu of recent arrival, and those who have lived in the town for a very long time but never gained patrician status. These houses tend to have a different plan to the stone houses, incorporating a central passage with rooms leading off on either side." In subsequent pages they are referred to as "'Bajuni' type", or "'Bajuni' plan". Shades of the sea nomad's long house?

11 Columbus noted the same technique in use by the Arawak Indians in Hispaniola. See also 'plantains' below

12 A. Horridge *The Prahu*. Chap 24 Table 1 No's 47 and 48 Outrigger boom: Buginese - *buratang*. Mandar - *baratang*. Baju – *baratahana*. Connector piece: Makassarese - *tengo*. Baju – *tetenkona*.

13 James Hornell. *'The Sea-going Mtepe and Dau of the Lamu Archipelago'*. The Mariner's Mirror ..., Vol 27 1941 pp 54-68. A *dau-mtepe* was used in 1866 by Dr Livingstone to transport his 'six camels, three buffaloes, and a calf, two mules, and four donkeys' from 'Stinkibar' as he called Zanzibar, to the mouth of the Rovuma River for the start of his journey to the interior. A *dau-mtepe* is a version that incorporates a number of Arabian dhow features. Both the mtepe and the *dau-mtepe* look slightly 'wrong' to my eye, and I sometimes wonder whether the *mtepe* was not originally a *prahu* with two steering oars mounted on a wide transom in lieu of its unwieldy looking rudder. The Indonesian *Pajala* hull whose design is "not far removed from the traditional boats of a thousand years

ago" is double ended like the mtepe: [see: Adrian Horridge '*The Prahu*'] Boats such as the old Bugis *prahu* were built in this manner; with either a platform or the simpler 'Mandar' rudder supports across the stern. Most, if not all, the traditional *prahus* of western Indonesian and the Philippines had tilted rectangular sails. See also a description in Horton/Middleton's "The Swahili" p.95. "Those [*mtepe*] encountered by Vasco da Gama in 1498 were described as 'large, without decks; they are not nailed and sail tightly bound with esparto cord; and their boats the same. Their sails are of palm matting and their mariners have Genoese needles by which to steer, and quadrants and sea charts.'"

14 V.L.Grottanelli. *Pescatori....* p15
15 A. Horridge. *The Prahu* 1982
16 Marco Polo. "*Travels*". Ed. W. Marsden 1946. In the index 'Madagascar' is written thus: 'Madagascar. See Magastar'. There is no further comment; but presumably it appears as 'Magastar' in the original. Marco Polo dictated his 'Travels' between 1296 and 1299 to a certain Rustician of Pisa when they were both in prison in Genoa. Though originally dictated in 'very bad French' (according to John Masefield in his Introduction) over a hundred different versions were subsequently published in French, Italian, and Latin '...and no two of them are alike.' The name Madagascar is generally assumed to be a corruption of Mogadishu. The English version referred to above makes no mention of any places called 'Mogadishu', 'Magadaxa', or 'Mogadoxa' as Mogadishu has sometimes been called. although there is obviously considerable confusion (his account is based on hear-say) between the Great Island' and the coast of Zanj on the other side of the 'prodigiously dangerous' channel between Madagascar and Africa, there is no obvious reason why there should, even in his confusion, be any connection whatsoever between Madagascar' and Mogadishu.

Chapter 11. More about the Malagasy
1 Jared Diamond *Guns, Gems and Steel.* P. 381 Vintage 1998
2 Horton and Middleton. *The Swahili.*
3 Raymond Kent. *Early Kingdoms in Madagascar* 1500-1700. Pp 263 and 247 respectively. I have quoted Raymond Kent's work extensively as he is one of the few people who has deeply researched the Indonesia/Africa links. and he has done so with more flair, courage and perspicacity than most of his contemporaries. No one is infallible, and Raymond Kent is probably no exception. His work has been frequently

excoriated by fellow academics. In a letter to Maurice Bloch in 1998 I rashly commented: "I have always rather assumed that he (Kent) is THE guru on Madagascar – apart from yourself." The reply came back: "Kent's book contains many valuable points and many fanciful ones. It is difficult to separate them. This perhaps explains why it is avoided." But Bloch's own views are open to criticism; e.g. on the Vazimba.(see note 6 below); and his own published studies of Madagascar are too narrowly focused to contribute much to my subject.

Far less acceptable, however, was an unnecessarily snide 1000 word footnote by Aidan Southall, then Professor of Anthropology at Wisconsin University, at the end of his chapter "The Problem of Malagasy Origins" in Chittick and Rotberg's 1975 East Africa and the Orient p.214. ... a sort of Uriah Heap effort that initially extolled Kent's researches that "provide the most impressive analysis and reassessment of Malagasy history which has appeared in English", then proceeded to take them apart in a 'Holier than Thou' manner which makes very unsavoury reading. Southall's own position (based more on speculation than detailed research) favoured the notion of direct voyages from Indonesia to Madagascar. "It still seems more logical and economical" wrote Southall, "to assume a first migration to Madagascar direct from Indonesia, laying the indelible foundations of Malagasy Indonesian speech, followed by migrations of Indonesians to the East African coast, who later brought domestic animals, customs and vocabulary items from Africa to Madagascar." Today Southall's own views are untenable; and it is sad that such people set out deliberately – and with considerable success - to damage Kent's reputation.

Raymond Knezevich Kent (b. 1929) is an active and emotional Serb nationalist, and minor member of the old Serbian 'Royal Family'. At the age of 15 he was expelled from school by the Communists authorities, and banned from further education for 7 years. He escaped from Yugoslavia in 1945, and found his way to the USA where (so it is said) he changed his name to 'Kent' because his place in the Serb Royal Family was roughly the equivalent of that of our own Duke of Kent in England. He is fluent in five languages. When his Early Kingdoms in Madagascar was first published (with a run of only 500!) it was largely ignored by Malgachisant reviewers; possibly (so I was told by a longstanding resident of Madagascar) because at the time he only had an American Political Science degree. (He subsequently earned one of the first Doctorates of African History in the US, and until retirement

Footnotes

in 1991 to concentrate on Serb affairs, taught at U.C. Berkeley).
Another informant, Mervyn Brown, (one-time British Ambassador in
Tananarive and author of the excellent Madagascar Rediscovered and A
History of Madagascar) described Kent (in a letter in 1979) as 'a
delightful and stimulating companion' whose researches were 'most
enlightening, although marred by his aggressive manner and almost
impenetrable style.' There is truth in the last remark; but for anyone
who takes the trouble to venture into his jungle there is a payload of
gold to be found.

4   Emil Birkeli. '*Les Vazimba de la Cote Ouest de Madagascar*'. in Memoires
de l'Academie Malgache Fasc. XX11. 1936 pp 7-65.

5   R. Singer, O.E. Butz-Olsen, P.Brain and J. Saugrain. '*Physical Features,
Sickling and Serology of the Malagasy of Madagascar*'. American Journal
of Physical Anthropology. XV 1. March 1957. Pp 91-124. Also (quoted
in detail in R.K. Kent): "The Possibilities of Indonesian Colonies in
Africa with special reference to Madagascar" in "Mouvements de
Populations dans L'Ocean Indien" Quatrieme Congres de l'Association
Historique Internationale de l'Ocean Indien, etc. 1972

6   Maurice Bloch. Personal correspondence. 10th Oct 1998. "There is no
reason to believe Vazimba existed. The word is used in different senses.
Of course the Vezo did and do exist."

7   M.E. Ralaimihoatra, '*Le Contexte et la Signification du Terme Vazimba
dans l'Histoire de Madagascar*' Bulletin de l'Academie Malgache. Sept
1971 p.183/4

8   *Madagascar: or Robert Drury's Journal during Fifteen Years Captivity on
that Island.* London 1790

9   Mervyn Brown. *Madagascar Rediscovered.* P 118

10 Mervyn Brown *Madagascar Rediscovered...* Chapter 10

11 R.K. Kent *From Madagascar to the Malagasy Republic.* Thames and
Hudson. 1962 p. 28

12 I received this information about the Mahafaly in a letter from the
British Ambassador in Madagascar, and realising that (to the best of
knowledge) this was not a Bantu custom, I wrote to Isaac Schapira to
find out if he had heard of it among the pre-Bantu peoples. A letter
came back simply referring me to page 295 of his book (*The Khoisan
Peoples of South Africa*). "If a cow refuses to give milk, as may happen
when its calf has died prematurely, it is induced to do so by the
substitution either of another calf sewn up in a skin or merely of the
stuffed skin, or else somebody stands behind it and blows hard into its

vulva while the milking is taking place."

13 R.K. Kent *'Madagascar and Africa: 11. The Sakalava, Maroserana, etc.'*
J.A.H. 1X, 4. (1968) p.538.

14 H. Rusillon. *La Tromba – une culte dynastique avec evocation des morts chezz les Sakalaves de Madagascar...* p. 43 (my translation)

Chapter 12 From Madagascar to Africa...

1 David Beach, *The Shona and their Neighbours* Blackwell. 1994. P 214 and: Peter Garlake. *Great Zimbabwe* 1973. P. 11

2 Peter Garlake. *Great Zimbabwe.* P.162

3 Charles Bullock. *The Mashona* 1928, Bullock, fluent in the Shona language, was a Native Commissioner in Southern Rhodesia.

4 Henry Rusillon. *Un CulteDdynastique avec Evocation des Morts chez les Sakalaves de Madagascar – Le Tromba.* Paris 1912. According to Raymond Kent (Early Kingdoms in Madagascar. Page 50) " ... *tromba* comes out phonetically *tumba* (*toomba* with a terminal 'a' barely audible). A Sakalava possessed by *tromba* is said to be 'like dead', or a 'living corpse', an accurate impression of pitch phase in the trance and a statement of representing the dead. This very meaning applies to *mTumba/kiTumba* in the Ki-Ngwana dialect of Swahili, used as a commercial language from the Congo to Tanganyika. We still do not know the precise linguistic birthplace of *tromba,* but the general area of Africa in which it is used cannot be disputed."

5 P. Garlake. *Great Zimbabwe.* Thames and Hudson 1973 P 29.

6 G. Caton-Thompson. *The Zimbabwe Culture.* p 94 footnote.

7 R.P.Azais and R. Chambard. *Cinq Annees de Recherches Archaeologiques en Ethiopie* Paris 1931. In Sidamo and Wallamo they are all over the place. In 1960, with my associate Chris Konarski, we photographed many more around Lake Abaya when we were filming for a BBC program. One, in particular, was almost identical to that I have illustrated from Azais and Chambard; but about half the height.

8 G.W.B. Huntingford. *The Hagiolithic Cultures of East Africa,* in "The Eastern Anthropologist; a quarterly record of ethnography and folk culture", v.3, no 4, June 1950: pp.119- 136. (Lucknow).

9 James Kirkman. *Some Conclusions from Archaeological Excavation on the Coast of Kenya;* 1948 – 1966 in Chittick and Rotberg. "East Africa and the Orient".pp 229/230. The drawing of the pillar tombs is taken from a photo in J. Kirkman. "Men and Monuments on the East African Coast." London 1964.

Footnotes

Footnotes For Page 108-125

10 Missionaries in Madagascar are good sources of information – people such as L.Dahle, E. Birkeli, H.Rusillon, W.Ellis, J.Sibree, J. Richardson, and, more recently, Jim Hardyman, who was a great help to me in correspondence. Ellis, Sibree, O.Dahl, Richardson published both books and article in such journals as the Antanarive Annual in English. Virtually no trained British anthropologists have contributed to this particular subject on the Madagascar side… and it would be true to say that Americans such as Linton and Kent have probably contributed more than the French! On the Africa side there are literally thousands of books and articles on every aspect of Zimbabwe and the people around it/them.

11 Charles Poirier. *Vatolahy d'Ampasampirafy et d'Ankazomiranga en pays Betsileo* . Planche X1. "Memoires de L'Academie Malgache." XXV111 1939. This version is translated freely and edited. I have concentrated on the Ampasampirafy site as it is more general. The other vatolahy is that set up by Princess Ralavao, a libertine who takes lovers galore, and as the story goes, has a passion 'enthousiaste et immoderee pour le phallus'.

12 Roger Summers. *Inyanga: Prehistoric Settlements in Southern Rhodesia* Camb. U. Press 1958 p.12.

13 Robert. Soper. *Pits, Tunnels and Cattle in Nyanga. Etc.* in: South African Archaeological Bulletin 52 pp89 – 94 . 1997

14 Roger Summers. *Ancient Ruins and Vanished Civilisations of Southern Africa.* and p.32 Robert Soper. *Nyanga* 2002. The longest such furrow he found was 2 kms; and as few are associated with terraces he believes the latter were only rarely irrigated.)

15 Robert Soper discusses the pits in his *The Role of Cattle and Manure in the Agricultural Systems of the Nyanga Terrace Complex.* Zimbabwe Prehistory. 2001. On pages 164 and 165 of my book "Sanamu" I have given a description of the miniature cattle (Bos Brachyceros - said to have come originally from Egypt), belonging to the Fon of Bum in the Cameroons. His herd consisted of six cows and a bull, and they were more dear to him than anything he possessed. Standing c. three feet, (90 cms) to the shoulder, they lived outside like any other cows; but - lured by a biscuit - they would happily follow him inside his palace when he wished. They were prized for their horns for drinking purposes. In 1959 they fetched about £10 each; but one in the old days might change hands for two slaves. If the Muozi cattle of Nyanga were prized for the same reason, a) they would not have been polled until fully grown, and

b) the tunnel entrances to the pits would not have been so narrow that the cattle risked damaging their valuable horns on the rock walls.

16 A. *Grandidier Histoire de Madagascar* Paris. Vol.4 Tom 111 p 58f

17 Caliuzac *Essai sur les institutions et les droit Malgaches,* 1900 … quoting A. Grandidier

18 M. Bloch. *The Placing of the Dead.* P.8, and sections dealing with the tanindrazana.

19 J. Sibree. *Madagascar Before the Conquest.* Fisher Unwin. London 1896 P.320 ff. Sibree and others remark on the astonishing skill of the Betsileo at quarrying – and moving - stone. Immediately following the passage quoted he goes on: "The tombs of the rich are sometimes 15 or 16 foot square, and are quite on the surface of the ground, and the four walls and roof are formed of five immense stone slabs, which are brought from great distances, and involve almost incredible labour. I measured one slab of granite which was more than 18 feet long, 10 feet wide, and nearly 3 feet thick in some parts. I was once in a tomb 18 feet long, 14 feet wide and 10 feet high, formed of 5 stones, in one of which, to the west, had been cut an opening, and a rude stone door, working in stone sockets, had been fixed there. The finest memorial stone I saw was almost circular, and was 4 ft in diameter, and about 20 feet above the ground. Sometimes these stones are covered with carved oxen and birds." Amongst many others, H. Lormian, in his *L'Art Malgache* illustrates two other types of Bestsileo tombs… one is a pyramid, or cone, of stones roughly 10 feet high; the second is a very neatly constructed rectangular tomb made of high quality dry-stone work, rising about 6 feet above ground level. Clearly Betsileo tombs varied in design and construction, and as Sibree points out, only the very rich could have afforded such amazing creations as he describes.

20 M. Bloch. *Placing the Dead.* London 1971. P 145 ff. *Famadihana* is varied and complex. For many tribes it involves the transference of a corpse from its first burial place (where the body has been allowed to dry out) to the family tomb, usually after two years or so. "But *famadihana* is a particular Merina (and to a less extent the Betsileo) custom does not necessarily involve moving the body to another place – although this happens necessarily when the person has died abroad or in a distant place far from the family tomb. It is the removal of the corpse or corpses already in the tomb (many of them buried there in the first instance) at regular intervals of a number of years, for a family celebration after which the remains are wrapped in a new funeral cloth

and returned to the same tomb." (M. Brown: correspondence).
21 John Mack's *Island of the Ancestors*. British Museum publication. 1986. P.789
22 Ralph Linton. *The Tanala. A Hill Tribe of Madagascar.* P.177 Chicago 1933. It is interesting reading Linton's *Tanala* alongside Stayt's *The Bavenda* and Bullocks *The Mashona* to note numerous similar customs relating to burials.
23 Susan Denyer. *African Traditional Architecture*, Heinemann 1978. pp 62, 65 and 142. From personal observation the Iraqw house also had a security value inasmuch as when approached from behind they were often invisible until you were standing on the roof. Those built completely below ground level (like the one shown on the right)were very rare
24 R. Summers. *Ancient Ruins and Vanished Civilisations of Southern Africa* 1971. P. 73
25 R. Soper. *Nyanga* p. 143 ... after a description of one partial skeleton buried at Nyangui: "No other burials have been reported firmly associated with the Nyanga archaeological complex, apart from two slightly flexed burials in passages in a pit-structure at Mkondwe (Martin 1937) which appear to represent a different burial arrangement, and a few bones of a very young child in an upturned pot in the passage of a small pit-enclosure close to the present Ziwa Site Museum".

Chapter 13. The Music Trail
1 From a letter home after hearing a Chopi xylophone orchestra in Johannesburg.
2 A.M. Jones. *Africa and Indonesia*. Leiden 1971. This is essential reading for anyone seriously interested in Indonesian/African discussion. Father Jones brought forward numerous arguments to demonstrate the relationship between the music of Africa and Indonesia. But they did not insulate him from vehement criticism. Most hurtful to him were several vociferous attacks by an old colleague, Professor Mantle Hood. However in 1967 Jones countered these criticisms in a paper presented at the Conference on "East Africa and the Orient" held in Nairobi,(see *"The Influence of Indonesia: the Musicological Evidence Reconsidered".* A.M. Jones 1967)) in which he was able to show that Professor Hood had clearly misread his arguments; and to reply convincingly to other criticisms of a different nature. Despite this, brickbats continue even after his death, viz the biographical entry in

The New Grove's Dictionary of Music and Musicians':- " ... He has been criticised for the selection and analysis of his evidence, as well as for his view (in opposition to historical evidence) that the xylophone was introduced to Africa from Indonesia." One has to ask the author of the Groves article: What evidence? In the 'List of Writings' Groves omits Jones' well reasoned 1967 rebuttal of his critics, ('The Influence of Indonesia: etc) further damaging his reputation posthumously. It is sad to see this sort of thing in such an authoritative work as Groves, which at the time of writing has shown little interest in correcting this or other mistakes in connection with African music (Panpipes). It is also ironic that, despite its attacks on Father A.M. Jones, the establishment seems now to accept the Indonesian origins of the xylophone!

3   Letter from Andrew Tracey (Hugh Tracey's son).

4   Hugh Tracey. *Chopi Musicians* 1948. According to legend (T.V. Bulpin *The Golden Republic* quoted by G.M. Thain in the JSAI of Mand M January 1974) the Shona also worked ancient gold mines near Malalene in South Africa, about 100 miles west of the Chopi's present homeland. The Chopi connection with the Karanga, or Mocaranga, was also made by two early Portuguese missionaries, Father Andre Fernandes in 1560 and Friar Joao do Santos in 1586 – the latter describing their instruments called *mbira* in some detail. See also *Chopi Musicians* page 9, lines 11 and 12 re: similarity of Chopi and Karanga musical terminology.

5   Raymond Kent. *Early Kingdoms in Madagascar* ...

6   In 1948, Hugh Tracey compared the tunings of a Chopi xylophone (timbila) and a Karanga hand-piano (mbira) and found that the average tuning of the Chopi xylophone in southern Mozambique was virtually identical to that of the Karanga *mbira* in Zimbabwe, viz ....

Mozambique Xylophone (Chopi)							Tested by:	Tracey
0	176	345	519	680	854	1029		1200

Zimbabwe Hand piano (Karanga)							Tested by:	Tracey
0	176	346	519	675	853	1032		1200

7   A.M. Jones. *Panpipes and the Equipentatonic Pitch.* African Music va/1 1980 62-69

8   Jaap Kunst. *Music in Java.* The Hague 1970. Note on page 30 and P 376. Kunst wrote: "The instrument seems to be of Central-Asiatic origin, and to have spread over parts of Austronesia (and of South America) during the Han period (206BC – 220 AD) as a consequence either of migrations or commercial traffic." One wonders whether there

Footnotes

is significance in the single base-note *Hatong honghong* and the base-
note of the Barwe mbira in Central Africa: *nyonganyonga*
9   Andrew Tracey *The Nyanga Panpipe Dance* African Music. Vol 5, No
    1,1971.
10 Hans Fischer. *Sound Producing Instruments in Oceania.* Institute of
    Papua New Guinea Studies. 1983. pp 112-116.
11 A.M. Jones *Africa and Indonesia.* General discussion.
12 A.M. Jones. *Africa and Indonesia* for B, C. and D. J.F. Carrington. *A
    Comparative Study of some Central African Gong-Languages.* Brussels
    1949, For A.
13 J.F. Carrington. *Central African Gong Language...*
14 J.N. Lo-Bamijoko, *Classification of Igbo Musical Instruments, Nigeria.* in
    African Music Vol V1. Part 4 1987 pp19-41. Also: Groves Dictionary
    of Music under IGBO.
15 Jaap Kunst. *Music in Java.* Also on several internet sites.
16 R. Dick-Read. *Sanamu – Adventures in Search of African Art.* Rupert
    Hart-Davis 1964.
17 Kon. Instituut v/d Tropen. Pic No: 726.121.312: 78 No 10. Borobudur
    – 1Bb 89

Chapter 14. The Darker Side of Life.
1   J.H. Hutton. *West Africa and Indonesia: A Problem in Distribution* The
    Everard im Thurn Memorial Lecture delivered to the Scottish
    Anthropological and Folklore Society on April 10th 1947.
2   N . Levtzion and J.F.P.Hopkins. *Corpus of Early Arabic Sources...* p 298
    Ibn Battuta's descriptions of cannibalism on the upper reaches of the
    Niger suggest a more casual attitude as expressed below, in chapter 17.
3   Information on the Nok is taken from: Bernard Fagg. *Nok Terracottas.*
    Nigerian Museum, Lagos. 1977
4   B.R. Laurence. *Elephantiasis and Polynesian Origins* Nature Vol. 219 No
    5154. pp 561-563 Aug. loth 1968. Also, Letter from Dr Laurence,
    1978; plus A.M. Jones: Elephantiasis and Music in "African Music" Vol.
    5 No 2 1972.
5   J. Vansina *Paths in the Rainforests.* U. of Wisconsin Press. 1990...p. 60
    In a letter to me dated 'Madison le 5 july 2003' Jan Vansina made these
    points. "The view that Air has been the earliest site for iron smelting in
    West Africa is still accepted. The dates for Gabon and Cameroun are
    also still correct. For their explanation see ... Raymond Lanfranchi and
    Bernard Clist *Aux origines de lAfrique centrale,* Libreville, (Sepia)

Footnotes For Page 139-147

1991. The explanation for the Gabon estuary sites probably is that the technology spread downstream along the Ogooue first – alternatively it could have reached these spots by sea from further north. Jan Vansina had not, to the best of my knowledge, ever considered the possibility that the technology might have come from the south, which still seems to me to be a very possible alternative.

6   R. Oliver *The African Experience* Wiedenfeld 1991 p. 72

7   J. Vansina *Paths...*

8   S.U.Deraniyagala. *The Prehistory of Sri Lanka.* To be found at www.the-prehistory-of-sri-lanka.de/index.htm The author (M.A. Cantab; Postgrad Dip @Inst. Arch. London; PhD, Harvard) was assistant commissioner of the Arch. Survey dept in Sri Lanka from 1968 – 1983, and its Director General since 1992. ... with specific interest in Early Historic periods c. 1000 BC – 300 AD. His massive book has been described in the 'American Anthropologist' as "...the benchmark study on Sri Lankan prehistory for a long time to come."

9   Carl Schuster and Edmund Carpenter. *Patterns that Connect.* P. 281 Harry N. Abrams. New York. They illustrate a fine pre-Hellenic board from Cyprus with a male figure at one end and a female figure at the other.

10 The British Museum has a particularly fine collection.

11 I found this on a seemingly authoritative 'encyclopaedia' website; but with no source reference.

12 E. Torday. *On the Trail of the Bushongo.* P. 144 London. 1925

Chapter 15. Plantains and Yams.

1   G.P. Murdock. Africa: *Its People and their Culture History.* New York. 1959

2   I am indebted to Dr Roger Blench for information and bibliography on Musaceae.

3   Jan Vansina. *Paths in the Rainforests* 1990. Curiously the generic term for bananas and plantains in Madagascar is *kondro,* among the Merina – the 'purest' Indonesian stock in Madagascar – it is *akondro,* pronounced *a-koondru* Vansina suggests that this could have been borrowed from Swahili. But, although the root –*ko*- occurs in northern Swahili – viz *ninko* on the Tana river – the standard Swahili words covering 'bananas' are: Fruit = *ndizi*; plant = *mgomba*; bunch = *chane;* stem of the tree = *mkungu.* Either the Malagasy *kondro* came from Indonesia; or - if it came from Africa - it is more likely to have been

Footnotes

borrowed from Central Africa. This would tie in with assertions (Kent, Birkeli and others) that Indonesians penetrated deep into Africa before peopling Madagascar. Paradoxically it is amongst the more heavily 'Bantuised' Sakalava that one finds the closest survival from Indonesia - *utsi* or *untsi*.

4 John Carrington. *A comparative Study of some Central African Gong Languages.* Brussels 1949.

5 Vrydaghs & E. De Langhe. *Phytoliths: An Opportunity to Rewrite History.* Sent to me by Dr Peter Robertshaw without any indication where it was published. The two authors were working with C.M. Mbida and C.M. Mindzie who have published articles respectively in the *Journal of Archaeological Science* 27:151-162 and *Vegetation History and Archaeology* 10: 1-6

6 R. Blench. Personal correspondence. N.W. Simmonds is the author of several definitive works on the banana: *The Evoloution of the Bananas* 1962. Bananas 1966. *Evolution of Crop plants* 1976. With R.H. Stover ... *Bananas* 1987.

7 In his book *Lords of the Tiger Spirit* about the Caribs of Venezuela and Guyana, Neil Whitehead noted that Oviedo y Valdes was struck by the abundance of bananas along the Orinoco in Venezuela in 1520, and that they seem to have been there before the 'Christians' arrived. I put the thought to him that those who brought them to Africa might have extended their voyages of exploration from West Africa to South America, a journey that would not have been difficult for sailors of their experience. In an e-mail reply, N. W. had this to say: "Bananas ... were assumed (by Simmonds) to have come to the new world from Asia in 1700's... However, as you noted from my book, there is certainly evidence of bananas in America before that so the issue is open as to when exactly bananas may have first arrived – I think the west African origin in pre-Columbian times is quite possible but as so often in the new world the destruction of native society has left us with only circumstantial evidence."

8 Roland Oliver and J.D.Fage, *A Short History of Africa* Penguin edition 1975 p.107

9 Richard and John Lander. *Journal of an Expedition to Explore the Course and Termination of the Niger.* Vol 1 1832

10 The story was told by M.D.W. Jeffreys in 1956, and quoted by Keith Ray in: "The Archaeology of Contextual Meanings" ed. Ian Hodder. Cambridge. 1987

Chapter 16. The Bronzes of Igbo Ukwu

1　Thurston Shaw .*Unearthing Igbo-Ukwu.* OUP Ibadan 1977

2　According to H.R. van Heekeren *The Bronze Age of Indonesia,* Gravenhage, 1959 pages 20, 23, the ancient Dong Son gongs were made in more than one piece and joined. Likewise metal drums in Java and Bali – "The kettle drums show two vertical cast-seams; they were cast in two halves which are soldered together" To find out more about this technique I consulted Richard Blurton and Paul Cradock at the British Museum, but neither of them seemed to know about it.

3　Reminiscent of a 5-handled 'mimbo'-bin to hold palm wine for the Fon's society {kwifon} that I collected for the Bamenda museum. Others in the collection were of wood with geometric and animal designs, some of pottery, and some of fine basketwork waterproofed on the inside with clay.　In most cases great care had been lavished on their decoration. Most Bamenda mimbo bins ranged in height from about 18" -36".

4　See: *Metal Sources and the Bronzes from Igbo-Ukwu,* Nigeria. Journal of Field Archaeology/ vol 24 1997. Joint authors: Paul T. Cradock, Dept. of Scientific Research at the British Museum; metallurgy section.Janet Ambers, -ditto -dating section. Duncan R. Hook, -ditto -analytical chemist. Ronald M. Farquhar , Professor of Physics, University of Toronto. Vincent E. Chikwendu, University of Nigeria, head of Archaeology Dept. Alphonse C. Umeji, -ditto -Head of Geology Dept. Thurstan Shaw, (when Igbo-Ukwu was excavated) Head of Archaeology at Ibadan University.

Chapter 17. Sources of Igbo Genius

1　Donald Harden. *The Phoenicians. Pelican Books* 1971 p 167 "The only extant manuscript is no earlier than the 10th century and has been garbled by much scribal copying", says Harden. "Yet the story is so interesting and circumstantial that it has been widely commented on in modern times. Most scholars accept the basic story, but when it comes to identifying the places Hanno mentions and deciding how far Hanno penetrated, opinions differ." P. 163 He also states: "However important the debate is for the story of Phoenician exploration, it has no bearing on that of Phoenician colonisation, for this part of the journey had no lasting effects." P. 169

2　Herodotus. *The Histories.* trans. Aubrey de Selincourt. Penguin Books. 1954. P 114.

Footnotes

Footnotes For Page 160-170

3   E.W.Bovill *The Golden Trade of the Moors* Oxford, 1958, with James Wellard's *The Great Sahara* London 1964 together provide a wealth of information on the history of Sarahan exploration. Wellard and Bovill are sometimes at odds; Wellard feels the Romans may have reached Lake Chad; he does not credit the Romans with making as much use of the camel as Bovill; he believes the Romans made greater use of Negro slaves from the Sahara. J. Fage in his *History of West Africa* gives yet another angle.

4   Graham Connah *African Civilizations.* P. 135

5   J.D. Fage *History of West Africa* Cambridge 1957 pp 13-18

6   N. Levtzion *Ancient Ghana and Mali* (quoted in Connah, African Civilisations . p 115)

7   J.D. Fage *History...* p.18

8   J.D. Fage *History...* pp 34-39

9   Nehemia Levtzion *Arab Geographers, the Nile, and the History of Bilad al-Sudan..* In H. Erlich and I. Gershone, *The Nile: Histories, Cultures, Myths.* 1999 pp72.

10 N. Levtzion and J.F.P. Hopkins *Corpus of Early Arabic Sources for West African History..* Cambs U. Press 1981. page 298

11 N. Levtzion *Corpus....* p. 287

12 N. Levtzion *Corpus...* Note 21 p 415. Since W.D. Cooley, in his *Negroland of the Arabs* (1841) 'took it for granted'(Levtzion's words) that Yufi was a corruption of 'Nufi' meaning modern 'Nupe', one of the Hausa states, located opposite Yorubaland in the 'Y' between the Niger and the Benue, this assumption has barely been questioned. But there are good reasons for thinking otherwise. First: There are no Hausa people as such; just loosely integrated groups of different origins speaking the Hausa language, and living the Hausa way of life. As J.D. Fage said in his *History of West Africa* (p. 34):- "The Hausa states were never much of political account. They were always small and divided, often fighting among themselves...." Or, as Sir Alan Burns put it (*History of Nigeria* p. 47): "Although each state was independent of the others, they appear to have been bound together at intervals for mutual defense in a loose confederation, but there were constant internecine wars in which the fortunes of each rose and fell, none retaining for very long its precarious pre-eminence." Nupe was never one of the Hausa Bokwoi – the seven 'senior Hausa states': it was one of the Banza Bokwoi, the 'seven upstart states' none of which were known to have been great powers in the 14th century when Ibn Batutta was writing.

Second: Islam began to spread rapidly among the Hausa in the thirteenth (Burns) or fourteenth century (Fage) and was probably established in Nupe by Ibn Batutta's time, when they would no longer have been a threat. Conversely, the Ile Ife civilization was by that time 'already ancient' (Fage). It was the earliest of the Niger states to emerge; and the most long-lasting. "At its peak, it probably covered a greater area and encompassed more people than did Benin, Dahomey and Ashanti". It was the greatest of the four great forest states. Furthermore, as we shall see in the chapter dealing with divination, the Yoruba people resisted Islamic influences until quite recent times. Thus 'Yufi' is altogether more likely to have been Ile 'Ife' than anywhere else on the Niger.

13 Richard and John Lander. *Journal of an Expedition to Explore the Course and Termination of the Niger.* 1832. On returning to England Richard Lander was the recipient of the first Royal Medal from the Royal Geographical Society which had been formed two years earlier. He returned to Nigeria for a Liverpool company to open up trade, but was shot and wounded by an Ibo gunman. He died in Fernando Po, where he had been taken to recuperate, in 1834. Brother John died in England in 1839 from a tropical disease he had contracted while in Africa.

Chapter 18 Maize in Yorubaland.

1 Frank Willett. *Ife.* P. 108

2 Ricardo J. Salvador, Iowa State University, in *The Encyclopaedia of Mexico* 1997.

3 M.D.W. Jeffreys. *How Ancient is West African Maize?* 1963. See also his *The History of Maize in Africa.* In the South African Journal of Science, March 1954

4 George F. Carter. *Maize to Africa.* 1963 (Not known what publication this article appeared in). Also: *Plant Evidence for Early Contacts with America.* Southwestern Journal of Anthropology. Vol 6 1950: and *Movements of People and Plants across the Pacific Ocean in Ancient Days.* Proceedings of the Pacific Science Congress 1962. G.F. Carter was Professor of Archaeology at Johns Hopkins University.

5 C.R. Stonor and Edgar Anderson. *Maize among the Hill Peoples of Assam.* Annals of the Missouri Botanical Garden. Vol 36 1949.

6 J. Needham. *Science and Civilisation in China* Vol 4. p.542 – 547 including the discovery of stone ship's anchors such as the Chinese used, off the coast of Peru and Chile.

Footnotes For Page 171-175

7   Stonor and Anderson. *Maize among the Hill People...* P 392

8   G.F.Carter. *Archaeological Maize in West Africa.* MAN May-June 1964.

9   J.H. Hutton; J.P.Mills – various, including Stonor and Anderson, *Maize among the Hill People....*

10 Frank Willett. *The Introduction of Maize into West Africa: An Assessment of Recent Evidence* J.I.A.I. January 1962. In 1954 "Mangelsdorf published evidence that maize is unquestionably an American plant."(Willett)

Chapter 19. The Yoruba – and their Beads.

1   Eugenia Herbert, in *Red Gold of Africa,* Wisconsin 1984, notes that the total weight of brass rods carried by a single caravan that came to grief in the sands of Mauritania in the 12th century weighed over 2,000 lbs. The total weight of bronze goods found at Igbo Ukwu amounted to only 155 lbs, and of brasses found at Ife 375 pounds. The likelihood is that there is a huge amount remaining undiscovered.

2   J.D. Fage *An Introduction to the History of West Africa* .Cambridge 1955 p.88

3   Sir Alan Burns. *History of Nigeria* 1969edition. P 28. Compare with the Malagasy lamba use in their burials, and also the fact that canoe burials ('Ships of the Dead') were once common among coastal Yoruba, as they are also in many parts of Madagascar. Both the quotation in the same paragraph and the Frobenius quote in the following paragraph are on p. 29

4   Frank Willett. *Ife in the History of West African Sculpture* Allen and Unwin 1969. Thanks to F.W. for the myths and legends quoted.

5   *The Niger Journal of Richard and John Lander.* Ed. Robin Hallett. Routledge and Kegan Paul. P. 88.

6   For information on beads I am primarily grateful to correspondence with Jamey Allen, Consulting Curator at The Bead Museum in Glendale, Arizona; Sonia Magnavita, of the University of Franfurt; Peter Robertshaw who, at the time of writing, is working on Nigerian Beads; Kwesi Amanfrofo for his article *Yoruba Glass Beads.* Also articles by the late Peter Francis on *Indo-Pacific Beads* (www.thebeadsite.com/UNI-I- P.html). There is an excellent description on this site of how glass beads were drawn in southern India); by Mark E. Hall and Leonid Yablonsky in the Journal of Archaeological Science No 25 1998 pp. 1239- 1245; and others. There is a huge amount of literature on beads; much is available on the

internet. Start on the website dedicated to Peter Francis mentioned above.

7   Samuel Kurinsky. *The Glassmakers.* Hippocrene Books 1991. Kegan Paul. P. 88

8   Alastair Lamb. *Some Glass Beads from the Malay Peninsular.* MAN. March/April 1965

Chapter 20. Shekels and Shells.

1   M. Hiskett. *Materials Relating to the Cowry Currency of the Western Sudan.* Bulletin of S.O.A.S. Vol 29. 1966

2   R. Mason. *Background to the Transvaal Iron Age, – new discoveries at Olifantspoort and Broederstrom.* Journal of the Institute of Mining and Metallurgy. Jan. 1974. "Dr van Genderen found at least one cowrie shell and one Conus hebraicus shell eroding from the Broederstroom soils, indicating contact with the coast."

3   M. Hiskett. *Materials Relating to...*

4   Sylvain Levi, Jean Przyluski, and Jules Block. *Pre-Aryan and Pre-Dravidian in India.* p.xiv. Translated from French by Prabodh Chandra Bagchi. U. of Calcutta 1929. See also: *Encyclopaedia Britannica* Vol 16, p 782.In China, by the 5th – 4th c. BC "Small change was supplied by cowrie shells, as it had been long before the invention of coinage; there was also an issue of bronze imitation cowrie shells."

5   M. Hiskett. *Materials Relating to.....*

6   T. Mackintosh-Smith. *The Travels of Ibn Batuttah.* 2002

7   N. Levitzion and J.F.P.Hopkins. *Corpus of Early Arabic Sources for West African History.*

8   Mungo Park. *Travels into the Interior of Africa* pub. Dent, 1954 p 355 - 362

9   A. Burns. *History of Nigeria.* 1929. p.96 . The Landers, Burns and others quote dozens of similar examples. When the Landers traveled down the Niger in 1839 everything had to be paid for with cowries which were needed in vast quantities:- "We brought a quantity of new shillings with us from England, which are vastly admired by all classes of people here, on account of their shining property; and whilst the Spanish dollar sells for fifteen hundred cowries only, one of these little pieces is purchased willingly at a thousand." But large bags-full were needed:- "When a free man forms an affection for a female who is a slave, and he has money sufficient for the purpose, he goes to her master, and informs him of his intention of taking the woman to wife,

if he will give him permission. Should the owner of the girl approve of the connection, the suitor pays him 20,000 cowries for his consent to the match..." But such a marriage did not break the bonds of slavery, for she was still obliged to serve her master as before, and any children of the liaison belonged to the slaves owner, not to the husband! See: Richard and John Lander – *Journal of an expedition to explore the Course and Termination of the Niger.* Vol 1. P 128/9 1832. And more... When the Chief Dosuma of Lagos was deposed in 1863 "petitions were addressed to Queen Victoria by Dosumu and his chiefs, but the former was satisfied by the fixing of his annual pension at 1,200 bags of cowries, equal at that time to about £1,030..."

10 E. Torday. *On the Trail of the Bushongo.* p.92ff. Torday recounted a Luba story of the Jackal and the Dwarf Antelope clearly indicating the use of cowries as money. It tells of the Jackal's greed:- "Off he went and found the jackal in front of his house counting a big bag of cowries. 'Hundred, hundred and one, hundred and two....' The little antelope's mouth watered at the sight of the tremendous amount of money." The Luba come from the area of the Upemba Depression between the Lualaba and the Lubilash rivers.

Note also: Graham Connah. *African Civilisations* p. 273, writing of the Upemba Depression's Kisalian and Kamilambian traditions dating back to the 5th century. "Social stratification was further indicated in the Classic Kisalian (c. 11th century) by the unequal distribution of grave-goods between the various burials. It was observed that the few graves that contained an unusually large number of pots also contained uncommon things like cowries ...." And for a reference to later years: D.W.I Piggott. Writing on the *History of Mafia* in the Tanganyika Notes and Records. "In 1850 Chole Island (Mafia) was visited by Krapf and he noticed that there was an important trade in cowries-shells. These were bought at the rate of two measures to one of rice and were shipped by traders to the West Coast as currency."

11 David Henderson-Quartey. *The Ga of Ghana.* 2001

Chapter 21. The Arts of Ife.

1 Frank Willett. *Ife in the History of West African Sculpture.* Thames and Hudson. 1967. This has been my primary source for Ife art.

2 H.R. van Heekeren. *The Bronze-Iron Age of Indonesia* Gravenhage. 1958. pp 14 – 23. Also: Charles Higham. *The Bronze Age of Southeast Asia.* Cambridge 1997

Footnotes For Page 191-195

3   I have illustrated the piece shown by Jones. But another example can be seen in a "A Handbook of the Collection" of the Herbert F. Johnson Museum of Art , Cornell University which can be seen on www.museum.cornell.edu/HFJ/handbook/hb92.html. The museum's example has a frame around it; and notice the eight-petaled lotus flower on the 'plume'.

4   A.M. Jones. *Africa and Indonesia – The evidence of the Xylophone and other Musical and Cultural Factors.* Leiden 1971. Connah makes no mention, either, of any of Raymond Kent's numerous publications without which it is impossible to get a proper understanding of Africa's relationship with Madagascar … and hence Indonesia. His book is another sad example of professional disinterest in the subject.

Chapter 22. The Art of Divination.

1   William A. Lessa. *Divining from Knots in the Carolines.* Journal of the Polynesian Society. pp188 – 203. 1959.

2   John Mack. *Telling and Foretelling – African Divination and Art in Wider Perspective.* Chap. 3 pp 34 –44 .

3   A.F.L. Beeston, in letters from St Johns College, Oxford. 22 and 25 .3.60.

4   Hellmut Wilhelm, Professor of Chinese history, Washington, in a letter to the author. In the same letter he added: "I have in the meantime looked at the book by Linton on the Tanala … In the divination ritual of the Tanala I found several elements which are decidedly reminiscent of Chinese useages. Within the whole system these elements are concededly minor; they are on the other hand so distinctive that they let one think of diffusion." (ref: note 5, below)

5   R. Kent. *Early Kingdoms in Madagascar* 1500 - 1700 Holt, Rinehart and Winston. 1970 p111. 'Flacourt reported in his *Histoire* COACM Vol V111 (1913) pp 279-280 that the beaten bark technique was employed in paper manufacturing, and that the bark itself came from the *avoha (Dais Glaucescens)* tree. D. Hunter, in *Papermaking: The History and Technique of an Ancient Craft* (1947) pp 29-47, attributed the beaten bark (*tapa*) to the Pacific Islands in general.'

6   John Pemberton. *Divination in Sub-Saharan Africa.* In 'Art and Oracle: African Art and Rituals of Divination' 2000. ed. Alisa La Gamma. Metropolitan Museum of Art, N.Y. p 11 col 2. Quote: "The 'sixteen signs' type of divination may have its origins in Islamic sand writing (*khayy ar-raml*), and its traces are found not only in Ifa and Fa but also

in divination systems in the Mande culture zone in Mali, in Madagascar, and among the Shona in southern Africa." Compare with Beeston and Wilhelm, above.

The Yoruba and the Shona (and some people immediately around them) also have in common the use of divining bowls or dishes, quite similar in appearance, with designs carved around the rims. The Yoruba read omens from 16 nuts scattered in sand in the flat bowls. The Shona and Venda filled their bowls with water and used to (these dishes did not survive beyond the 1930's) make interpretations from maize or other seeds floated on the surface. (See Anitra Nettleton. *Divining Bowl* (*ndilo*). in "Africa: Arts and Culture." Ed: John Mack. 2000. British Museum, London.). One famous dish found in Zimbabwe in the 19th century was surrounded by designs that were, quite reasonably, interpreted as Signs of the Zodiac. In view of the probable relationship between the Zimbabwe Culture and Madagascar, and the Arab-influenced Anteimoro, this may have been an exception to the general rule of 'no Arab influence in Central Africa'.

7   Ralph Linton. *The Tanala*. Marshall Field Expedition to Madagascar. 1926. P. 203 and also in the appendix.

The Tanala pattern names are as follows: (with a few obvious Swahili intrusions):

1. *Taley* = first; or head of the family. 2 *Mady* = wealth, or medicine, something good. 3. *Fahatelo* = third; significance of relative of the sick. 4. *Bilady* = land, country, native place. 5. *Fianahana* = children. 6. *Abidy* = old woman. 7. *Betsimishe* = wife. 8. *Fahavalo* = enemy – only in the sense of illness. 9 *Fahasicy* = ancestors. 10. *Ombiasy* = The person who has made the sikidy. 11. *Haza* = food. 12. *Andriamanitra* = God, or Zanahary. 13. *Sholtana* = very old person. 14. *Shedy* = young person. 15. *Safary* = road or journey. 16 *Trano* = house, home or dwelling.

8   R. Kent *Early Kingdoms in Madagascar* 1500 - 1700. . p. 111 and pp 88-115.

9   P Azais & R . Chambard. *Cinq Annees de Recherche Archeologiques en Ethiopie - Province du Harar et Ethiopie Meridionale*. Paris. 1931.

10 Grottanelli, V.L. *Pescatori dell'Oceanoo Indiano* Rome 1955. P. 51 and elsewhere.

11 S.S. Dornan, *Divination and Divining Bones*. South African Journal of Science. XX 1923 pp504-511.

12 Rev. Noel Roberts. *A Few Notes on To Kolo, a System of Divination practiced by the Superior Natives of Maloboch's Tribe in the Northern*

Footnotes For Page 198-208

Transvaal. Unfortunately I do not know where this article was published; nor do I have a date. But I suspect it must be very early 20th century.

13 Not everyone agreed with Dornan. viz: I. Schapera argued that that the Bushmen must have got their knowledge from the Bantu. See: *The Khoisan Peoples of South Africa.* Keegan Paul 1930. P.200.

14 William Bascom. *Ifa Divination: Communication between Gods and Man in West Africa* Indiana University Press. 1969

15 N. Levtzion and J.F.P.Hopkins. *Corpus of Early Arabic Sources for West African history* p, 298 See also the 'Trade Route' map.

INDEX

Index

Due for publication later in 2005

"Sanamu: Adventures in Search of African Art"

by: Robert Dick-Read

Paperback; 304 pages; 72 drawings by the author; 34 photographs; 5 maps; £14.99

Later this year Thurlton Publishing will be reprinting *Sanamu*, first published in 1964 by Rupert Hart-Davis, with an additional section discussing the changes that have taken place in the African art world during the 50 years since Robert Dick-Read first went in search of Kamba carvings for his new shop, "African Art", in Mombasa.

Wars, famines, floods and disease, plus social changes since independence, have inevitably caused a collapse in the traditional arts that still just flourished when the author set out on his journeys across nineteen African countries, buying arts and crafts, filming, and establishing a museum in the art-rich Cameroons.   The picture today is in stark contrast to the waning days of the colonial era.   In many ways it is exciting and full of hope for future generations; in others it is a lament for the past, when the arts flourished as an integral part of age old social structures.

One of the author's concerns is that Africa's young artists will be sucked into the shallow, get-rich-quick orbit spun by many of today's galleries; and that the craftsmanship that once characterised so much of Africa's ancient artwork will be subverted and forgotten.   He warns against the dangers of imposing on modern African art the phoney aesthetic values that often define today's taste, and how they could stifle the huge well of originality that Africa has to offer.

This new edition brilliantly highlights the contrasts between Africa today and fifty years ago; and not least, perhaps, the changing attitudes of the author himself.

ന ന ന ന ന

If you are interested in receiving more information
nearer the date of publication, please email:

thurlton.publishing@ntlworld.com

or write to:

Thurlton Publishing, 5 St James Villas, Winchester, Hants, SO23 9SN, England.

ന ന ന ന ന